ALIVE AND KICKING

ALIVE AND KICKING

Legal Advice for Boomers

Kenney F. Hegland
JAMES E. ROGERS PROFESSOR OF LAW
UNIVERSITY OF ARIZONA

Robert B. Fleming
ATTORNEY AT LAW
ELDER LAW SPECIALIST

CAROLINA ACADEMIC PRESS
Durham, North Carolina

Library of Congress Cataloging-in-Publication Data

Hegland, Kenney F., 1940-
  Alive and kicking / by Kenney Hegland, Robert Fleming.
    p. cm.
  ISBN-10: 1-59460-322-7 (alk. paper)
  ISBN-13: 978-1-59460-322-8
  1. Right to die--United States--Popular works. 2. Advance directives
(Medical care)--United States--Popular works. I. Fleming, Robert B.
II. Title.

  KF3823.Z9H44 2007
  344.7304'197--dc22

                                                        2006038318

Cover by Perry Woods, pwink3@excite.com

CAROLINA ACADEMIC PRESS
700 Kent Street
Durham, North Carolina 27701
Telephone (919) 489-7486
Fax (919) 493-5668
www.cap-press.com

Printed in the United States of America

To those of us who still sing in our chains like the sea.

Summary of Contents

Contents

PART 3   TROUBLE: GETTING IN AND GETTING OUT

Part 6   Death in the Family

PROLOGUE:
NOW YOU'RE 64, GIVE OR TAKE

Will you still need me,
Will you still feed me,
When I'm 64?

The Beatles

Remember when? Then 64 was a myth, something lurking at the outer edge of our imagination. We had better things to do: schools to finish, careers to start, mates to find. Etcetera. Sure, our grandparents were old, but they had always been old, preferred being old, chose to be old. Curious choice. Not ours.

A blur of momentous events. Viet Nam, civil rights, Berlin Wall, goings-on in the Oval Office, 9/11; meanwhile, we finished school, started a career, found a mate, not to mention Etcetera. We didn't start the fire, but it has consumed us. Suddenly, quite suddenly, we just turned around, and, hey, it's us. Sixty-four, give or take.

Growing old isn't as bad as we feared. Most of us will stay in good health and find engaging things to do in our retirement. However, growing old is not eating a peach. It's not for sissies. It won't be for us. It won't be for you. This book will help you, and it will help us.

The problem is this: There are a lot of things you need to know now in order to avoid trouble. On the other hand, there are things you don't need to know unless you're in trouble. It's good to think about living wills now, but you need not worry about fighting age discrimination unless and until it happens to you. What's a poor boy to do?

Divide the book. The first part of the book, *Training for Ill*, is designed to be read. It deals with a ghastly range of topics: living wills, the aging process, and, on a lighter note, protecting your identity and avoiding scams. There will be advice on how to stay mentally active, perhaps staving off senility by doing crosswords, and advice on how to recognize one of the plagues of growing old: strokes. Finally, as retirement isn't always all that it is cracked up to be, we offer some advice on coping with existential angst. (Remember when that was something we puzzled over in the afternoon, before going to that night's party? Which was it: existence precedes essence or essence precedes existence?)

You may think, "I can skip that part. I already know about living wills, hospice, and the virtues of exercise." But Samuel Johnson was right: people more often need to be reminded than informed.

Training for ill isn't pleasant. We would all prefer to go to the beach, to get around to it tomorrow. Training for ill today will allow us to avoid it tomorrow or, if we can't, to better cope with it. Resist your Little Voice shouting, "You don't have time for this now. Maybe tomorrow." Take a deep breath, sit down and read. On the bright side, not every bad thing we mention will happen to you.

The rest of the book can wait until you have specific questions. Our later topics:

- Retirement: finances, housing and health insurance.
- Family matters: divorce and remarriage, grandchildren, financial obligations.
- Trouble: elder abuse, bill collectors, and age bigots.
- Estate planning: wills, living trusts, trusts for special needs, probate.
- Bad times: disability and death in the family.

And, in a shameless ploy to sell more books, we have devoted a chapter to sex. Good news on that front.

We were going to call this book *Geezer Law* (cooler heads prevailed). Why? We're invited to parties. "Come to Larry's 65th. Please, no serious presents." Our goal with *Geezer Law* was to overtake adult diapers and capture the joke-gift market. But we had loftier, more respectable goals as well. In the Civil Rights Movement came a sharp defining moment: "We're not Negroes, we're black." Everything changed.

We're not senior citizens, we're not elders, and we aren't living our golden years: we're geezers and here we come, ready or not.

Finally, style.

We won't write down. You're probably smarter than us. Editors, mostly in their thirties, have advised:

"Kill the jokes, the poetry, the background stuff. Just tell 'em how to stretch their Social Security check."

Despite what these whipper-snappers may think, us geezers don't shuffle over to the couch, sit blankly before a static TV, drooling oatmeal. We still have our humor, our curiosity, our intellectual excitement. We'll come and go, talking of Michelangelo, telling bad jokes, and reciting wonderful poetry. If you're in it just for the information, you've picked up the wrong book. Not that there's no information here—we just think you need a spoonful of humor with your maturity medicine.

Legal prose is pretty deadly. A law professor (from Yale!) once wrote:

> *There are two things wrong with almost all legal writing. One is style. The other is content. That, I think, covers the ground....*
> *Readers like a dash of pepper or a dash of salt along with their information. They won't get any seasoning if lawyers can help it. Lawyers would rather be dignified and ignored.*

This book will to help you; it will help your family. We won't let you ignore it; we'll put on lampshades, paint our noses red, and do back flips.

OK. No back flips.

PART 1

TRAINING FOR ILL

CHAPTER 1

TRAINING FOR ILL

Since the world has still
Much good, but much less good than ill,
And while the sun and moon endure
Luck's a chance, but trouble's sure,
I'd face it as a wise man would,
And train for ill and not for good.

A.E. Houseman

In the chapters that follow we'll deal with living wills (which, if done right, require us to confront the prospect of our own death), the aging process (which, like it or not, happens—and, as they say, is better than the alternative), and consumer scams (which, unlike death and age, you can avoid). This chapter introduces the necessity of training for ill (trouble's sure) and covers a potpourri of ills which, while significant, do not warrant separate chapters: the existential anguish of retirement, the constant threat of stroke, the fear of disability and death, the need to have an unpleasant (at first) talk with your family.

Training conjures grunts and sweats. And that's a nice transition into an optimistic aside. While death may be sure, disability isn't. In fact, the rate of disability, defined as the loss of one major life function (such as the ability to dress or feed oneself) has been falling among the elderly: among folks over 85, it is only one in five. Improved medical care has played a role, as has improved nutrition and, indeed, so have grunts and sweats.

On the Virtues of Pumping Iron and Working Crosswords

If you stop exercising, you get weaker; if you stop pushing yourself mentally, you get dumber. Studies show that learning new things is good exercise for the brain. Consider adult education, programs like Elder Hostel, not only for their intrinsic fun, but as a method of maintaining mental agility. Don't be a passive student.

Question what you learn. "How could a study show that learning keeps you alert? Are these guys just making up studies as they go along?"

> *What's the cube root of 27? Who said "Fee, fie, foe, fum, I smell the blood of an Englishman"? Explain chaos theory. Coherently.*

There are computer games for grown-ups designed to test and push your intellect. Ask your grandkids.

Travel helps, too. Going to new places is a mental challenge: making plans, reading maps, finding good restaurants, learning how to ask "Where's the bathroom?" in Greek. Even at home, varying your schedule can help. If you are in too much of a routine, you do it without mental effort. Try taking the dog for a walk *before* breakfast (yours, not his—let's not live *too* dangerously); try denouncing the government *after* lunch. Variety, variety, something different.

As to physical exercise, yet another study showed that surprisingly little effort can produce surprisingly much reward. A hundred men and women in their 80s and 90s, most so frail that they needed walkers, increased their strength 118% during a ten-week exercise program. They could walk faster and climb stairs more easily. Some, so taken with their new persona, even began snarling: "Fee, fie, foe, fum ..." Oddly (and frighteningly) a follow-up study showed that when the support staff of professional trainers were removed from the equation, nearly every participant stopped exercising—even though the equipment was still there, even though the results had been phenomenal, even though the participants had all been trained on how to manage their own exercise regimen. So hire a trainer, join a club, start a group to work out together. That's the basic premise behind the "sport" of mall-walking: groups of mature adults meet every morning to walk in air-conditioned comfort, window-shop and gossip. And walk.

According to Blue Cross, Blue Shield, walking 10,000 steps a day will help you lose weight, lower cholesterol, and reduce your risk of heart attack. If everyone did it, the claim is that it would reduce health care costs $77 billion a year. Blue Cross, Blue Shield, in addition to saving billions, have no idea what they are on to: consider the fabulous impact on your mental abilities, the concentration required to count all those steps, "Eight thousand, five hundred, fifty-one; eight thousand, five hundred, fifty-two; eight thousand, five hundred, fifty-three; eight thousand, five hundred, fifty ... fifty? Darn! One; two ..."(A cartoon shows aerobatics in Hell with the leader saying, "OK, now

10,000 deep knee bends.") Most of us can reach the magic figure of 10,000 steps by adding a 30 minute walk to our daily routine.

On Existential Angst and Retirement

We have only two questions: What shall we do and how shall we live?

Tolstoy

We spent, what, eight, ten, twelve hours at work each weekday? There was no question as to our place in the universe: butcher, baker, candle-stick maker. How are you going to fill all of those hours? With the label gone, from whence your sense of self-worth? Of belonging?

Retirement can be rocky. Many wish they never retired and spend their golden years watching daytime TV (which is a fine choice, provided you really like it). After Dylan Thomas died, his widow wrote *Leftover Life to Kill*. Many turn to booze; some to violence. Many suffer physical and mental abuse at the hands of their spouse. Be aware of the dangers and, if they befall your lot, there are specific ways to deal with them. We will discuss them later in the book. But here, the root problem: what will you do and how will you live?

Sports agents advise their clients to keep a diary during their playing years noting what they like to do in their off time. Editors advise budding authors, "Don't write about what you know, write about what you *don't know* you know." Our advice is similar. Sit down and write out how you will spend your time and where you will get your sense of self-worth. You probably know but you don't know that you know. Don't just *think* about these questions, write. We think too fast; writing slows the mind and allows ideas to bubble. And don't be too serious, "I will find ways to serve mankind." Try instead, "I'll run off and join the circus." Silly ideas lead to good ideas, "I'll have to go to clown school. That's stupid. But, wait, how about cooking school? My pancakes have always been a hit!"

On Strokes: STAT

This topic does not fit with our poetic forays nor our philosophic musings. But nothing ruins a good retirement like a stroke.

Strokes can lead to death or severe disability. The good news is that, if the victim receives medical attention within two or three hours, most of the damage can be avoided. The bad news is that often the victim is unaware of the stroke and does not seek medical help. There may be no catastrophic event—perhaps only a stumble, a sudden dizziness.

Someone falls, gets up, and seems OK. Suspect stroke. Recite STAT.

"S" – ask the person to Smile.
"T" – ask the person to Talk.
"A" – ask the person to raise both Arms.
"T" – ask the person to stick out their Tongue. If it goes off to one side, rather than straight out, it is a sign.

If the stumbler flunks one test, call 911. Call 911 even if they pass all four if you still suspect a stroke.

How can you recognize that **you** have had a stroke?

- Sudden numbness or weakness of the face, arm, or leg, especially on one side of the body.
- Sudden confusion, trouble speaking, understanding.
- Sudden trouble seeing in one or both eyes, double vision.
- Sudden trouble walking, dizziness, loss of balance, or coordination.
- Sudden severe headache.
- Sudden drowsiness, nausea, vomiting.

In short, *suddenly something is amiss.* Err on the side of caution. Call 911 immediately. With each passing minute, more cells die.

On Death

Death is overrated. In a famously searing couplet, Dylan Thomas cries to his dying father:

Do not go gentle into that good night.
Rage, rage, against the dying of the light.

What a powerful phrase—the dying of the light. One almost chokes. But that's young Dylan's view of death; was it his dad's? What do those who have almost died tell us? They report feeling a sense of calm and acceptance; many report on seeing a bright light rushing toward them. A surgeon visits his patient and is told:

"Lying on the operating table, I knew I was dying. You and the others were trying to save my life and that was O.K. But it was also O.K. if you didn't."

When he was a young man, the 16th-century French essayist Michel de Montaigne was thrown from his horse, sustaining serious injuries. He was a bloody mess.

It seemed to me that my life was hanging only by the tip of my lips. I closed my eyes in order, it seemed to me, to help push it out. I took pleasure in growing languid and letting myself go. I was not only free from distress but felt that sweet feeling of sliding into sleep. I believe that is how people feel whom we see in the agony of death. We pity them without cause, thinking that they are troubled by grievous pains or have their souls full of distressing thoughts.

So what of Dylan's father?

"That's O.K. Dylan. Everything will be fine. Now wipe away your tears and go back to bed. I want my rest."

The fear of death, the denial of death, prevents us from living to the fullest. In *tuesdays with Morrie*, Mitch Albom writes of his Tuesday afternoon visits with his former professor. Morrie, dying of Lou Gehrig's disease, talks about denial:

"Everyone knows they're going to die, but nobody believes it. If we did, we would do things differently.... To know you're going to die, and to be prepared for it at any time. That's better. That way you can actually be more involved in your life while you're living. Once you learn how to die, you learn how to live."

On Talking to Your Family

Gruesome stuff: the angst of retirement, the threat of disability, the certainty of death.

As you train for ill, there is more to come: your final illness, and the process of aging. Don't face all of this alone. Talk to your family. Down the road you and your family will face difficult times and difficult decisions. Training for ill means getting the team on the same page.

If you don't discuss these issues, they will not go away. One of our basic fears is dying alone. We tend to think of this in physical terms, focusing on the importance of having family around us. However, when the time comes, emotional isolation is just as frightening. Have your family emotionally around you as you face the future.

These conversations will bring your family together: they acknowledge the elephant in the room. They can even be fun, with recollections from the past, "Remember the motel and the big black bug in the shower and Dad going in?" The hardest part is *starting* the conversation. As we go along, we offer some opening lines.

Please, not a somber affair, in a well lit dining room, with lists, and Mozart's *Requiem* playing in the background. Please, something more casual and more spontaneous, with the Beatles or The Mamas and The Papas. And, as long as we are quoting Houseman, recall his famous couplet:

> *Malt does more than Milton can,*
> *To justify God's way to Man.*

Training for Ill

In the poem with which we began, A.E. Houseman advises us to face reality directly, even though it may be painful. Does training for ill work? You bet! Houseman tells of King Mithridates. He knew his enemies were plotting to poison him. Training for ill, he prepared himself by taking small dosages of poisons to get used to them.

> *They put arsenic in his meat*
> *And stared aghast to watch him eat;*
> *They poured strychnine in his cup*
> *And shook to see him drink it up;*
> ....
> *—I tell the tale that I heard told.*
> *Mithridates, he died old.*

Quick! Repeat the mnemonic device for recognizing a stroke. Feel smarter?

CHAPTER 2

LIVING WILLS

I don't mind the idea of my death. I just don't want to be there when it happens.

Woody Allen

No doubt you've heard of Living Wills and might even have one. Of all the planning documents, such as Wills and Durable Health Care Powers of Attorney, they are probably the least important and, for that matter, the least effective. Why would we devote a chapter to them in our ever-popular "Training for Ill" series?

In our last chapter Morrie told us, *"Everyone knows they're going to die, but nobody believes it. If we did, we would do things differently."* Fine, well and good. But he didn't tell us how to go about it. Writing your own living will, thinking long and hard about your last illness, might get you part way there. And, as Morrie tells us, *"Once you learn how to die, you learn how to live."*

And, in our last chapter, we stressed the importance of having a conversation that matters with your family. We even promised opening lines. Here we give you one: *"I just wrote my living will. I need your input, and you need to hear my views. Let's talk."*

Living Wills promise that we can decide what medical treatment we will receive during our last illness. Although one can insist that everything be done to prolong life, generally Living Wills are intended to curtail treatment—the guiding and terrifying image, the stuff of countless TV shows, being hooked to machines in ICU for weeks, dying a slow, painful, and expensive death.

Living Wills aren't very effective. Studies show that they have little impact on the medical treatment one actually receives. If your Living Will insists on "no heroics" but your family insists upon them, most likely you will get them. Doctors realize that it is much easier to defend a "wrongful life" lawsuit than a "wrongful death" one.

Is this a problem?

Not really. Living Wills are too casual, too vague, and too speculative to be taken too seriously. Many are of the "Check the Appropriate Box" variety and, in confusing legalese, tend to boil down to two choices:

❑ "No, I don't want to be hooked up to a lot of machines," or
❑ "Yes, keep me alive as long as possible."

Boxes are checked in crowded hospital waiting rooms, when you have more pressing matters, or in a lawyer's office, as part of your estate plan. With the meter running, there is no time to dally with stupid questions like, "Box 3(a) talks about 'a persistent vegetative state,' and just what is that, anyway?"

Life and death decisions should not be flip. But let's put the hurried and non-reflective Living Will aside. Say you brooded long and hard and, with appropriate angst, finally checked "No heroics." When the time comes, if your family and physicians decide that heroics would be best, what then?

The root problem, the unsolvable problem, is that Living Wills are written long before they come into play: We are asked to decide *now* what we want *then,* and usually we don't have a clue. The stuff of Greek tragedy, especially since we *think* we have a clue—we are clueless about our cluelessness.

Putting aside the inherent problem of changes between now and then, such as advances in medical treatment and pain control, if you found yourself dying and *you were able to communicate,* would you automatically reject (or automatically insist upon) all heroic medical interventions? Of course not. You would talk it over—with family, religious counselors, doctors. Are you 63, 73 or 93? How certain the diagnosis, and how great the pain? How costly the stay, how rich your family? How sharp your mind? Do you need more time for final goodbyes? And, finally, of course, who's left?

We misjudge the future. When I was a teen, I firmly believed that sitting in an office all day, writing stuff, would be a fate worse than death. I no longer *firmly* believe this.

Healthy, visualizing our ourselves lying in a hospital bed, hooked to machines, we think, "I would rather be dead." When and if we get there, would we rather be dead? When we are green and golden, singing in our chains like the sea, we might check, with great bravado, the "Rage, rage against the dying of the light" box. But, when the time comes, will we want to hang on?

That you cannot predict the future does not mean you shouldn't have a Living Will. However, consider one less dogmatic, less demanding, less legalistic. Consider something more humble, more folksy, a letter sharing your thoughts with family. You also can address things that might skew the decisions away from your best interest: family guilt and physicians' fear of legal liability. Here's one possibility:

A Letter to My Family, My Friends and My Health Care Providers Concerning End-of-Life Matters

This letter addresses medical issues that may arise near the end of my life. I request that those involved in making decisions for me at that time do so only after careful consideration of what I say here. As no one can predict specific circumstances, I do not wish to bind those decisions in any way but to request that they be made in light of my preferences, in light of my best interests, and in light of the best interests of my family.

It is my hope that those involved, after carefully listening to each other, would come to agreement as to the best course of action. If division persists, I hereby appoint _____ as the final arbiter and as my health care power of attorney. If _____ cannot serve, then I appoint _____.

I fully appreciate that your decisions may hasten my death. No one should feel guilty in making such decisions or feel that the only way to show love for me is to prolong my life as long as possible. The opposite may be true.

Pain. Health care providers may fail to administer adequate pain medication in fear that it might addict or kill. My request is that I receive medication adequate to relieve my pain even if that runs the risk of creating addiction or hastening my death. I further request that none of my family or friends institute any action against any of my health care providers premised on the notion that I received too much pain medication and, furthermore, that they resist any governmental action against my health care providers, whether by prosecuting or licensing agencies, premised on that notion.

End-of-Life Medical Treatment. I do not want my life extended by medical interventions if my prognosis is grim in terms of my ultimate recovery and the quality of life. I realize that some health care providers, fearful of malpractice claims, may pursue aggressive treatment even if that is unwarranted. I request that none of my family institute any malpractice action premised on the notion that the treatment I received was not aggressive enough.

As a general matter, I disfavor cardiopulmonary resuscitation in any form and artificially administered food and fluids. I expressly authorize my family to reject, on my behalf, any form of resuscitation and to decline or later remove any forms of artificial administration of food or fluid. I want my family to know that death due to lack of *hydration is not a horrible way to die; in fact it is rather peaceful and painless.*

Furthermore, I would prefer not to be taken to the hospital.
<u>Death</u>. *I would much prefer to die at home or in a hospice. I do not want to die alone or among strangers. I do not want to die in an intensive care unit or in a nursing home. If I am in intensive care for more than one week, then I strongly suspect that my life is being artificially extended.*

I consent to organ donations and to an autopsy realizing that much can be learned from it to understand the cause of my death and to help others. Though I want to help my fellow humans, I am somewhat leery of experimental treatments and research studies.
<u>Burial</u>. *I prefer cremation and an Irish Wake.*

I intend that this letter, which I shall sign before witnesses, shall be as legally binding and as enforceable as my Living Will and Appointment of Health Care Agent as is provided in any state in which I reside at the time that this letter would be effective. Furthermore, I intend that my wishes be binding on my estate.

Signed:
Dated:
Witnessed by:
We, the author's family members, have read and discussed this letter with the author. We understand it and agree to follow it.
Signed

Don't copy this out, rewrite it. Or at least tailor it to your own preferences. "Sitting Shiva" might replace "Irish Wake." Write your own. Writing, as we have observed before, slows the mind and insures reflection—and that is a good thing. Not to put too fine a point on it, you owe your dying self, and you owe your distressed family, an hour of serious thought.

When you're done, go over it with your family. As you have given it serious consideration, it will go better than, "Persistent vegetative state? I don't want to be hooked up to a lot of machines!" "Me neither; what's on Channel 4?" As Death is a reluctant topic, remember that malt does more than Milton can, to justify God's way to Man.

Note that family members sign off on the letter. This is not required for Living Wills and, indeed, is rather novel. It is a wonderful idea.

Everyone advises that you discuss your specific wishes with your family; this advice probably doesn't even make your "To Do" list. This approach *requires* this discussion. And it is simply easier to start with "I need you to do something for me" rather than "Do you have 30 minutes for a dismal discussion about my death?"

Having family members agree to follow your wishes should prevent horrible family fights when the time comes. It is also an important prophylactic. As you want to convince health care workers that they will not be sued if they give too much pain medication or too few medical interventions, the agreement of your family to follow your instructions will help. Would such an agreement bar litigation? As us lawyers like to say, "Maybe, maybe not." It would turn on a complex assessment of contract law, tort law and health care law. Down the road courts may have to grapple with the issue. For now, realizing that drafting can take us only so far, let's trust our relatives and do what we can.

Once you have written out your preferences, and discussed them with family, you should also sign a more traditional, formal health care power of attorney. Your state law may use different language ("health care surrogate," for example), but the point is that someone should have the *legal* authority to sign the hospital's consent forms—that really will increase the likelihood that your wishes, and those of your family and loved ones, will be honored when the time comes. More on this in Chapter 23.

Some will object that the letter doesn't save loved ones "the anguish of making the tough call," the lurking fear, "Maybe we pulled the plug too soon, or too late." By describing my fears and wishes, my letter goes a long way to direct and support their decision.

In any event, anguish and guilt cannot be avoided. A living will, which dogmatically asserts "No heroics," *might* be better in this regard. Of course, nothing is perfect. In all but the most extreme cases, there will be room to argue, and hence room to regret. "Yes, Dad wanted to die under those circumstances, but a good daughter would have challenged the doctors more— maybe he wasn't in a persistent vegetative state."

Leaving the tough decision to my family seems right, not only pragmatically (they will probably have to decide anyway), but philosophically. We are not islands, not in our lives and not in our deaths. Our families are part of us; they need time say goodbye, to comfort us, and to be with us.

But the value of the letter is *now*, not *then*; the value is the simple message "I love you, I trust you, and it's time to spend a few minutes talking about my final illness; it's really nothing to dread, pass the wine."

Tell your family this *now*. As to *then*, as to the tough choice, it probably won't ever come up; you'll probably be run over by a bus.

CHAPTER 3

GROWING OLD: WHAT TO
EXPECT AND HOW TO COPE

*Three tough things about growing old. First, you're not as spry. Second,
you forget things.*

The third stop on our ever-popular "Training for Ill" series is "Growing
Old." It's like puberty: a lot of physical, mental and emotional changes are
going on. It helps to anticipate and it helps to know you are not alone.

The good news is that people are living longer and living in much better
health. But we have not come to praise old age. Overall the news is not good:
physically, we will lose prowess; mentally, we will lose some memory and will
have more difficulty learning new things; socially, things may go badly and,
worst of all, psychologically, we may begin to loathe ourselves.

Why is it that we cut so easily? Why is it that our faces wrinkle? That our
skin seems blue? Fewer cells. Babies are so cute, so plump, so lovable, because
they are bundles of cells. Cut them and they heal instantly. Over time, cells
die. This does not mean that we can't be buff—a friend, a ninety-pound
weakling his entire life, started lifting when he turned 70. Now he wears mus-
cle T-Shirts and, after all these decades, he got his gal back (or at least we like
to think). With exercise, the cells we have can be made larger, but those we
have lost cannot be replaced.

Along with cell loss comes a general decline in physical prowess—our
hearts and our lung capacity shrink, we become less sure on our feet, we tire
quickly. Slowly making our way to the supermarket check-out line, middle-
aged folks, wearing nifty sun visors and dressed in fashionable exercise garb,
pretending not to be looking the other way, cut in front us. Our solace: the
process of physical decline begins around age thirty—their smugness is illu-
sion, and the clock, not us, will exact the revenge we only dream about in a
civilized society. Evolutionists tell us that this makes sense—by thirty we have
had our children and raised them to the point where they can bring on the
next generation. From an evolutionary point of view, after thirty, we aren't

15

needed. An interesting question: if we are obsolete at age thirty, why do we go on living well beyond that age? Probably the answer is "excess capacity": when we send a rocket ship into space, we install two computers just in case the one goes bad—to make thirty, we are equipped to go much further.

You'll get fat. As we age, our metabolism slows. Looking at the generation before us, we might get it wrong and conclude that one loses weight as one ages—"Those folks are skinny." What we fail to realize is that that generation was always skinny (unlike, alas, us). To use cross-generation comparisons to make predictions is dangerous: doing so in Miami, for example, one would conclude that most folks are born Cuban and die Jewish.

Expect a loss of hearing and vision. There are things to be done, but vanity may get in the way. 'Fess up and get a hearing aid.

Children tend to believe that the old always were and that they chose to be that way. Childhood beliefs die hard. Remind yourself that decline is not your choice, your fault, something to be embarrassed about. Don't panic—the decline is gradual: the first incidence of losing one's balance does not announce impeding doom. (Strokes are not gradual; know their signs and know what to do.)

You are not alone. Everyone your age is going through pretty much what you are. That's reassuring. At dinner parties one is apt to look around the room and think, "Oh no, everyone here is so confident, so self-possessed, so fluent and brilliant in making small talk! Oh woe is me, I'm a nervous wreck with absolutely nothing to say, no clever stories to tell." It helps to realize that everyone at the party is feeling the same way, and, looking at you, thinking, "That person is so confident, so self-possessed, so fluent and brilliant in making small talk."

Viagra and scores of "Dirty Old Man" jokes attest that sex is well and thriving. In nursing homes this presents something of a problem (or not). And, of course, the odds have shifted substantially: there are usually four or five widows for each "eligible" man.

One way to cope with this inevitable decline is not to deny it, is not to fight it, but is to study. Morrie, in *tuesdays with Morrie*, said "I know what it was like to be thirty. Now I can find out what's it like to be seventy." What a fabulous perspective!

Mental powers will decline. As you age, you will do less well on IQ tests and have a harder time learning new tasks. But, then again, you have much less need to do well on IQ tests and much less need to learn new tasks: experience and knowledge trumps mental agility—take that, whipper-snapper!

Expect some short-term memory loss—"Senior moments." We can wish we had that excuse for all of the stupid gaffes committed by our younger selves.

(One thing about aging, though: gaffes, falls, and lost keys are no longer shrugged off as they were before; they now seem to signal ominous things.) You can combat memory loss by writing lists and being a tad more conscious of the need to remember things. Rather than just parking your car at the mall, confident that you will remember where you parked, recite to yourself "I am leaving the car in the third row about halfway down." And don't panic, the mere fact you can't remember where you left your keys does not mean that soon you will not know where you live. While advanced dementia is terrible, it is not inevitable—many people are mentally active and agile in advanced old age.

Exercise helps the mind as well as the body: "Use it or lose it." Forcing yourself to learn new things, to do crossword puzzles, to read up on geezer law, will help. If you insist on sitting in front of the TV, drinking beer and smoking Camels, make it the Discovery Channel. Unfortunately, the History Channel becomes less challenging when you've already been through the subject material once—yes, that was us, and yes, we did wear those funny clothes.

Expect social changes. You may become grumpy (like our co-author). Pain trumps charm. Yet another explanation, a favorite of economists, is that there is less need for charm as you age. You no longer need to impress neighbors or even friends. I guess the notion is that you aren't getting grumpy at all; you were always grumpy but previously covered it up. We refuse to believe this (except about our co-author).

Perhaps related to grumpiness, perhaps not, you will begin to feel more comfortable with lawyers and doctors of your own age, being slightly suspicious of younger professionals who "don't know what it's like." You will also begin to notice fewer and fewer professionals of your own age.

Worse than how you treat others is how they treat you: waitresses call you "dear," cheerful young men hold open the door, and family members think all you are interested in are Social Security and your grandkids—never mind politics, books, movies and, yes, sex. (Have you ever told a dirty joke to either your child or your parent?) Suddenly, quite suddenly, you are no longer a "player." This can lead to one of the most horrible aspects of aging: self-loathing.

We, as a society, do not value the old. In some societies, at some times, elders were highly respected; they were consulted; they were wise. But now there are so many more of us; we are no longer novelties, we tend to get in the way (not to mention bankrupting Social Security). As to our wisdom, yes, we are wise but *not* wise enough *not* to write down what we know. We are no longer needed: we published (foolish us).

At bottom we are all "ageists." It is natural to flee the infirm, the sick, the elderly. Before we were them, we were uncomfortable around the aged, put off by their wrinkles and frailty, resentful of their ability to remind us of our mortality. Our attitudes do not change as quickly as our age. We tend to freeze our self-image in time—no matter what our children and grandchildren see, we still see the long hair, the tie-dyed shirts and the bell-bottom pants of our youth. Now we look in our mirrors and see our parents; it takes a moment to make the mental adjustment, and we have to make it each time. Because our parents are also frozen in memory, we suddenly notice that we are actually older than them. (Have you gone to a high school reunion only to notice that everyone invited their parents—while they, themselves, went to the real party, with all the cool kids?)

We're not ugly; we're just old. OK, older. We can try to minimize it, and its effect, but, to paraphrase the bumper sticker, *aging happens.*

Feeling ugly, frail, and slow, you may want to isolate yourself, perhaps moving into a retirement community where everyone is ugly, frail, and slow (in the land of the ugly, frail and slow, the merely slow can be king); or perhaps just staying home watching the Discovery Channel. While these choices are fine, there are costs: hanging out with younger folks (and learning first-hand how much more important experience is than mental hops), staying part of the community, going to interesting events, hearing new jokes, meeting people who just might be worth the effort. Isolation is dealing with the symptom, not the cause: self-loathing.

Cosmetic surgery can help. If you can afford it, go for it. We know folks who have and they emerge bubbly.

More basically, overcome loathing. Some of the most contented folks we know are hospice volunteers, bedside as individuals they know, they helped feed, they listened to and cried with, die. Hang out with folks older than you. Play Canasta. Get behind the wrinkles, the frailty, the reminder of your own mortality; look at the person and realize: "There, *with* the grace of God, go I."

Pretty grim stuff, thus far. *It won't be as grim as you fear.*

Christopher Reeve believed that he was better off after his crippling fall; Lance Armstrong is glad to have had cancer; Anthony Perkins believed himself blessed with AIDS; and cancer patients tend to be more optimistic than healthy folks.

The encouraging truth of the matter is that what we dread turns out to make us less unhappy, and for a shorter period of time, than we feared. (The discouraging news is that what we look forward to often turns out to make us less happy than we thought.)

Nancy Mairs is paralyzed from the waist down and has lost total control over one arm, partial over the other. She has fallen from her wheelchair and has been unable to get up, lying there until someone happened by. She cannot feed herself, and someone must dress her.

A fate worse than death? It seemed like that to us, but we were wrong. In *Waist-High in the World* she writes:

> *There are readers who need, for a tangle of reasons, to be told that a life commonly held to be insufferable can be full and funny. I am living that life. I can tell them.*

Growing old, commonly held to be insufferable, can be full and funny. Millions are living that life. They can tell you.

So don't lament. Studies have repeatedly shown that older folks are generally happier than younger ones; the odds are you will be, too.

Why not? You are free from the restraints of adulthood. You are no longer the teacher on the playground, you are yet again the kid. Free to sleep in, free to wear your trousers rolled, free to eat a peach, and free to disturb the universe (or perhaps, less grandly, the neighbors). Follow poet Jenny Joseph and go out in the rain with your slippers on, take flowers from other people's gardens, and "learn to spit."

But despite vitamins, aerobics, and spunk, there will come a time when we will slow down. That won't be so bad, either. In *The Brothers Karamazov*, an old man reflects:

> *The old grief, by a great mystery of human life, gradually passes into quiet, tender joy; instead of young, ebullient blood comes a mild, serene old age; I bless the sun's rising each day and my heart sings as before, but now I love the setting even more, its long slanting rays, and with them, mild, tender memories, dear images for the whole of a long and blessed life.*

CHAPTER 4

IDENTITY THEFT AND SCAMS

It's a haggard, frazzled, despondent Tarzan who swings up to his tree house. "Jane, I need a drink. It's a jungle out there."

After chapters on stroke, angst, and death, you will no doubt rejoice in a chapter on how people are, as we speak, hatching clever plots to steal everything you worked for. Although not of cosmic proportions, identity theft and scams fit nicely into our Parade of Woes that you need train for. While you can't stop "time's winged chariots hurrying near," you can slow down cheats. If only they had real jobs.

Crooks count on us taking our lumps, blaming ourselves, "I must be getting senile. I don't want anyone to know how stupid I was. I'll just take my lumps." Realize this: you are not alone. Graduates of Harvard's Business School, by their own reckoning quite brilliant, get taken just as us people on the pavement do. The only difference is that they get taken for a whole lot more.

a. Identity Theft and Credit Reports

To protect your identity, take time to smell the roses, march to a different drummer, do it your way, don't sell out to Corporate America to become one of those faceless men and women in grey flannel suits. (Oops: wrong book, wrong decade.)

To protect your identity:

Right now: Look in your wallet or purse. If you find your Social Security Card, you bad. Take it out and store it in a safe place. Cancel unnecessary credit cards.

If you shop online, use credit cards, not debit cards (which put your entire bank account at risk). Buy a shredder (they're not just for corporations and politicians). Keep important documents (tax records) in locked files. (In addition to huge multi-national corporations, identity thieves may be relatives, colleagues, visitors or, we kid you not, plumbers!)

Get a locked mailbox. As to your Social Security Number, forget it (the upside of Senior Moments). Short of that, if a business asks you for it, ask to use other identification. Check your credit card bills. Under the Federal Fair Credit Billing Act, you have 60 days to report billing errors, including unauthorized charges, situations where the goods or services were not delivered or accepted, clerical errors, and failure to indicate payments made.

Check your *bank statements* when they come in. Under the Uniform Commercial Code, if you report a forgery within 30 days after you receive your statement, the *bank will pick up the loss*. After 30 days, the bank need not pick up the loss unless you can prove that it was negligent. This will be an uphill fight.

Credit Reports. Identity thieves, once they have your Social Security number and other information, will open credit accounts in your name (but not with your address), run up big bills and, unless they are very new to the game, neglect to pay them. These false accounts will show up on your credit report.

Your credit report will show all of the accounts in your name with outstanding balances. You are entitled to a free credit report per year; if you are clever, you can get three. The *only* website authorized by the government to fill orders for your free credit report is www.annualcreditreport.com. (Avoid other sensible-sounding websites like freecreditreport.com.)

The law requires *each* of the three nationwide consumer reporting agencies to provide you with one free credit report per year. Go to www.annualcreditreport.com and *(after* you indicate your state but *not* before), select one of the reporting choices: Equifax; TransUnion, or Experian. They will try to head you off into buying something, like your *credit rating* or email alerts. Keep going, unless you are convinced, and eventually you will get to your free credit report. Check for fake accounts. Four months later, repeat with a different choice.

Once you have done all this, you are entitled to take some time to smell the flowers. Then come back to learn about popular scams.

b. Internet Scams

Scams enlist the little larceny in everyone's heart.

Dear Sir or Madam. You have been referred to me by a Distinguished and Most Honorable friend. I know that you too are Most Distinguished and Most Honorable. My father was the treasurer of a small

*African country that you and no one else has heard of. He was mur-
dered most foul by ugly rebels shouting lies about corruption. Lies, all
lies. Before his death most foul he was able to deposit $25 million (U.S.)
in a Swiss bank. Honorable American friend, a land I have always
loved. I need your help in getting that money before it falls into the
hands of the ugly rebels most foul. If you help me I will give you half.
Please answer this email.*

Answer it and you will discover that either you must send money to cover as-
sorted costs (brides for unruly warlords) or that, more simply, you need only
send your bank information to facilitate the transfer. Once you are in a little,
these people keep coming at you for more. We know one university professor
who has lost tens of thousands of dollars. (We hasten to add, a Professor of
English, not Law.)

Scams play on your fears.

*Alert from Chase Bank Security. Third parties have attempted to access
your account. We will have to suspend your access to your accounts, unless you send us, immediately, your Social Security number, your account
and PIN numbers, your date of birth, your mother's maiden name, and
your favorite flavor of ice cream.*

This is known as "*phishing*" for your credit card and other financial information. The bait comes in many forms: "alerts," "updates for your credit
union," "unauthorized activity warnings," "immediate cancellation of your
trading privileges." Scammers write much more believable prose than we do
(that's why we had to take day jobs). Their emails look quite official and
some purport to be from the U.S. Government. Some even repeat the information we provide here, and offer easy links to check your credit report
or your online account security. Those links do not take the gullible victim
where they say they will, and soon personal information is in the hands of
thieves.

It is easy to be fooled and the scammers don't need to fool many. Charities that send out solicitation letters do very well if they get a 3% response:
if you are sending zillions of email at virtually no cost, you need very few
bites.

No bank, seller, financial institution, or governmental agency *will ever send
you an email requesting that you respond by giving them financial information.*

Another internet fraud (don't these people ever sleep?) involves "hot stock"
tips. You get an unsolicited email, touting a very lower price stock which is
about to "take off," "explode," "go through the roof." These schemers buy cheap

stocks, send out their emails to drive the price up, and then dump their holdings, collapsing the price. Enron Light.

c. "You've won!"

A cartoon shows a hotdog next to his mailbox. He is reading a letter. "Congratulations, you may already be a wiener."

It has been said that the chances of winning a state lottery or Powerball are the same whether you buy a ticket or not. (The odds of winning the Powerball jackpot are 1 in 146.1 million which means that, if you bought 73,050,000 lottery tickets, it would be even money that you would *still* lose, and, even if you won, good luck finding the ticket!)

You receive a letter or email announcing that you won $2,000 in the Canadian lottery. In your excitement you skip over the fact that you didn't enter the Canadian lottery. No matter. All you have to do is send back $200 to process the award. The letter may even contain a very official-looking cashier's check in the amount of $2,000, but, you are instructed, to cash it you must first wire back the $200. The check is phoney.

Or you may be asked to send your bank account information so that your winnings can be wired directly to your account. If you do, you will be cleaned out.

If you haven't entered a lottery, a vacation contest, or a "new car" drawing, you ain't going to win.

d. Home Repair Scams

A friendly man, whom you might mistake for Will Rogers, comes to your door to offer a free inspection of your roof, or perhaps your heating system. Tell him *"no thanks."*

Dollars to donuts he will find that you need a new roof, or a new furnace, which of course, he can supply.

A particularly repulsive variation of this scam is recounted in Mario Puzo's *The Godfather*. After tearing the furnace apart, the burly repairmen would explain "It's broke. Pay us $500 and we will fix it and put it back together. Otherwise, we're out of here."

"An offer I cannot refuse." This did not set off the necessary bells: they were talking to the Godfather. "I will go get the money."

He did not return. His henchmen did. Every now and then, simple justice!

Folks may claim to be city or county inspectors. After inspecting they find violations that need to be repaired immediately. *Don't let them in your house.* No government official has a right to enter your home without a *search warrant.* (That was what the American Revolution was about—that, and if we recall correctly, tea.) Take their card and phone the city to see if they are for real. If they are for real, they can come back.

e. Home Mortgage Scams; Bill Payer Loans

Targeting cash-strapped seniors, crooks offer loans which seem too good to be true, requiring only low monthly payments. *Don't bite.* Many have lost their homes, others fell into a spiral of increasing debt. Lower payments do not mean lower interest; they mean a longer time paying back the loan, a longer time your house will be at risk. If you get behind, you may be forced to refinance at still higher interest rates or risk losing your home when the lender forecloses. These are not nice people.

Loan offers may come door-to-door, by mail or through the internet. While first mortgages, those that finance the purchase of your home, are extensively regulated, second mortgages, home improvement loans, and home equity accounts are much less regulated. This gives crooks their opening. If you have to borrow against your home, risky even in the best of times, always use reputable, established banks: folks who have been in town a long time. It is always best to have any loan or mortgage agreements reviewed by someone independent, such as an attorney. On getting money out of your house, see Chapter 9.

Bill Payer Loans should be avoided. Sure, they consolidate your debt and lower your monthly payments. What's not to like? First, they lower your payments by extending the length of the loan and hence the time you will be paying interest. Overall you will pay more than you would sticking with your old creditors. Second, they may take a security interest in your home. Most of the folks you owe money to (credit cards, doctors) are *unsecured creditors* which means they can't take your house; secured creditors can.

f. Annuity Scams

With an annuity you give the financial institution a bundle of money and it agrees to pay you a certain monthly amount for either a term of years or for life. Many financial advisors believe annuities stink; they *really* stink in the case of seniors. Of course, they sound good when they are pitched: guaranteed monthly payments sound terrific. Some presenters use blackboards so that their promises and projections can be simply erased when the meeting is over.

Don't buy annuities. At most they offer security. If you are risk-averse, buy treasury notes. Given all of the hidden charges with annuities, treasury notes may actually pay more; in any event, you can get your money when you need it. With annuities, you will have a hard and expensive time getting your money out to cover emergencies.

g. Income Scams

The pitch here is that you can earn substantial amounts, usually in your spare time, often from the convenience of your own home. Of course, to show your good faith, or to help offset some of the costs, an investment on your part is required. Be leery. Postal officials claim that they are not aware *of one* of these offers that actually lives up to its claims of profits. Not one!

Higher end investment frauds include franchising and distributorship frauds. Under a franchise agreement, an individual gets the right to distribute the franchiser's product or service in a local area. In return, the individual (the franchisee) pays fees and, usually, purchases equipment and supplies from the franchiser. These are common in fast-food restaurants, vacation and travel agencies, and other service agencies. Distributorships are quite similar, involving an individual purchasing the right to distribute certain products, such as vending machines, in particular areas.

Many of these are great investment opportunities, *but go slowly*! Hundreds have been bilked out of their life savings in phony or shaky franchise and distributorship deals. The Federal Trade Commission requires that, as a potential investor, you be given a great deal of information. Contact it.

h. Investment Scams

We've already seen some of these in "super stock tips" over the internet. You may get them over the phone as well. Here we deal with the infamous *Ponzi Scheme*.

The brilliant thing about Ponzi schemes is that the crook does not immediately run off with your money. In fact, he gives it back to you, often doubled. It begins with a plausible plan to make money. In the 1930's, Ponzi claimed he could make huge profits trading foreign currencies across the international dateline. Sounds good to us. The mark (that's you) was asked to invest, usually not much. Ponzi did not simply get on a boat and leave. In a few days, he would come to the mark:

"Here is your investment. Doubled. Thanks."

"Wait! Wait! Keep my money. Here's some more. I want to reinvest."

The money was what other people invested. After thousands had invested, Ponzi took the boat.

i. Obituary Scams

Reading the obituaries, cheats send fake bills to the decedent hoping the family will pay. Often they are for pornography. As we advise in our chapter on death in the family, don't pay any of the decedent's bills until the immediate crisis has passed.

j. Health Care Scams

Apricot pits don't cure cancer, Compound Q doesn't cure AIDS, and Snake Oil doesn't cure much of anything. Fraudulent cures cost money, may delay an actual cure through traditional medicine, and may kill you.

No matter your ailment, from cancer to wrinkles, from alcoholism to ulcers, someone will offer you a cure. The American Medical Association advises extreme caution if the cure is claimed to be quick and easy or that it involves a "secret" formula or machine to cure disease. Some scammers even try to sell their product by claiming that the health care industry and the government are conspiring to suppress it.

Before taking any new form of medicine, at least talk to your pharmacist! *Drugs can interact in bad ways.* You can also get advice from local offices of the American Medical Association, the American Dental Association, the American Cancer Society, the Arthritis Foundation or similar organizations.

Be leery of the word "natural." Without getting into a philosophic discussion of what is natural (and the fallacy that "natural must be good" — cancer is natural), just realize that before a drug is approved by the FDA, it goes through millions of dollars worth of tests, looking for side effects and effectiveness.

"Natural remedies" generally have not been tested for either effectiveness or side effects. Personal testimonials mean little because you don't know (1) whether anything was ever wrong with the person; (2) whether what was wrong with them is wrong with you; and (3) even if they got better, why they got better; it could have been for a host of other reasons.

k. Timeshare Scams

If you have a timeshare you wish to sell, be cautious of ads that seem to promise that they will sell it for you. There is often a substantial "listing fee" involved; and, we hate to tell you, the market for timeshares is not strong.

l. The Nibblers: Phone Solicitations, Door-to-Door Sales, Home Shopping Channels

Telephone Fraud

Consumers are bilked to the tune of $40 billion annually by telemarketing scams. (Again, you're not alone.) If you haven't already, get on the Do Not Call List: www.donotcall.gov.; 1-888-382-1222, TTY 1-866 290 4236.

Charities can still get through. If you are interested in contributing, it's best to say, "I never contribute over the phone. Send me some literature."

Remember the following points:

- Never agree to make a purchase or give money on the first call. Insist on thinking it over. Resist the "Limited time" offer. Legitimate sellers will give you time to think.
- Never give your credit card number to a caller.
- No one *ever* wins a free trip to Hawaii.

Door-to-Door Sales (and Three-day Cooling-off Period)

What do you know about door-to-door purchases?

- Before you answered the door, you didn't even know you needed the product.
- You have little idea as to what is a fair price or as to whether competing models have better features. (*Consumer Reports* would come in handy.)
- You don't know anything about the seller or even where to find him if the product never gets there or breaks when it does.

As to the "substantial savings" you get because the seller doesn't have to maintain a retail store or engage in advertising, the commission structure on door-to-door sales offsets these amounts. Salesmen pocket a large part of the purchase price.

Bottom line: *never,* well almost never, buy from door-to-door sellers. (Two thumbs up, however, for Girl Scout Cookies.)

If you do purchase from a door-to-door seller, you have *three days* to cancel the sale under a rule of the Federal Trade Commission. You have the right to cancel any *credit* purchase (as opposed to *cash* purchase) *for any reason you want.* This rule applies even though the goods have been delivered to you. You simply have to write the seller by midnight of the third business day after the contract was signed. The seller must give you a "notice of cancellation" to use for this purpose. (Some dishonest sellers won't give you this.)

The cooling-off period does *not* apply to cash purchases, internet sales, sales that were first discussed at the seller's place of business, telephone orders, mail orders, or emergency home repairs.

Most states have statutes which parallel the federal rule.

"Home Shopping" Channels

Here the problem is not getting cheated; it is spending too much. "Those nice folks on TV seem to be talking to me; and when I call them, they do." If your parent or spouse continues to overspend, phone their 1-800 number and follow up with a letter.

> *Please be advised that my mother is 83 and has made several substantial purchases from you which she does not need. She no longer has contractual capacity. From this time on, I will refuse to allow her to pay you on credit card charges. When the bill comes, I will dispute it by enclosing a copy of this letter to you.*

m. If You've Been Cheated

The main thing these crooks count on is that you will simply blame yourself and do nothing. Our advice: scream!

Start with the Consumer Affairs Office of your state's Attorney General's Office or that of your County Attorney's Office. If they can't help, they can point you on your way; there are a plethora of laws and agencies that might be involved: State Unfair and Deceptive Practices Laws; Section 5 of the Federal Trade Commission Act; U.S. Post Office (mail fraud); FDA (foods and drugs); Securities Exchange Commission (stock and bond frauds).

Consider a lawyer. Laws prohibiting consumer fraud may give victims not only the right to get their money back, but also to sue for money damages, punitive damages and statutory penalties. Attorney fees may be recoverable if you win. Even if you were not cheated out of a great deal of money, a lawyer might take your case if a lot of other people were also cheated by the same person or company: class actions are possible.

If the amount is small, consider filing a complaint in *Small Claims Court*. The forms are easy to fill out and you don't need a lawyer. You just go to court and tell your side of the story and the other side does likewise. Then the judge rules. On your way out, you stand before a TV camera and are asked what you think of the judge's decision. (Oops, wrong show.)

The main point of all of this is—Scream!

> *"Hello. Office of Consumer Fraud. May I help you?"*
> *"Yes, I've been cheated."*
> *"Sorry, you will have to wait. I have three Harvard MBA's on hold."*

PART 2

LET THE GOOD TIMES ROLL: RETIREMENT

MONEY, HOUSING, MEDICAL CARE

Introduction

We have only two questions: How should we live?
What should we do?

Tolstoy

Law doesn't answer the important questions, but it helps. No matter *how* we choose to live, no matter *what* we decide to do, there will *always* be tax consequences.

Chapter 5 is an overview to retirement. There is some good news in terms of health, housing, working, volunteering or simply sitting back and smelling the flowers.

If you are already retired you can safely skip Chapter 6 (*Social Security*) unless you are raising your grandkids, as they might be entitled to benefits. Chapter 7 deals with *pension plans* and will be helpful if you have yet to retire.

Even if you are already retired, and surely if you are still considering retirement, take a look at the remaining chapters in this section:

Chapter 8: Retirement Finances
You'll have less income and some new expenses, mostly in the area of medical care and insurance. Should you keep your life insurance? What about withdrawals from IRA's and the exciting new possibility of converting your IRA's into Roth IRA's? We'll discuss investment options as well.

Chapter 9: House Rich, Cash Poor
How can you get cash out of your house without selling it? There are several methods, including *reverse mortgages* where the *bank pays you* a monthly payment. We'll also look at the options of renting or selling your house. We have some great news in terms of capital gain taxes.

Chapter 10: Retirement Housing
Should you join us in the Southwest? The issue may be getting help in your own home or moving to an *assisted-housing* facility. We look at the options and consider pros and cons. Nursing homes are discussed in Chapter 33.

Chapter 11: Medicare and Health Insurance
What are your insurance needs before the magical year of Medicare Eligibility (65)? After 65, there is *Medicare*. What does it cover? More importantly, from a planning perspective, what *doesn't* it cover? Should you get additional insurance or join a new Medicare HMO? What about drug coverage? We close with some tips on buying insurance.

Chapter 12: Long-Term Care
Long-term custodial care can trigger major financial problems. We will discuss a relatively new form of insurance: long-term care insurance. We will also look at the federal *Medicaid* Program—which does pay for long-term care—and how you might make yourself eligible without first bankrupting your family. This is sometimes referred to as *Medicaid Planning*.

Chapter 13: Tax Breaks for Seniors
You (and your children) may be missing some benefits. Discover just one and you have more than paid for this book.

CHAPTER 5

Retirement: An Overview

"How's retirement going?"
"Wonderful. I absolutely love it."
"Keeping busy?"
"Busier than ever."
"What do you do?"
"Well, let's see. I get up, have coffee. Read the paper. Go for a walk.
Maybe an afternoon movie."

We have spent a lifetime accomplishing things.

"What did you do today?"
"Took to the kids to soccer. Got them into college. Engineered a hostile
takeover of NBC."

Never:

"What did you do today?"
"Not much of anything. I had a marvelous time."

Retirement will require a major shift in our thinking, a major shift in how we see ourselves in the world.

In Chapter 1, *Training for Ill*, we discussed the possibility that, during retirement, existential angst might actually be real. (Remember the salad days of Philosophy 101 and the wondrous times lamenting the essential tragedy of life with friends, music and etcetera?)

To cope with retirement angst, we recommended that you sit right down and write yourself a letter: "These are some of the things I can do during my retirement." (Put a lotta kisses on the bottom; you'll be glad you got 'em.) In addition there are books filled with good ideas for successful retirement, mostly written by driven and compulsive folks who have *never* taken time to smell the flowers, but who hope, as do we, to retire on their royalties. Be care-

ful, though; most of our peers report that they find themselves busier in retirement than they ever were in their careers. How can this be true? It may be
a result of planning to do too much, flush with the excitement of having nothing that must be done.

Before we discuss your basic choices (work, go into business, volunteer, or
simply smell the flowers), some common questions and fears about retirement.

a. Questions about Retirement

1. When can I retire?

You can begin drawing Social Security at 62 and under many pension plans,
you can retire well before then. On the other hand, if you go on working after
62—or simply delay drawing on your Social Security, even though you may
be "retired"—every year you work (until the age of 70) will increase your Social Security benefits and your benefits under most pension plans. *Mandatory
retirement is illegal* in most occupations. See Chapter 21-f.

2. How much income will I need?

To maintain your pre-retirement life-style, as a rule of thumb, you'll need
pretax retirement income equaling about *70 to 80 percent* of your pretax working income.

Expenses go down: no more saving, no more college tuition, and no more
work expenses (work clothes, business lunches and Mylanta). One expense
that will go *up* is medical insurance even after you are eligible for Medicare at
age 65.

We'll spend a lot of time in chapters that follow discussing the financial side
of retirement: Social Security, pension plans, getting money out of your
house, and financial planning and budgeting.

3. How about medical insurance?

Medicare is a marvelous program providing for hospital care and doctor's
visits, plus some of the costs of drugs and medical supplies. However, *you will
not be eligible for Medicare* until you are 65 and thus medical insurance may
be a major expense if you retire before then (and lose your employment-based
medical coverage). As we will indicate later, you will probably be able to keep

up your insurance from work to cover you before you turn 65 but only by paying a premium—possibly a hefty one.

Medicare, the basic Medicare, known as Part A, does *not cover* many routine medical expenses such as doctor's visits and prescriptions. You'll have to buy additional insurance or enroll in an HMO. There are many choices and we describe them in Chapter 11.

4. What about housing?

Many move to more forgiving climates—here or abroad—and may buy into Retirement Communities. There are both legal and emotional ramifications of such moves as well as substantial risks which we will discuss in Chapter 10.

As we get older, health and medical concerns must be considered in relation to housing. We'll look at making your own house safer or moving into a Continuing Care Retirement Community.

b. Retirement Fears

Death is on the doorstep.

Most people will spend *15 to 19 years in retirement.* That's a lot of time; consider that in your first 15 to 19 years, you learned to walk, you learned to talk, you got acne, you cursed your fate, and, if you were one of the lucky ones, got a date.

Current Life Expectancies

Age	Men	Women
50	26.0 more years	31.0 more years
55	21.9	26.7
60	8.2	22.5
65	14.8	18.7

I will get sick.

A recent study: 37% of retirees showed no change in their health; *40% got better.*

And you haven't been reading the daily newspaper if you are unaware of the numerous studies showing the remarkable benefits of physical exercise programs. These programs can be started anytime—except tomorrow.

I will get senile.

Senility is not a disease. It is a symptom of different medical conditions, many of which are *treatable*. We discuss this in Chapter 29.

Retirement will create a void. Working keeps us on our mental toes. Science shows that our *minds*, as well as our biceps, *need exercise.*

Take classes at community colleges. Learn a new language. Work crosswords.

There are now "adult" computer games which tax the intellect (not to be confused with those "adult" games that tax other parts of the anatomy).

For couch potatoes all of this means both bad news and good news: the bad news is that they'll get fat; the good news is that they won't realize it!

Now let's return to our existential choices.

c. Working, Opening a Bookstore, Tax Implications

- Folks who continue to work part-time are healthier than those who don't.
- Mental abilities tend to remain strong if used; by continuing to learn new things, memory is improved. (We have said this before. True or False?)
- Retirement jobs can be *more fun* because they are *less filling* (who cares if you don't get promoted).

Dare to eat a peach! No need to do the same old stuff. Raise chickens. Teach children. Rob trains. We're kidding about that last one, of course—trains no longer carry much wealth, so you'll have to rob espresso bars, where the real money is.

Getting a job. Small companies are best. They are more flexible in terms of working conditions and in recognizing and using your talents and experiences. However, some large companies go out of their way to hire seniors (they tend to show up).

Some jobs take *advance planning*. Learn the computer. Many consider "going into teaching". Teaching certificates are required for public school teaching. Community colleges, elder hostels and other community education programs may welcome you with open arms. Teach a class on contract bridge; teach kids to weld.

If you have a hard time finding work, then maybe you have been discriminated against because of your age. Age discrimination in employment is generally illegal. See Chapter 21.

Starting your own business.

"They see the bookstore, but not the inventory."

Joe Tolstoy, Leo's Great Grandson

While this is not a book of literary criticism, we think that young Tolstoy's deep meaning is that running a bookstore is a whole lot more complicated than simply talking with teary customers about their favorite romance novel.

Look before you leap. Opening a business is *risky*. You can lose your life's savings. Unless you are a corporation, or flee to Brazil, you will be personally liable for the debts your business runs up. And, despite what you may think, opening a restaurant is risky, even if you went to cooking school.

Be leery of retirement work *scams*. Folks selling *franchises* and *home work opportunities* make their money selling to *you*. Sharks circle, offering exciting, *can't miss*, big buck opportunities. Work at home! Open your own franchise!

Ask for references—people who have already invested. In retirement you cannot afford the risk of losing your shirt.

Of course, it always *costs* money to get into the business, either to buy supplies or to show "commitment," but be very suspicious of any *opportunity* that costs you to get in.

Never, ever cash in your retirement or your savings to invest in a business unless you are very, very sure. Run opportunities past your most cynical and pessimistic friends or past a professional well trained in both attributes, i.e. your lawyer. Even if everyone tells you to take the chance, wonder why they are not putting *their* money into the sure thing.

Get disinterested advice. The person offering you the opportunity is *never* disinterested. That person is a salesman. If they have a secret way of always making money in real estate, don't you think that they would be doing it?

SCORE, the Service Corps of Retired Executives can put you in touch with people who have "been there" and "done that".

Tax Implications of Working. If you retire before your "full retirement age" (65 to 67, depending on your age), the amounts you earn over $12,480 (as of 2006) will be subject to a rather stiff tax: a reduction in your Social Security check of $1 for every $2 you earn until you reach your full retirement age. We'll go through the painful details in the next chapter.

d. Volunteering or smelling the flowers

George Bernard Shaw wasn't one to sit on the sidelines:

> *I am of the opinion that my life belongs to the whole community and as long as I live, it is my privilege to do for it what I can. I want to be thoroughly **used up** when I die, for the harder I work, the more I will live. I rejoice in life for its own sake. Life is no brief candle for me. It is sort of a splendid torch which I have got hold of for a moment and I want to make it burn as brightly as possible before handing it on to future generations.*

Wow! That's why he's George Bernard Shaw. (At the opening of one of his plays, answering the call "Author! Author!" Shaw came out to take a bow. Thunderous applause. After several minutes, it began to die down. A guy in the front row was then heard booing. Shaw acknowledged him, "Sir, I quite agree with you. But who are we two against all the others?)

There is a lot to be said for Shaw's approach. Helping others, being of service, is deeply human. Many tell us that their volunteer work is the most rewarding of their lifetime. And it needn't be full-time!

You have a lifetime of experience. Many in your community could use it. Most locales have *Volunteer Clearing Houses*. In addition there is the RSVP (Retired Senior Volunteer Program) in nearly every community. You really can make an important difference in the lives of children, seniors, shut-ins and others in all sorts of programs in your area.

And we're not talking about your specialized knowledge. Sure, even if the good folks of McCallsburg, Iowa, have no need of a hostile take-over specialist, if you can drive a car you may find opportunities to transport seniors who can't. Contact *beverlyfoundation.org*. Or you can help kids learn how to read. Contact *experiencecorps.org*. We hope you get the idea: there are lots of folks who need your help regardless of what your training and experience might have suited you for, or failed to suit you for, prior to retirement.

The best place to start is at your local *Area Agency on Aging.* There are over 650 such offices throughout the United States; every community is served by one because it is required under the Older Americans Act. In fact, there are all sorts of good things going on at your Area Agency on Aging, and throughout this book we will refer you again and again to this wonderful agency.

Gail Sheehy, in *New Passages*, calls the years between 45 and 85 a "Second Adulthood" and details many of the exciting possibilities once the responsibilities and worries of one's "First Adulthood" are gone. As she points out, many do their best work after the age of 60, including Winston Churchill, Earl

Warren and Ronald Reagan. Grandma Moses gave up embroidery in her 70s because of arthritis, and took up painting. You may have heard of the favorable results.

But don't expect contentment to drop in your lap! Retirement is hard work. We cannot stress enough the need to confront and overcome your fears about aging. We have had many clients who just gave up. Soon what they feared became a self-fulfilling prophecy. Alcoholism and depression are common (and often confused by relatives as senility).

Robert Louis Stevenson wrote:

> *The world is so full of a number of things,*
> *I'm sure we should all be as happy as kings.*

If you're not, get out a pen and start writing about how to have a terrific retirement. You may get a novel out of it and, yes, more tax consequences.

CHAPTER 6

SOCIAL SECURITY

a. Important Tidbits

- If you are working and become disabled, you may be entitled to disability benefits under Social Security. If you die before retirement age, your family may be entitled to monthly payments.
- Family members may be entitled to monthly payments when you retire.
- Divorcees who are not eligible for their own Social Security may sometimes qualify based on their ex-spouse's work history.
- You need 40 calendar quarters of work history to qualify for retirement benefits (fewer for disability, depending on how old you are when you become disabled). If you are close, try to get the 40 quarters; while you may not get a big retirement check, you will be eligible for Medicare (otherwise it will cost you a bundle.)

All of this, and much, much more, will be explained, in painful detail.

b. Social Security: Contents and Discontents

Social Security, child of the Great Depression, folks selling apples, losing farms, praying that things wouldn't get worse. Franklin Roosevelt is elected President and reassures the nation *"The only thing we have to fear is Fear itself."*

Social Security has prospered.

- The poverty rate among folks over 65 is no longer 70% as it was before Social Security; it is now 12% (about the same rate for people under 65).
- 90% of retired folks draw benefits.

- Of those drawing benefits, 65% receive more than half of their income from Social Security.
- In addition to retirement benefits, Social Security protects young folks by providing both life and disability insurance.
- Its administrative costs are about *1%* (compared to around 15% for private pension plans).

The bad news: monthly benefits are low. Social Security was *never intended* to be a full retirement plan. In fact, at the time it was passed, most folks died before reaching retirement age of 65, and planners of that day loved to talk about the "three-legged stool" of retirement—with private wealth and individual pensions intended to provide the two strongest legs of the stool.

Benefits are calculated so that lower income workers receive a higher percentage return than do higher earners. Workers who have earned only half the national average will receive about 56% of their average salary, average workers about 42%, while folks at the high end typically get about 28%.

For a comfortable retirement you should arrange to earn about 70% or 80% of your pre-retirement income, not 56%, 42%, or 28%. It is a *serious mistake* to think that Social Security will maintain your standard of living.

If you aren't making ends meet, *Supplemental Security Income (SSI)* pays additional benefits to people who are 65 or older (or blind or disabled), *and* have very limited income and property. See Section (i) in this Chapter. Also consider Veterans' Benefits, Section (h).

And we all know that Social Security is *going broke*. Well, it isn't. And not for a long time. Currently Social Security is *making* money—collecting more from workers than it pays to retirees. It is financed by a payroll tax of 12.4% on the first $94,200 of earnings (split between worker and employer). (Medicare payroll tax is an additional 1.45% with no wage cap.)

In *2017*, give or take, Social Security will begin to *lose* money, paying out more than it collects. However it will still have an initial surplus of $3.3 trillion.

> *Big numbers like $3.3 billion are essentially meaningless. We have no idea what they mean, only that they are a lot. Why not, after say 100,000, just one number: "lotsa"—"The moon is lotsa miles from the earth" "McDonald's has sold lotsa hamburgers."*

If the lotsa surplus is actually *there* at the breakeven year, Social Security will remain solvent for another decade or so. (We will see why the money might not be there in a moment.)

Why will Social Security begin to lose money? The number of workers paying into Social Security, compared to the number of retirees taking from Social Security, is falling—from 5 to 1 in 1960, to 3.3 to 1 in 2006, to 2.1 to 1 in 2031. This is because folks are living longer *and* because the birth rate is falling. Note that the worker/dependent ratio is not as stark as it may first appear—with falling birth rates, current workers, while supporting more retirees, support fewer kids.

Where is the lotsa surplus? Not under the President's pillow. It's in government bonds (government IOU's). Currently Social Security can *only* put its surplus in government bonds. The government uses this money for other programs; the fear is that when the time comes, in 2017 perhaps, the federal government will not be able to pay back the money it has borrowed from Social Security, or will have to raise other taxes, or cut other programs to do so.

Bottom line: today there are 48 million recipients; in 2030, an anticipated 83 million. Solutions to the crisis are the stuff of daily newspaper editorials and Presidential Commissions: raise social security taxes, reduce benefits, raise the retirement age, allow for *privatization,* either by allowing individuals to invest some of their Social Security dollars in the stock market *or* by allowing the Social Security Trust Fund to play the market. One objection to privatization is that politics, rather than financial judgments, may dictate investment decisions.

Currently there is a general political attack on "entitlements." Some attempt to foment generational hostility by convincing younger workers that Social Security will not be there for them and that, while they toil, retirees play golf in Florida. That image, besides being unfair and inaccurate, misses several other points.

The cost of caring for the elderly will not go away. Shift it from Social Security and it falls on sons and daughters, or the elderly will return to poverty and government welfare benefits.

Besides, Social Security is not just retirement benefits. Of the more than 48 million currently receiving benefits, one-fourth are the families of workers who have died or become disabled.

However, we have come to praise Social Security, not to solve it. Solutions are, as we academics (who haven't a clue) like to say, "beyond our scope." The nitty-gritty isn't.

c. Eligibility and Computation of Benefits

You must have paid into the system for *40 calendar quarters* (generally a *ten-year* work history). These quarters need not be continuous. Some government work is not covered by Social Security, nor are some forms of private capitalistic endeavor, such as drug dealing (reason enough to go straight).

Every year, about three months before your birthday, you will be sent a statement estimating your monthly retirement amount, and indicating what you have contributed in prior years and what benefits your relatives may be entitled to. And you can get one by calling *(1-800-537-7005)* or requesting one on the Internet: http://www.ssa.gov.

Check that your wages have been reported correctly. This is important as benefits are calculated on your earnings. Generally you have *3 years* to make corrections—but if you find that an employer simply didn't report any income, you can have this corrected at any time.

How does Social Security compute your benefits? Pretty much this way:

> *A train leaves New York going West at 60 mph. Two hours and 13 minutes later, another train leaves Los Angeles going East, at 62 mph. What is the capital of Nova Scotia?*

The basic idea is to figure out how much your *average monthly salary* was while you were working and then give you a *percentage of that figure*. It is assumed that you worked *35 years*: your total earning will be spread out over this period. Some really good news: the calculation of your earnings history is adjusted for current average earning levels, so that your thirty-year-old income may be multiplied by somewhere between 5 and 7 in determining your work history. Even though you will be *eligible* for Social Security after 40 quarters, *the longer you work and the more you earn, the greater will be your benefit.*

The key figure is *Primary Insurance Amount (PIA)*, the monthly amount you will receive at *full* retirement. If you retire early, you'll get less; if you retire late, you'll do better.

d. Early, Late, and Full Retirement

When you reach your "full retirement age" you will receive your full PIA. What is your full retirement age? It is going up.

Year of Birth	Full Retirement Age
Before 1938	65 yrs
1938	65 yrs and two months
1939	65 yrs and four months
1940 (Year of the Dragon)	65 yrs and six months
1941	65 yrs and eight months
1942	65 yrs and 10 months
1943–1954	66 yrs

After 1954, it goes up two months every year until, if you were born after 1959, your full retirement age will be 67. *Put another way*: if you turned 65 before 2004, that birthday was your "full retirement" age. If you will turn 66 between 2009 and 2020, or turn 67 after 2026, those birthdays will be your "full retirement" age. For everyone else, you get full retirement benefits on a day other than your birthday.

Early Retirement

You can retire at 62 and get a monthly check. *There are prices to be paid.*

You still won't be eligible for Medicare. You have to wait until 65, so your health insurance will still be a concern. Under a program called *COBRA* you will be able to continue your employer's health insurance but you must pay the premium. See Chapter 11 for more details.

Your monthly check will be a little lighter. If you retire at 62 (the earliest age you can begin receiving benefits), there will be a *permanent* reduction of *25% to 30%* in your monthly benefits. The reason for the range of reductions: although the full retirement age creeps up by two years over the next two decades, the *early* retirement age does not change. The retirement benefit reduction may sound like a lousy deal, but remember: you will be getting those checks, albeit smaller ones, for a longer period. The closer you retire to your retirement age, the less will be the reduction.

Your earnings from outside work will incur a penalty. There will be a rather stiff tax on amounts you earn over $11,280. Your Social Security check will be reduced $1 for every $2 you earn over that amount until your full retirement age (the benefit reduction ends when you reach that magical age of full retirement).

Before taking early retirement from Social Security, check its impact on your private pension plan. Some private pension plans have what is known as an *integration of benefits* clause which operates to *reduce your pension payments* in light of what you receive from Social Security. Depending on the rate of reduction, it might be well to delay taking Social Security as long as possible.

On the other hand, there may be *financial incentives to retire early*. If you have a *child under 18* or *a spouse over 62*, when you retire *they can begin* drawing benefits from your Social Security. This may increase your family take by as much as 150% to 180% of your monthly benefit.

Even if you do not begin drawing a Social Security check at age 65, *you are still eligible* for Medicare at that age. If you go on working after age 65, you can increase your monthly check at the time of your eventual retirement. If you wait until 70 to begin drawing your benefits, your checks may be between

24% and 27.5% higher. After the age of 70, there will be no further increase in benefits—virtue finally then becoming its own reward.

e. Income Taxes and Your Benefits

A portion of social security payments may be taxed as regular income. If you have no income other than Social Security, *none* of it is taxed. If you have substantial income (from all sources, including, alas, royalties—and also including nontaxable earnings like interest on municipal bonds), then up to 50% of your Social Security Benefits may be counted as income.

f. Family Benefits:
Spouses, Kids and Grandkids

The basic notion is that when you retire your income will go down. If you have a family to support, you will need more money. The following people can begin drawing benefits when you do:

Spouses. Your spouse, if 62 (or younger, if caring for one of your children under 16) can draw a benefit of up to half the amount of your monthly check. Of course, many spouses age 62 will qualify for Social Security in *their own right.* Social Security will automatically pay the higher of the two amounts. On your death, if your spouse survives you, he or she will be eligible to receive the full amount of your benefit. That may mean that on retirement your spouse qualifies for his or her own benefit because it is greater than one-half your retirement, but then get an increase to your retirement amount on your death. Be careful about explaining the incentives to your spouse.

Kids and Grandkids. Your unmarried and dependent kids (adopted, out-of-wedlock, whatever) under 18 (or 19 if still in high school) are entitled to draw up to one-half your monthly benefit. So too older *disabled* children, if they were disabled before they turned 22. *Grandchildren,* if they are "dependent" upon you, may also draw benefits.

Payments to these folks *will not* reduce your check. There is, however, a *family maximum*: the *combined* payments to your spouse/kids will *not be allowed to exceed 150% to 180% of your monthly payment.*

Finally, if you defer your retirement beyond 65, these folks *cannot* receive benefits until you do.

g. A Note to Divorcees

At the time of a divorce, the family's assets are divided. Pensions create problems. How do you divide something that has yet to mature? (We aren't talking about your ex-spouse; we're talking about his—or her—pension.) Divorce lawyers get rich figuring this one out.

Social Security has an automatic solution. As an ex-spouse, if you were married *at least ten years,* you are entitled to a benefit equal to one-half of his or her full retirement amount. You must be 62, or younger if you are providing care for a dependent minor.

Your take *doesn't* reduce your ex-spouse's check—Social Security ain't perfect.

h. Veteran's Benefits

In recognition of their service to the Country, the Federal Government has an extensive program of veteran benefits, including monthly compensation, pensions, medical and nursing home care, and support services in the home.

Most benefits are available only if you have seen active service and were not dishonorably discharged. Benefits are available if you have a service-connected disability or are low-income with a non-service-related disability. Spouses, dependent children and survivors may also draw benefits.

The Department of Veteran Affairs publishes a yearly edition of *Federal Benefits for Veterans and Dependents.* Local offices have copies, or you can obtain it online at http://www.va.gov

i. Safety Nets for Low Income Folks: SSI, Medicaid, and Help with Medicare Premiums

SSI stands for Supplemental Security Income, a program run by Social Security which pays monthly checks to the elderly, the blind, and to people with disabilities who don't have much income or property. If you are entitled to SSI, you usually get food stamps and Medicaid which helps pay hospital and doctor bills.

To qualify you must be 65 *or* blind *or* disabled (if blind or disabled, you are eligible at any age). Disability means a physical or mental problem that is expected to last at least a year or result in death, and that makes you unable to perform any "substantial gainful employment".

As of this writing, the base monthly payments are $603 for one individual and $904 for a couple if both are eligible. These amounts may be higher in some states or lower if you or your family has other income coming in.

Even if you are over 65 (or blind or disabled), to be eligible you cannot own much and cannot have too much income.

Property. Generally, personal items and the value of your home or car are not counted. Cash, bank accounts, stocks and bonds are counted. At this writing, for a single person, they cannot add up to over $2000; for a couple, $3000.

Income. Basically everything coming in is counted: Social Security, pensions, earnings, and even the value of food, clothing, and shelter that you receive. The amount of income you can have and still be eligible depends on the state where you live.

Call Social Security at

> 1-800-772-1213
> Hearing impaired: 1-800-325-0778

You should also ask these people about Medicaid and those programs that help low-income folks pay premiums for additional Medicare coverage, like payment of Medicare Part B (doctor visits) or Part D (prescription drug) premiums.

CHAPTER 7

PRIVATE PENSION PLANS

The powers not delegated to the United States by the Constitution, nor prohibited by it to the states, are reserved to the states respectively, or to the people. (10th Amendment, United States Constitution)

The federal government has the power to build post offices, make war, and, as we all know, grant letters of marque and reprisal. But the Constitution doesn't delegate pensions to the United States. So how come most pension plans are governed by Federal law?

What the federal government cannot do directly, it can do by way of Big Carrots and the Internal Revenue Code. If a business wants to deduct its contributions to pension plans, those plans must conform to Federal requirements. If the plans do, employee contributions are deductible from current income.

A rule of thumb about retirement accounts: *"Deduct now, pay later."* If money going into your pension fund was deductible from your income tax, when you draw it out, it will be taxed. This usually works well. When you are working, your income (and tax rate) is higher. "Deduct now, pay later" tends to even things out.

Compare this tax treatment to money you set aside in a savings account. As these were *post tax* dollars, when you take them out, they do *not* constitute income. Visualize yourself as an apple; the IRS cannot take two bites.

a. Pension Plans: Defined Benefit, Defined Contribution, 401(k) Plans

Pension plans vary a great deal. In general:

1. They favor, unlike Social Security, higher paid employees.
2. They favor long-term workers; the longer you work, the more you will get.
3. The normal retirement age is 65.

4. Your employer is obligated to give you a yearly statement of where you stand.

There are two kinds of basic pension plans.

Defined Benefit Plans

Under these plans, your retirement payments are based on a percentage of your earnings (usually the average of your last three to five years of work). The percentage goes up the longer you have worked, say 2% per year. If you have worked 30 years, you might get 60% of your average earnings over the last few years.

Defined Contribution Plans

Under these plans, retirement contributions are put in a retirement account. This amount is invested. If the investments do well, your retirement benefits will be high; if the investments do badly, you are in trouble.

In a defined *contribution* plan, the employee takes the risk of market variations; in a defined *benefit* plan, the employer takes the risk. It is also worth noting that contribution plans are not insured while benefit plans usually are.

401(k) Plans

These plans are like defined contribution plans, but give the employee somewhat more flexibility as there are no fixed contributions. The employer may match an employee's contributions up to a certain amount. 401(k) Plans can be risky. First, they depend on how well the investments do, and second, they are not insured. On the other hand, depending on the market, they can do much better than defined benefit plans.

Before Enron, companies could insist that all of one's 401(k) contributions went to buy stock in the parent company. Now more flexibility is allowed. In a word, *diversify.*

What type of plan should you have? You generally don't have much of a choice in the matter; you take the kind of plan your employer offers.

Assuming you are locked into your pension plan, what do you need to know?

1. *Before you retire*, you need to know if you are *vested*.
2. *When you retire*, you need to know your options on taking your money.
3. If there is *trouble*, you need to know where to look for help.

b. Vesting

If you have made contributions to your retirement account, you are entitled to get them back, no matter what, whether you were laid off, quit, or fired. However, you will *not* be entitled to your *employer's* contribution until your rights *vest*. (This amount may be substantial.) Most plans vest after *five* years, but this varies widely: some vest in a month, some in seven years (the maximum length allowed under federal tax law).

Before you quit a job (or retire), make sure your rights have vested. Check your *Individual Benefit Statement* (a document your employer will give you). If you only have a year or so to go before vesting, stay. For older employees, rights vest at the normal retirement age, even if they haven't put in the traditional number of years. Get a job at 62. If the normal retirement age is 65, you can retire at 65, and be entitled to your pension even though it usually takes longer for it to vest. (But the pension won't pay very much.)

Some employers, to get their money off the table, fire folks shortly before their retirement rights vest or, in the alternative, make their jobs so miserable that they quit. This is known as a "constructive discharge." If you think this is happening to you, a legal consult is in order.

c. Choices at Retirement: Cashing Out or Buying an Annuity

Some plans (such as *401(k) Plans*) allow you to *cash out* when you retire. That is, you can take all of the money in your account. This can be *very dangerous* even if you don't take the Red Eye to Vegas. Unless you do it right, you will have to treat the entire amount as current income and your tax bill will be *staggering*. However, if you do it correctly, it might be a good idea to roll the money over into a traditional IRA or a new Roth IRA. See Chapter 8(c). Consult your fund manager or an accountant.

Most people don't opt to cash out. Rather, they take an *annuity*. Basically you give all of your accumulated retirement benefits to a bank or other financial institution and it agrees to pay you a certain monthly amount for a certain number of years, perhaps until you die. There are several variations.

Fixed Term Annuities

These pay monthly payments over a fixed period of years. The risk is that you will outlive the fixed period and then you will be in a fine kettle of fish.

However, if you have assets to cover this possibility, a fixed term annuity may be the way to go; monthly payments will be higher than with a *life annuity.*

Life Annuities

Payments continue until death.

Joint and Survivor's Annuities

Here monthly payments are made to you and, after you die, to your designated survivor, usually, but not always, a spouse. Because the annuity is now betting against two lives (so to speak), the monthly payments will be less. Another alternative is the *joint and 50% survivor's annuity,* which pays half the monthly amount to the designated survivor.

Under federal law, *if you are married*, you must elect a joint and survivor's annuity, with the survivor getting at least 50%. A single life annuity (one paying only you, leaving nothing for your spouse at your death), is possible *only* if your spouse agrees in writing.

A *single life annuity*, which will pay the highest monthly payments, may make sense *if* your spouse has adequate retirement income *or* is in such bad health that it is unlikely he or she will outlive you.

If you are in the fortunate position *of not needing all of your pension*, consider making your *children* the surviving beneficiaries. This will probably take a big bite out of your monthly check, but it will provide your children with monthly payments long after you have gone. Who knows? They might actually thank you.

d. Pension Troubles

The newspapers are full of stories about pension plans reducing benefits, cutting out health care, and even going broke. The legal principles are quite complex and beyond the scope of this book. Here are some basics to get you started.

Your plan goes broke.

Defined benefits are usually insured by the Pension Benefit Guarantee Corporation (800-400-PBGC). *Defined contribution plans* are not. Even in those plans which are covered, some of the plan's benefits may not be, such as disability and early retirement.

Your employer changes the plan.

If your employer changes the plan to your detriment, first make sure that the plan allowed him to do so. Get a copy of the plan. This is a tricky, fact-specific area. If changes in benefits are substantial, consult a lawyer who specializes in employment or pension law.

Your individual claim for benefits is turned down.

Plans will tell you how to appeal. Again, some lawyers specialize in pension law.

You get divorced.

You will probably have to divide the worth of the pension—and this gets complicated. See Chapter 20-a.

You forget where you worked.

Remember after the War? You spent four or five years with that little company outside of town. What was its name? Did it have a pension plan that you just forgot? Old tax forms will give the employer's tax number and perhaps the number of the retirement plan. If you haven't kept old tax forms, for a fee the IRS will provide a copy. Once you have these numbers, perhaps the Pension Benefit Guaranty Corporation can help you (800-400-PBGC). www.pbgc.gov.

You may be looking at Bank Error in Your Favor! Don't fall over backwards.

CHAPTER 8

RETIREMENT FINANCES

Wives make the little decisions, like what to have for dinner, who to have over Friday night, when to go on vacation, and where the kids are to go to college. The husbands make the big decisions, like whether Red China should be admitted to the U.N.

This is a pre-Nixon gag; things were different in our parents' time. Often the husband made the money decisions and, if your parents fit that mold, and realizing that men usually die first, encourage mom to get involved in the financial side of things. She should be subtle, not "Dear, you're not looking good today; tell me about our investments." Community colleges might offer courses and one good website is WIFE (Women's Institute for Financial Education). www.wife.org.

This chapter will help (even men, despite the fact that they never need directions).

a. Rethinking Money

Retirement requires a *major* shift in thinking about money.

Working, you could count on occasional raises and could ride out new roofs and old cars on borrowed money. No more. Credit recedes and raises become fond memories. What you got is what you have. Three questions:

1. How much income will you need?
2. If you have some left over, how should you invest it?
3. If you fall short, what cookie jars should you open first?

A few quick pointers.

1. As to income stream, it should exceed your expenses, some advise by 150% to 200%. This will give you a cushion against all those things you didn't anticipate. (Ben Franklin once said that, to have a good vacation, figure out precisely how much it will cost you and then double it.)

2. As to investments, *inflation happens*. Assume, in 1975, you decided you would need two postage stamps per year and you set your investments to cover their costs—20 cents. Six years later, you could buy only one stamp and, today, half a stamp. *Moral*: invest with an eye to growth.

3. As to cookie jars, some are more breakable than others.

First we'll look at budgeting, a major new item to include, health insurance, and one you might consider dropping, life insurance. Then we will look at cookie jars, saving accounts, IRA's and Roth IRA's. If you find yourself running short, we warn of two dangers: invading capital and going for broke on "hot" stocks. Finally we will look at investment alternatives. In our next chapter, we will review ways you can get cash out of your house—without having to turn over all the cushions on the living room sofa.

b. Budgeting: Big Ticket Items, Life and Medical Insurance

Time to make a budget. Work expenses will be gone: professional dues, fancy clothes, business lunches and, if you were a lobbyist, bribes. Some expenses will go up—you may have to purchase services, yard work, home repair, that the younger you did yourself. There are no doubt computer programs and scores of budget books, with blanks to be filled in, long depressing lists of expenses we don't even know we have. (In fact, at least one of your authors has no real sense of *any* expenses he has: his wife pays the bills, and makes all the decisions, the little ones and the big ones—China's in.) Here we flag some special items to consider at retirement.

Big ticket items. Think ahead. Will you need a new car in a few years? A new roof? A new furnace? It is probably safe to predict that you will need at least one of each of those during your retirement years—perhaps more than one—and the challenge is to budget for how many and when. You will find it more difficult to borrow money *even though* you may have good security. Lenders look not only at security but also at income stream. Will the person be able to repay the loan without selling other assets? Budget for big item purchases *before* you buy, putting aside a little each month (and earning, rather than paying, interest).

In this regard, *age discrimination* in lending money or extending credit is unlawful. See Chapter 21-c.

Life insurance. When our children were young, we purchased life insurance in case "something might happen." Many retirees cancel life insurance: their children are grown, many have jobs, and some have even moved out. (*"Son, your mom and I would like a little time by ourselves before we die."*)

If you get your money out of life insurance, you can move it to something producing income or into a kind of insurance you might need: *long-term care insurance.* See Chapter 12. On the other hand, life insurance is a good way to pass on money to loved ones. See Chapter 25-d. This is complicated and you need to consider such issues as the tax benefit of keeping the policy, the option of borrowing against it, or even making it a gift. Also realize that premiums are likely to go up, way up. Talk to your lawyer, accountant or financial adviser (or buy a more helpful book, although many will applaud us for not drowning them in a sea of details). Our general thumb-rules: life insurance is primarily useful to take care of your young children or to pay your estate tax costs. With your children all grown up and the estate tax tapering down to a small shadow of its former self, you may not need either kind of protection.

Health insurance and medical costs. Medical costs will be a *major* new hit on your budget. If you retire before age 65, you will need to *purchase* health insurance to cover what you lost when you retired. This costs a pretty penny. At 65, likely you will have Medicare, a great program but one covering mostly just hospital stays. Most everyone will get some additional coverage by joining a Medicare HMO or staying with the basic Medicare plan by purchasing Medicare Part B (doctor visits) and Part D (some drugs). These additions can run several hundred a month. We discuss medical insurance in Chapter 11.

But even if you insure yourself to the hilt, you will face additional medical costs in terms of hearing aids, dental work, eye glasses, and over-the-counter medications. These can run into thousands of dollars per year.

Finally, you may want to purchase long-term care insurance. See Chapter 12.

c. Cookie Jars: Saving Accounts, IRAs and Roth IRAs

Individual retirement accounts (IRA's) were created by Congress to encourage savings. They are better than traditional saving accounts in two important aspects: contributions to them are *deductible* from income tax and the taxes on interest earned on the contributions is *deferred.* Say what?

Say you want to save $5,000 a year (which is the maximum, in 2007, that you can put in an IRA). Put it in a regular savings account, it costs you $5,000. Put it in an IRA, it costs $3,500 (assuming a 30% income tax rate). This is because you can *deduct* the contribution ($5,000) from your taxes and, at a 30% tax rate, that would save you $1,500 in taxes. Sweet. Over the long run, *deferral* of taxes on interest is even sweeter.

Assume you earn 5% on your savings. Interest earned on regular saving accounts is taxable income: at 30% tax bracket, you would pay $75 tax on the $250 earned. This leaves you with a balance of $5,175. If the money was in an IRA account, taxes on the earned interest would be deferred: the balance on your account would be $5,250. At the end of year two, your savings account would stand at $5,426 and your IRA at $5,513. Over time these small gains lead to big ones.

Depending on your income, your marital status and your spouse's contributions to a retirement plan, you may not be able to fully deduct your payments to an IRA. Even if you can't deduct them, however, the IRA's income will be tax-free until it is withdrawn (you can just imagine the complexity of the tax calculation when you do start receiving your IRA accumulation). An IRA account can hold, buy and sell stocks, bonds and mutual funds which promise further growth. *If you are still working, open an IRA.*

The unhappy ending to this wonderful story is that when you take money out of your IRA you must pay income taxes on it. The general idea is, however, that when you retire you will be at a lower tax rate—if you deducted the $5,000 at a 30% rate, you saved $1,500; when you withdraw it, at 20% rate, you pay only $1,000 in income taxes. This leads to:

Rule One re Cookie Jars:

Make your IRAs the last one. Money you take from traditional savings accounts will not be taxed and money you leave in your IRA will continue to accumulate tax deferred income.

Note: if you are younger than 59½, first our congratulations, second our condolences: you cannot withdraw money from your IRA with incurring a substantial penalty—currently an excise tax of 10% on the amount withdrawn. There are several exceptions to this rule, but the important message should be: leave your retirement accounts untouched if it is at all possible.

> *When was the last time you added "and a half" to your age? Sure, "Five and a half" makes sense but not so "Sixty-five and a half." Thus the Internal Revenue Code doth make children of us all.*

There are two problems with traditional IRAs. First, you must start withdrawing money from them after you turn 70½. Maybe you don't need the money and don't want to pay income tax on the mandatory withdrawals. Second, and alternatively, you may need as much money as you can get in your retirement years and would prefer to pay no taxes on withdrawals. The *Roth IRA*, created in 1997, solves both problems.

Roth IRAs, like traditional IRAs, have the wonderful feature of deferring taxes on interest earned, which makes them grow much faster than traditional saving accounts. However, unlike a traditional IRA, you need not withdraw money at any time: the money you don't need continues to grow. This is a particularly good feature if you are using your IRA as an estate planning tool.

Further, the money you do withdraw comes tax free; not only is the money you contributed tax free, but also the *interest* your account earned is tax free *if* the withdrawal is made after you are 59 ½ and you have had the account for five years.

With all that good news, you just knew there had to be at least one catch, didn't you? There are at least two: you don't get to deduct the payments into a Roth IRA when you make them, and you may not be able to contribute at all if your income is too high. But assuming you don't need the income tax deduction and you qualify, the Roth IRA may make more sense than a traditional IRA. When you write the check, reflect on the late Senator William Roth of Delaware, who figured out that getting a bridge named after him wouldn't protect his legacy nearly as well as having a financial instrument coveted by every American taxpayer.

Rule Two re Cookie Jars:

You might want to rearrange the cupboard (*Rule One re Writing*: don't let your metaphors force you into ridiculous binds). Consider *converting* traditional IRAs into Roth IRAs. Although you will have to pay taxes on the conversion, this may make sense, particularly if you are thinking of using a Roth as a estate planning tool. See your accountant. She will probably tell you that the only way the conversion makes sense is if you can pay the income taxes without having to use the IRA proceeds to do it. This leads to:

Rule Three re Cookie Jars:

Consider making them part of your estate plan. However, with traditional IRA's *don't designate your estate, nor, necessarily, your spouse as beneficiary.* When money comes out of these accounts it is taxed as regular income. If they empty into your estate at the time of your death, *all* will be taxed at that time. Bad idea. If your spouse will not need the money, designate one or more of your children or grandchildren.

A good idea: if you intend to leave anything to charity, your IRA or qualified retirement plan makes the best possible gift. Although your family will have to pay income taxes as they withdraw money, the charity will not. Be careful, and seek professional help—but consider this less-known benefit to retirement accumulations.

d. Running Short: A Rock and a Hard Place

If you are running out of money, there are two dangers: the danger of invading capital (the rock), and the danger of going for broke (the hard place).

The Danger of Invading Capital. You've done your budget. Social Security and your pension leaves you $11,000 short. You have $100,000 in a CD which pays 6% or $6000 per year. The first year, you withdraw $5000 of principal to add to your $6000 of interest to get to your $11,000.

Well and good. But note what happens.

Next year you will have only $95,000 in CD's and thus they will pay only $5,700 the next year. You will have to *invade principal a tad more* next year: $6,300. Now your balance is $88,700. You get our drift—downward. And this analysis does not include inflation—it has been running nearly 3% and hence will trigger higher expenses. And historically, medical expenses—of which you might now have a lot—have increased faster than the general rate of inflation.

$600,000! Now that's a nice nest egg. Something to be proud of. However, if you have invested at 5.5% and must invade it at $17,000 a year, what with the dwindling principal and inflation fueling increased needs, *you will go through the $600,000 in 14 years.*

There are two ways to avoid this unhappy result, unless, of course, you are a Member of Congress which will mean that the first choice is not available to you: Cut expenses. The second choice: invest some of your savings in assets that will grow or at least keep up with inflation. Stocks, mutual funds, and real estate are possibilities. But don't over learn this lesson and dump into a hard place.

The Danger of Going for Broke; Stock Frauds. Some folks, realizing that they don't have much of a nest egg, put most of their savings into risky investments, hoping to make a killing. Don't. Because you no longer have an income stream, losses now will be permanent and you may not be able to ride out bad turns in the market.

As Lincoln said (or maybe it was Yogi, but we are pretty sure it wasn't Woody Allen), it is better to spend down your principal over 14 years than it is losing it in one.

Guard against stock fraud. You will get a call from a "broker" who will be a tad vague about how he got your name. He will tell you of a very hot stock out there, one which will greatly out-perform the market. Usually the stock is in a small company—which allows for price manipulation.

Computer owners beware. A popular fraud is to send "hot stock tips" on stocks that are selling quite cheaply ($0.28) but have "incredible potential" ($150.00) in a mere week or so. Perhaps these stocks don't even exist—the con just wants your credit card information. If the stocks do exist, the con buys them low, sends out the email, drives up the price and then dumps what he has which causes the market to crash driving the price below $0.28.

e. Investment Options

Get investment advice. We recommend this for folks who have investments of $100,000 or more. *Professional financial planners* are preferred: they work on a *set or hourly fee* (and not on a commission which will skew their advice to buying and selling). Insurance agents, stock brokers, bank advisors will naturally steer you to their own products. Dispassionate advice is what you need.

It is extremely difficult to outsmart the market. (It is not difficult to write books or put on programs to outsmart the market—but, if the authors could do what they claim, why are they wasting their time writing books and putting on programs?) New Yorkers who play the market went to business school to learn how and they have devoted their allotted time on earth to the ridiculous pursuit of money. Give them their due—they will outsmart you—they even get up earlier.

Overview of options. Some basic investment options. We have already discussed traditional saving accounts, IRAs, and Roth IRAs. If you are investing with an eye to leaving your kids cash, life insurance is another option. We discuss estate planning in Chapters 24 to 28. Here are other options.

Annuities. There are two types, *immediate* and *deferred* annuities. With an *immediate annuity*, you give an insurance company a bundle of money and it guarantees you monthly payments, for a set number of years or for your life. You can have a secondary beneficiary, your spouse or child, who will receive payments when you die. The longer you are projected to live, or the longer your beneficiary is, the smaller the monthly payments.

Many brokers do give annuities low marks, particularly for seniors. First, although they promise security, they are only as secure as the institution that issued them. Second, they tie up your money. If you suddenly need some of your bundle, you can't get it back—you can with IRAs, CDs, stocks and bonds. If you have chosen a life annuity, when you and the designated beneficiary die, that's it. There will be no money left over for your estate—the bank keeps it.

There is a new and quite unethical "annuity" *scam*. Older seniors, in their 80's or 90's, are sold lifetime annuities. Some provide that payments won't start for a couple of years and, in any event, promise large monthly payments. The reason is that the company, knowing the individual's life expectancy, is counting on keeping most of the bundle for itself. Again, there will be nothing left over.

Deferred annuities. The investment idea pushed by your local banker when you complain about low interest rates on deposits will probably be a *deferred annuity*. You agree to put your money in an insurance company affiliated with the bank, and not to withdraw it for some number of years—typically seven. If you do need your money back before that date, you will have to pay a penalty—typically beginning at 7% and shrinking by 1% each year—for the early withdrawal. In return, the insurance company promises you extraordinary rates of return, and no income taxes until the annuity matures.

Beware. Deferred annuities are unsuitable investments for most seniors. If that were not obvious, the rate of commissions paid to the salespersons should convince you: as much as 10% of your investment will go into the pocket of the friendly saleslady. And though you buy the annuity at your bank, it doesn't actually have anything to do with the bank itself—it is sold by an insurance company through the bank's securities department. It is not insured like bank deposits, and there is even an annual management fee tacked on top of the commission costs.

CD's. Certificates of deposit pay less than annuities as they do not consume the principal. They allow for more flexibility as you invade capital when they mature. Many retirees split their "nest egg" into various CDs, at different banks, so that all of their money is insured.

Although it is important to be careful not to exceed the $100,000 per account insurance limit, there is no advantage to having dozens of $10,000 accounts scattered all over the country. We frequently see estates where the decedent shopped carefully for the highest interest rate available on the internet every time he scraped a couple thousand dollars together, and the result is that the cost of figuring it all out, closing all the small accounts and calculating the taxes and estate division dwarfs any small increase in return during their life.

Bonds and Stocks. Here the tradeoff is safety versus return. In the market today, you can probably find stocks and bonds that are quite safe. Be *cautious.* Choose your investment counselor or broker carefully. Many seniors have lost everything when their brokers put them in high-risk stocks. Again, we advise financial counselors who work for a flat fee.

The problem with CD's and safe market investments is that, while they guard the principle investment, they do not account for inflation: after a period of time, the purchasing power of the original investment will be less than it was originally. Recall our 20-cent stamp fund.

Your house. Of course, the biggest nest egg is the nest itself. How can you get money out of the nest? Turn the page.

CHAPTER 9

House Rich, Cash Poor

If you are having a difficult time making ends meet, you may wish to get the money out of your house and into your pocket. There are three ways: borrow against it, sell it, or rent it. In this chapter we'll flesh out these options, including *reverse mortgages*. In the next we tackle the question of retirement housing: staying put, seeking warmer climes, or smaller digs. First a few warnings for homeowners.

Crooks target your home. They come offering free roof inspections only to find that you need major repairs; they come offering you loans, secured by a second mortgage on your house. *Never, ever,* sign any paper giving someone a security interest in your home unless it is a bank. For more on these despicable types, reread our Chapter 4 on Scams.

One piece of good news. Some locales give property tax breaks to seniors. Check.

a. Traditional Borrowing

The great advantage of borrowing money, rather than selling or renting, is that it allows what most of us want: to age in your home. The problem is that, if you can't pay back the loan, you lose your home. (On a foreclosure, your house would be sold and your creditor would take off the top what you owed; if there is any remaining, you would get the balance.)

Rule one: don't borrow against your home unless you have to. *Don't* borrow to go on a cruise. *Don't* mortgage your home without first seeing if you are eligible for *SSI, Medicaid* or another welfare type program. See Chapter 6-i.

Traditional mortgages and the newer *Home Equity Accounts* (essentially a line of credit secured by a mortgage on your home) are harder to arrange once you have retired. Loan officers usually look to income flow. One advantage of such loans, however, is that the amount you pay in interest is tax deductible. The amounts you pay in interest on credit cards, car loans and other consumer purchases are *not* deductible. (Note: you cannot deduct interest payments on home equity loans over $100,000 unless the money was for home improvement.)

b. Reverse Mortgages

Reverse mortgages offer a great opportunity to get some of the growing equity out of your home without requiring you to move. The lender pays you a monthly amount—hence the "reverse" moniker. The loan grows over time (rather than shrinking, as a regular mortgage does, with monthly payments to the lender)—the loan does not have to be repaid until you move or die. The money you receive is not taxed and will not impact either Social Security, Medicare or Medicaid. There are no out-of-pocket costs, with closing costs being picked up in the loan. Title stays in your name.

The federal government's Home Equity Conversion Mortgage Program, the principal, and most principled, of the reverse mortgage offerings, is regulated by the Department of Housing and Urban Development-HUD. There are no income limits on who can apply. The owners must all be 62 or older. Basically any kind of house can qualify, from mansion to house trailer, with the exceptions being cooperative apartments and newly-built (less than a year) dwellings. One of the best elements of the federal program: every borrower must first complete a free reverse mortgage counseling program. In our experience, the counseling program shows many, perhaps most, of the interested prospects how to better arrange their finances without going through the reverse mortgage—and that's a sign that the program is more interested in good results than in closings. Beware, however—there are reverse mortgage scams in the world, and not all lenders are scrupulously honest and careful about your best interests.

Eventually the money borrowed in a reverse mortgage must be repaid, with interest. The interest rates will vary and are usually adjustable rather than fixed. You can terminate the loan when you wish and repay it at that time. When you die, if your spouse is on the deed, the loan payments will continue. If not, your house goes to your heirs with the mortgage lien upon it. Your heirs can either pay off the loan and keep the house, or allow it to be sold. If the selling price exceeds the amount due under the loan, that money goes to the heirs.

You must continue to live in the house at least half time and reverse mortgages, due to the paperwork and costs, aren't a good idea if you plan to move. Talk to a specialist in the area. To find one, contact your Area Agency. On the AARP website you can find a wealth of information on reverse mortgages, from eligibility, basics, and lenders, to options and loan calculations.

Reverse mortgages will be the wave of the future. Currently they are grossly underused. Although 21 million homes are owned by folks over 62, representing zillions of dollars of value, at this writing, there are less than 200,000 reverse mortgages in place.

c. Selling Your Home

The value of your home has probably gone up since you purchased it (unless you live in our neighborhood—we'd like to apologize for that right now). There is good tax news. Since 1998, there are no federal capital gains taxes on the first $250,000 of profit ($500,000 for married couples). *However,* you must have lived in the home for two of the previous five years. This, incidentally, is the major danger of renting—if you rent your home out for three years, you will no longer be able to meet the two-of-the-last-five requirement, and suddenly all the appreciation in your home's value will be taxable if you sell it.

A major legal drawback to selling is that your home is generally an *exempt* asset; the money you receive from it isn't. In most states, a homestead can be filed (or may exist automatically, without even needing to be "filed") to protect your home from creditors (they cannot seize it and sell it); on the other hand, once you have sold it and put the money into bank accounts or stocks, creditors can get it by obtaining appropriate court orders. (The folks who hold the *mortgage* on your house can go after it even if it is homesteaded.)

Similarly, most welfare programs (*Medicaid, SSI* and the like) allow you to *keep* your home but not much of your cash. If Medicaid is a possibility, don't sell.

d. Renting or Leasing Your Home

This might be a good choice if you are moving to smaller digs, particularly if it looks like there will be no need to sell the house in the near future. Moving from the house for more than three years (assuming you have lived there for at least two years already) will mean that you will not be entitled to the exemption from capital gains taxes which was described in the last section.

As to the hassles of renting, thankfully there are management companies that will do the heavy-lifting—collecting, making repairs, etc.

With a little creativity, you will be able to avoid *income* taxes on most or all of the rents you receive (there may be local *sales* taxes on rentals; those will be hard to avoid and you should set the rental rates accordingly). Rental income is taxable income. Management fees and costs of repairs (and *rental insurance*, a must) are *deductible*. As you actually pay out these amounts, there is no real savings. However, now that your house is income-producing, you can *depreciate* it. A depreciation allowance allows you to reduce the income tax you pay on the rent you receive without actually paying out money.

A *depreciation allowance* is given to income producing assets (such as factories and building) in the recognition that, in 20 or 30 years, they are likely to wear out and must be replaced at that time. It is assumed that the owner is spreading the replacement cost across the life of the asset by putting money aside. *However*, there is no requirement that you actually put money aside or pay out anything.

The way the government gets its money back is to reduce your *basis* by the amount you took in depreciation. Say what? Assume you purchased your home for $100,000 and that you subsequently sold it for the same amount, $100,000. There would be no capital gain. However, if you rented the house and took a total of $40,000 in depreciation to offset your rental income, your basis would be $60,000 and thus, when sold at $100,000 there would be a capital gain of $40,000. One nice thing, however, is that if you leave the house to your kids, they will get a *stepped-up basis*—the amount the house is worth at the time of your death. So they won't have to worry about capital gains; regrettably, you won't either.

Complicated stuff. Talk to an account. The IRS has pamphlets:

527:    Residential Property
946:    How to Depreciate Property

We can't leave you without a moral. "Finally, after all these years, it is fine to talk to strangers; but don't give them a security interest in your house."

CHAPTER 10

RETIREMENT HOUSING

House too big? February too cold? Bathroom too dangerous? Lawn too thick? Despite all of the problems, most of us want to stay put. We'll look at some of the issues surrounding that choice and then those associated with moving. Then we will look at the plethora of new housing options created for seniors, including CCRC's: continuing care retirement communities.

a. Staying Put (with a little help from our friends)

Some move because they think they cannot afford not to. Take a look at our discussion of reverse mortgages in the last chapter. Others move because they fear that they won't be able to manage. While this may be true, consider your options in getting help in your home when and if you need it.

- *"Meals on Wheels"* and other forms of home services, such as minor repairs and upkeep, are provided by community and non-profit groups under the federal Older Americans Act of 1965. Check with your Area Agency on Aging.
- *Hospital beds* and other kinds of *medical equipment* can be rented or purchased. Check with Medicare to see what they will pay for.
- *Home nursing* services are available. In a few circumstances, Medicare will pay. Otherwise you will have to look to your long-term care policy; many, perhaps most, cover home care. Finally, if you must pay out of your own pocket, you may be entitled to deduct the expenses from your income taxes. See Chapter 13.

You can hire folks to help you. Sometimes children or other relatives move in to help out. There may be an understanding that, when you die, they will get the house. This might make a great deal of sense. But *don't put the title in their names now!* If the house is in their names, their creditors might be able to reach it. And there are tax consequences. It is generally a *bad* idea to make a lifetime gift of your home to your children (they will *not* get a stepped-up basis, and you may incur a gift tax). It is better to give it to them at the time of your death under your Will. See Chapter 25.

Rather than giving them the house now, you can make a formal contract to do so. In return for described services, you promise to give them the property by your Will. To be enforceable, the contract must be in writing and signed by all parties. Best to see a lawyer. If you don't see a lawyer now, the caretaker child or all of her (it's always "her," isn't it?) brothers and sisters will be seeing a lawyer—and paying a lot more—after your death, because they will disagree on what you intended to do.

Hiring help is another option. As these people will have the run of your house, best to seek advice as to hiring trustworthy and competent people. Want ads aren't a good idea. And pay a fair wage. It is a bad idea to give caregivers extra money or the loan of your car. It tends to blur the lines of ownership. Likewise, when caregivers explain that they need just a few thousand dollars now to fix their own car so that they can get to work to help you out— just say no, and get some assistance from family or friends to protect you from the possibility of financial exploitation.

One danger with having in-home care is that of possible abuse. We discuss abuse in Chapter 14; here we make one essential point. Always maintain and insist upon contacts outside the home: the favorite ploy of abusers is isolation. Have a weekly bridge game, hair appointment, or other regular weekly activity. If you can't get out of the house, make sure you are visited weekly by friends or relatives and insist on talking with them privately.

If you're planning to stay put, it is never too early to make your house safer. We have some suggestions in 32-b.

b. Moving to Warmer Climes

Golf, sunshine, and bridge. Not a bad combination, that. The salespeople are marvelous—ever sign up for a free vacation trip with the only obligation being to sit through a short *timeshare* presentation (which you knew you would easily resist)? (If so, do you still have it?) *Go slow.* Many buy into a retirement community only to find:

- that it is on shaky financial ground and that many of the promised benefits are in jeopardy;
- that they miss their friends and family and even the shrieks and laughter of the neighborhood kids; and

- that their slice is incurable and, as they always suspected, their spouse compulsively overbids.

Trying to resell, they find the bottom has fallen out. *Rent* in the new location before you buy. If you do, you may want to rent out your own house back home. In the previous chapter, we discussed some issues surrounding renting your house. Check with your insurance company to see if your home is covered for renters.

So, where to go?

Lake Woebegone and *Margaritaville* will immediately come to mind, although not to the same mind. Alas, neither exist. And, if that weren't bad enough, winters and hangovers both get worse. (Trust us.)

David Savageau's *Retirement Places Rated* can provide you with good information about different locales. Many move to such places as Mexico, Costa Rica, Canada, and Ireland where the cost of living is less. Check the quality of medical care, whether your insurance will pay (Medicare won't), and the cost of airfare back to the States.

If you are going to buy a new home, even if you are extremely active now, you may not be later. If looking for a new home, make sure it will accommodate possible disabilities. Are the hallways wide enough for a wheelchair? Is the house located near shopping? Medical facilities?

Finally, *transportation.* There will come a time when you will be unable to drive. If you are buying a new house, how will you get around when that time comes? We cannot stress this enough. Unless there is public transport or things are within walking distance, the inability to drive will mean staying at home and, isolated, life becomes quite burdensome. See Chapter 17 on the problem of driving.

Whether you stay put or move to a new home, at some point you may decide that maintaining your own home is too much work. You might want to move to a facility where you don't have to do all the cooking and cleaning, and where there are new people to meet and new opportunities to explore.

c. Assisted-Living Facilities

The housing options for older persons are quite numerous, not only in size and location, but also in the level of support they offer. The questions, however, are the same:

- What are the costs?
- What are the conditions?

- What programs and services are offered?
- How much independence will you have?
- How about complaints? What have they been and how have they been answered?

Shop around, visit at least two, visit at different times of day, and talk to residents as well as officials. Many states license these facilities, usually the Department of Public Health or similarly-named agency. On their websites there will be a list of facilities and a searchable database of past enforcement actions.

Your options run from essentially *boarding homes* and *assisted-living facilities* (apartments with various levels of support services), through the newer *continuing care retirement communities (CCRCs)*. CCRCs claim to provide extensive care, support, and nursing facilities on site. Many purport to guarantee care for life, first in an independent unit, then, if necessary, in the nursing or intermediate wing.

d. Continuing Care Retirement Communities (CCRCs)

Most assisted-living facilities charge by the month; others insist on a *buy-in*. Be careful buying in.

- Some have bought in with their life savings ($300,000 to $500,000) only to have the facility go broke.
- Others have bought in and died in the first year, with the facility keeping all of their money.
- Others have bought in while healthy and vital only to find, when they need it, that kinds of care they need are not covered in the contract.
- Others have found after ten or so years that they want to move, but all of their money is tied up.

There are about 1,200 CCRCs nationally and there are *no* federal regulations. Some states regulate them. To get into such a facility, one must be in relatively good health, and often pay a hefty up-front payment (from $300,000 to over $500,000 per person). There are set monthly fees and perhaps additional charges for nursing care.

Some points to consider:

- Treat the move as you would a major investment. Ask for an audited financial statement. Have your accountant review it. A guarantee of life-care is only good as long as the facility does not go bankrupt and as long as it maintains adequate beds in various levels of care.

- Once you buy in, it may be difficult to get your money back if you don't like it. Before buying in, *hang out*. Ask other residents about the facility.
- Are the medical facilities and services up to what is advertised?
- Are there enough physicians? Are there long waits? Are specialists covered or must you pay for them yourself?
- What is the policy about moving residents into the nursing wing? There have been complaints that some facilities do so quickly, so that they can then sell the individual's apartment to someone else. Along these lines, what are the policies about the institution seeking guardianship over residents?
- If a spouse dies, must the survivor move into a separate single's unit? A forced move at this time can be traumatic.
- Will the facility take Medicare payments? Some will not.
- What is the refund policy? If you die relatively soon, do your heirs get any of the money back?

e. Section 8 Housing for Low-Income Folks

If you are age 62 or older and have an income below the median in the area, you may be entitled to *"Section 8" rent subsidy* for certain independent facilities. Under it, you will pay only a certain percentage of your income as rent with the federal government picking up the difference. Although many Americans hold onto images of government housing being clustered into substandard buildings in dangerous neighborhoods, Section 8 subsidies today may be available for rental units pretty much anywhere in town.

f. More Info

The American Bar Association *Guide for Older Americans* has a nice checklist of questions concerning assisted living and continuing care facilities. It is published by Time Books, a division of Random House.

The American Association of Homes and Services for the Aging publishes *The Consumer's Directory of Continuing Care Retirement Communities*. 800-508-9442; *www.aahsa.org*.

The *AARP* has several publications:

Staying at Home Selecting Retirement Housing
Housing Options for Older Americans
800-424-3410
http://www.aarp.org

And your local Area Agency on Aging can help too.

CHAPTER 11

MEDICARE AND HEALTH INSURANCE

Medicare, Parts A, B, C, and D; Medigap policies; long-term care insurance; dread disease insurance; disability insurance, and, oh yes, COBRA. If you believe, as we do, that tough mental exercise makes you smarter, trying to figure out how to present these choices has made us geniuses. So we don't rob you of this wonderful opportunity for self-improvement, we will be a tad obtuse.

What medical expenses can you expect?

Hospital stays.
Doctor visits.
Prescriptions.
Dental, glasses, hearing aids.
Long-term care.

Whatever insurance you purchase, know this. Medical expenses will be much higher as you age. Historically, medical costs have increased considerably more rapidly than the rate of inflation, and long-term care costs even more rapidly than that.

In the pages that follow, we will look at how your various insurance options respond to those expenses. Before looking at your Medicare choices, first, what are your insurance needs *before* you turn 65?

a. Insurance Needs before 65

Disability Insurance

If you are still working, a bad back at age 58 can prevent you from reaching retirement in good financial shape.

Don't rely on Disability under Social Security. Under Social Security, your disability must be severe and the payments will be small. Social Security pays only if you are unable to perform any substantial gainful employment—even as cashier at a self-service gas station, or a crossing guard.

COBRA

If you retire before 65 and lose your health insurance, COBRA can help.

"COBRA," like life itself, is full of sound and fury, signifying nothing. (Actually it signifies "Comprehensive Omnibus Budget Reconciliation Act"— which, in turn, signifies nothing.)

If your employer has 20 or more covered workers, COBRA is the federal law that allows you to continue your employer's health plan if you lose coverage because of early retirement or layoff. You can continue the policy for up to 18 months, but must pay the premium (usually the same rate charged the employer plus a 2% administrative charge). This is known as Continuation Coverage.

If the first 18 months doesn't get you to the magical year of Medicare coverage (age 65), you have a right to convert the policy but at a higher premium and with more restrictions. This is known as Conversion Coverage. Professional organizations, service clubs, and the AARP offer group policies that will likely save you money.

If you had to retire because of disability, it may be possible to obtain COBRA coverage for longer than 18 months.

A related program protects you if you change jobs. The Health Insurance Portability and Accountability Act of 1996 (HIPAA) allows you to take your health insurance eligibility with you if you change employers. That means you cannot be denied coverage under your new employer's health plan. However, your coverage may not be with the same insurer or under terms as favorable as your former employer's health coverage.

Long-Term Care Insurance

We will see that Medicare does not cover most nursing home expenses. They can bankrupt a family. In our next chapter we discuss this problem. For now, if you decide to purchase a long-term care policy, the earlier the better.

Dread Disease Insurance

These policies are usually offered on late night TV by aging actors. Usually they are not a good deal as a lot of what they cover will be covered by Medicare or, if not, are extremely rare.

b. Turning 65: Medicare Part A

Medicare is a marvelous program. The basic plan, Part A, covers most hospital costs. It has kept countless families from bankruptcy and has given millions more peace of mind: "If I get sick, at least I will not bankrupt my family."

With daily hospital charges ranging from $500 to $1,500 per day, this is a very real possibility.

To be eligible for Medicare, you must be 65 (or disabled or blind). In addition to being 65:

- You must be eligible for Social Security (that does not mean you have to be *receiving* Social Security—just that you must be eligible); or, if you aren't,
- You must be a spouse, widow, or widower of an eligible member. Ex-spouses, if married for more than ten years and not remarried, can also qualify.

If you don't fit into one of these categories, and are 65 or older, you can still purchase coverage. The current premium is $309 per month. This figure gives you some idea of how much insurance coverage Medicare provides.

While you may want to put off taking your cash benefits from Social Security at age 65 (to get larger cash payments later), and while you may want to delay signing up for other Medicare Programs (because you are otherwise covered), there is *no* reason not to sign up for Part A when you turn 65. Apply for Medicare through your Social Security Office three months before you turn 65.

Medicare Part A basically covers most hospital costs, many skilled nursing facility care costs, some home care costs, and hospice. All of this gets quite technical and you will receive a booklet explaining the ins and outs—*Medicare and You*. But, for now, you don't need to know the details of what Part A covers; what you need to know is what it *doesn't* cover:

Doctor Visits
Prescriptions
Dental, Hearing, and Eye Care

As for *long-term nursing home care* costs, Medicare Part A provides a very limited benefit. Limitations are imposed on how you get to the long-term care facility (you have to be hospitalized for at least three days first); how much Medicare will pay (there are significant co-payments required); how long the coverage will last (the maximum coverage period is 100 days) and the type of care covered (Medicare pays nothing—that's $0—if what you need is "custodial care"). To a considerable extent, you'll have to self-insure ("go bare" as those wild and funny insurance guys like to say), or buy separate insurance, or make yourself eligible for *Medicaid* (note that this is not *Medicare*). More on these choices anon.

c. Basic Medicare Choices

To get coverage for routine doctor visits, prescriptions and dental, eye care and hearing, you have two basic choices, staying with Medicare and adding to its coverage, or opting for a Medicare HMO. Two points before we begin.

It will cost you, no matter which way you go. You already paid for hospital coverage (Part A) through your payroll taxes, but you must purchase additional coverage.

Second, you should make your decision as soon as possible. If you wait too long after you become eligible (usually three months after you turn 65), you will have to pay more for the same coverage. The higher premium protects Medicare from "adverse selection" (not buying insurance until you are sick, not placing your bet until the ball has stopped bouncing). The *only time you should delay* is where you are covered by a better health plan after you turn 65, through either your or your spouse's insurance.

d. Doctor Visits: Medicare Part B or HMO

Medicare Part B covers doctor visits and helps with outpatient hospital services (including emergency room visits), ambulances, diagnostic tests, laboratory services, some preventive care such as mammography and Pap smear, outpatient therapy services, durable medical equipment and supplies, and a variety of other services. It also picks up some home health care services.

You pay a $124 deductible per year and 20% of the other charges. You may have to pay more if your doctor does not agree to accept Medicare approved limits on charges.

When you sign up for Medicare, unless you opt out, you will be automatically enrolled in Part B. You will pay a monthly premium, at this writing, of $88.50 per month. It will be taken from your Social Security check. It is a great value. In fact, the federal government is required to peg the premium at 25% of the cost of the care provided to all participants—so you can expect that comparable coverage in the private market (if you could buy it) would cost about four times as much.

The other way to cover doctor visits is to sign up for an HMO under the "Medicare Advantage" program, sometimes referred to inaccurately (but with alphabetic consistency) as Medicare "Part C." You will have to sign up for Part B as well. The way these HMO's work is that you assign your rights under Parts A and B to them—and they in turn get paid by Medicare for providing medical care to you and folks like you.

Part B does not cover prescriptions, dental, hearing, or vision services. Some Medicaid Advantage HMO's do. Here is where things get very complicated, as purchasing this coverage will vary.

e. Prescriptions

Part D of Medicare, enacted in 2003 and started in earnest in 2006, provides for a voluntary outpatient drug benefit. Private insurers provide these benefits and the premiums and extent of coverage vary with each. There will be yearly deductibles and co-pays. There is also what is known as the "donut hole." You will be covered until your out-of-pocket expenses have reached $2,250. After that you will have no insurance coverage until your out-of-pocket has reached $3,600. Some policies, at an additional cost, will cover the "donut hole."

To all these variables add the number and kind of prescriptions that you will need filled. Choice becomes something of a nightmare. (Are we the only ones who long for the good old days when there were only Chocolate, Vanilla, and Strawberry? Did everything start to go wrong with the advent of Neapolitan ice cream?) Go to www.Medicare.gov and access its Prescription Drug Plan Finder. You can enter your specific needs and it will calculate your "Estimated Annual Cost," and then give you two or three plans to choose from and tell you how to contact them. Some good questions to ask:

Can I buy the drug I want or must I try another drug first?
Does the plan have to approve the drug before I buy it?
Can I buy drugs through the mail? Can I use drug stores not in the network?
What if I travel a lot?

Instead of using Part D, your HMO program may offer drug coverage. Here you would have to compare costs and coverage. If your pre-existing drug coverage is as good as or better than the Part D benefits, you should have gotten a letter from your current insurance plan letting you know that there is no need to look further.

Even with Part D, you're not home yet.

f. Dental, Glasses, Hearing Aids: Medigap Policies

Neither Parts A nor B covers services not related to treatment of illness or injury, such as dental care or dentures, cosmetic surgery, routine foot care, hearing aids, eye exams, or glasses. Except for certain limited cases in Canada and Mexico, Medicare does not pay for treatment outside of the United States.

You can purchase Medigap policies, which cover some of these gaps and provide coverage for some of the co-payments and deductibles in the Medicare programs. In order to simplify purchasing and make it possible to make meaningful comparisons, the federal government restricts Medigap insurance plans to one of ten basic policy benefit lists—your first step should probably be to figure out which plan type you want and need, and then to comparison shop among companies offering that plan. The HMO you join may cover some of these gaps as well, and may obviate the need to investigate further.

g. How to Decide

Again, your two basic options:

1. Staying in Medicare program: Part A and B, a drug policy under Part D, and a possible Medigap policy.
2. Joining a Medicare HMO under Part C.

One big advantage of staying with the basic Medicare program is that you are free to choose your own physicians and other health care providers. Many HMO's, though not all, restrict your choices.

First talk to your current health care providers. If you go with an HMO, will you still be able to see them? If you go on straight Medicare, same question. Some physicians, due to the fact that Medicare is notorious in paying late, are refusing to see Medicare patients.

Next, figure out what coverage is important in terms of the drug benefit and the incidental benefits under a Medigap policy. How much will they cost? Armed with this information, you can approach the numerous HMO choices under Part C. Ask their representatives to compare their drug coverage to what you could get under Part D and then ask for the same comparison of dental, hearing and vision coverage that you could get in a Medigap policy.

You will get a whole lot smarter.

h. Where to Get Help

There are insurance counseling programs, public presentations, and other resources available to those about to turn 65, older beneficiaries, and family members who are forced to make the choice for a Medicare recipient. There are great websites explaining much of this information—among the best of government websites is the one laid out by the Medicare program at www.medicare.gov. But for our money, the absolute best resource (other, of course, than this book) for your inquiry—and a fair number of other topics covered in other chapters—is your Area Agency on Aging. Every region of the country has one, and you can find yours by looking in your local telephone book or visiting the Administration on Aging's website at www.aoa.gov.

Unfortunately, you're still not covered for long-term care. But this chapter has been too long, too boring, as it is. But read on, no time to say "enough".

> .... *lay on, Macduff;*
> *And damn'd be him that first cries, "Hold, enough."*
> Macbeth

CHAPTER 12

Long-Term Care

Nursing homes have something of a bad rap, with images of folks zonked out in front of static TVs, drooling oatmeal. Not necessarily so, though the stereotypes do exist. There can be new friends to meet, games to play and, yes, even sex (we are, after all, talking about humans). Chapter 33 is devoted to nursing homes; here we discuss paying for them.

Long-term care can bankrupt. Yearly costs can exceed $100,000 and stays of five years or more are possible. *Medicare* and *Medigap* policies will cover only a *small* portion of these costs. This is a particular problem for women, since men are more often cared for at home (by their women) and women live longer.

What to do?

Long-term care insurance is now available. And once a family has exhausted its own resources, *Medicaid* is available. We discuss both.

Note: If your family is currently paying large nursing home bills, they may be deductible from Federal Income Tax. See Chapter 13.

a. Long-Term Care Insurance

This is a new and tricky area. Get advice. Do you need it? How much should you pay? What is the best policy for you? States regulate long-term insurance and have free or low-cost insurance counseling programs. To run down the one in your area, contact your Area Agency on Aging or call

Eldercare Locator 1-800-677-1116

There is also *A Shopper's Guide to Long-Term Care Insurance* put out by the National Association of Insurance Commissions. It even has a worksheet and may be available at local libraries or at your Area Agency.

Long-term insurance may not be for you. Like all forms of insurance, it is a gamble. Maybe you will never go into a nursing home—most people never do. Estimates vary. A study in the *New England Journal of Medicine* projected that of those who turn 65 in 1990, 67% of men and 48% of women will never enter a nursing home. Of those who enter a nursing home, many will stay less than a year (45%) but a large number will have extended stays, more than five years (21%). Obviously these are simply educated guesses and your odds will depend on current health, family history, and luck.

You may be rich enough to be self-insured or poor enough not to care. The latter sounds a tad cruel, but the truth is that insurance in essence protects your estate from being devoured by nursing home costs before you turn to Medicaid. If you don't have a lot to protect, then insurance may not be needed. Put another way, the classic candidate for purchasing long-term care insurance is a middle-class individual (or couple).

Assuming you are in the market, the earlier you start, the lower the premium and the better the coverage. Also, if you wait until your 60's or 70's, a medical condition may lead the company to deny your application—they have that right.

On the other hand, any policy will be canceled if the premiums are not kept current. If you are buying a policy early, be sure you can afford it later. If not, you will forfeit your coverage. To give you some idea of costs, a policy today at age 55 is around $1500 per year—though even suggesting this figure is dangerously simplistic, since the extent of benefits, your health condition, the area of the country where you live, and the benefit restrictions you choose will all have a huge impact on the actual cost of your policy.

Other desirable features in such policies include:

- Protection against inflation—if the benefits remain constant and the cost of care doubles before you need it, you are in trouble.
- Coverage of all levels of nursing care (skilled, intermediate, custodial).
- Home and assisted care coverage—you don't want the policy to cover only your last choice. Most policies today will pay as much for home care as for care in the nursing home, though the actual costs of care in the home will probably be higher. Look for restrictions on who can provide the care in the home, or the effect of using the home care option on the remaining term of your coverage.
- Low deductibles and not too difficult prerequisites—such as hospitalization.
- At least one year maximum benefit period, preferably at least 3 years—and 5 years is better, particularly if you are expecting the policy to cover your care while your family waits out the Medicaid ineligibility period occasioned by transferring your assets (more on that later).
- Coverage of dementia, like Alzheimer's disease.
- A forgiving pre-existing conditions limit—no longer than six months.

You might also want to glance at our list of points concerning buying insurance. See Chapter 11-g.

b. Safety Net of Medicaid; Medicaid Planning

Our worst nightmare: we wake up sick and alone, on a dirty city back street. *Medicaid* guards against that: you will not be thrown out of your home to wander the streets just because you are broke and need medical care.

In 1965, Congress passed Medicaid (known in California, in an apparent effort by state law makers to steal the credit, as *MediCal*). This program is designed as a health care safety net for poor folks, providing a full range of benefits, from doctors' bills to hospitalization. It *will* pay for custodial (nursing home) care in some situations.

Medicaid is for the poor, for those who cannot afford to pay for their own care. Live long enough, however, and you probably will be poor, especially if you are paying several thousand a month for nursing home care.

Medicaid coverage is only available if you have insufficient resources to pay for your own care—though the government's definition of "insufficient" may not match your own. There is some state variation, but the general rules are federal: some assets will not be counted—usually your home, your car and most personal items. Your *spouse* may be obligated to pay for some of your care but he or she will not be left destitute: there are property and income exemptions. Your children are *not obligated* to pay. In most states, if not all, children have no duty to support their parents, even if their parents are destitute. (In other countries, and in earlier times in this country, children did have that obligation, and some state laws still address the concept, but are not generally enforced or enforceable.)

Rather than spending their life savings on nursing home care and hoping to leave their children a little something, some middle-class folks take steps to get themselves eligible for Medicaid if the need arises. This is known as *Medicaid Planning* and, as with triple bypass operations, should not be attempted at your kitchen table.

It entails shedding yourself of the assets and income which would make you ineligible; in other words, making yourself poor. The downside, of course, is that you will be poor.

You'll have to give most of your life savings away. If you need them for an emergency, or for a fling, the money won't be there. Most people give their assets to their kids, counting on them to bail them out if need be. But even if your kids are more graceful than Lear's daughters and drink less than Falstaff, their creditors can get what were *your* assets. How's the kids' driving?

To guard against all of this, you may decide to play it cagey: keep your savings until the very last minute. Alas, the Feds have seen you coming. Transfers you make within five years of seeking Medicaid assistance will delay your eligibility. Further, and it's our job to remind you of unpleasant possibilities, when the very last minute comes you may have lost your shrewdness … if you then lack legal capacity, you can no longer give away your stuff. To deal with this possibility, we recommend a durable power of attorney (Chapter 23-c). Add a provision, not included in most, that your financial agent can make gifts—otherwise your agent might not have the legal power to do so.

One step you can take without running the risks inherent in giving your savings away is to convert them into exempt assets. In lay terms, sell your stocks and buy a fancy house. (Of course this move has its own dangers: lack of liquidity, income stream, and possible growth.) The Feds have seen you coming here, as well—Medicaid rules now restrict the value of your home as an exempt asset, though the $500,000 limit can still buy a pretty fancy crib in most states. Warning: although having a home may not keep you off Medicaid, it may be that the state has a claim against your estate—including that house—when you die after receiving Medicaid benefits. The rules are complicated and getting more complicated, so you can begin to see why we strongly suggest you get professional help in this area.

Medicaid planning is tricky and is getting more so every year as Congress tries to close loopholes. Mistakes can be quite costly. Find a lawyer who specializes in the area. For a referral, contact the National Academy of Elder Law Attorneys. 520-881-4005 or www.naela.org.

One final concern: Will you get worse care if you are a Medicaid patient? Often Medicaid will choose the home and the doctor. In most cases (and in most states) Medicaid patients are cared for side-by-side with private-pay patients. Some even believe that you might get better care as a Medicaid patient as you will be assigned a case manager to oversee your care. One problem: as Medicaid costs increase and states find themselves more financially strapped by their share of the program's cost, their largesse may continue to shrink, and the quality of care may suffer in the future.

CHAPTER 13

TAX BREAKS FOR SENIORS

Taxes are certain ... and *complicated*. Here we flag some tax benefits you may be overlooking. For specific questions:

- Call the IRS. 1-800-829-1040 (Ed. note: Cute, "1040," very cute!) http://www.irs.ustreas.gov
- See an accountant. Fees paid for tax advice and help are deductible.

a. If Your Children Are Supporting You

If your children are supplying more than one-half of your support, they may be entitled to significant tax breaks. They may be able to claim you as a dependent (and thus get an additional *dependency exemption),* and may also be able to claim head of household status (and thus increase their *standard deduction* as well as taking advantage of the *head-of-household* tax rate). Finally, if you have substantial medical expenses, they might be able to deduct some of them.

b. Federal Tax Benefits

Let's define some terms and show their impact on your tax bill. *Deductions* reduce your taxable income. They reduce your tax bill, but not by the full amount: only by the amount that would have been taxed had the deduction been included. Assume you are paying taxes at the 28% level: a $700 deduction will translate into a tax savings of $196 (28% of $700).

Exemptions work the same way. If some of your income is exempt, it need not be reported and hence will not be taxed.

Tax credits are better (and rarer). They reduce taxes dollar for dollar: a tax credit of $500 would reduce your tax bill by $500.

What federal tax rules might be of most interest?

Standard Deduction

Turning 65 entitles you to an additional amount if you are taking a standard deduction and *not itemizing* deductions. Additional amounts can be taken if the taxpayer is blind.

Personal Exemptions

Regardless of age, every taxpayer is entitled to a personal exemption. In 2006, it was $3,300. This exemption is not increased at 65 nor for blindness. You can take this exemption whether you itemize or not.

Medical Expense Deduction

If you have *significant* medical expenses for yourself, your spouse, or a dependent, some may be deductible. *You must itemize to take them.* Medical expenses not compensated by insurance are deductible *in excess of 7.5%* of adjusted gross income. This is the major limitation; most people never get up that high. When they do, only the amount over the 7.5% threshold is deductible.

And what counts toward that 7.5%?

- The costs of medical care including "diagnosis, care, mitigation, treatment, or prevention of diseases ... affecting any structure or function of the body." This includes medicine, prescription drugs, medical transport, glasses, seeing-eye dogs, artificial teeth, and artificial limbs.
- The costs of *medically required home improvements,* prescribed by a physician, to the extent their cost exceeds the increased value they give the house. For example, if a $1,500 elevator or therapy pool increases the value of the home $600, then $900 would be counted as a medical expense. (The $600 would be added to the basis of your house and thus, when it is sold, would not represent a capital gain.)
- The costs of nursing homes can be included, but only if the primary reason was medical care, as opposed to custodial care. This is generally not a difficult deduction to make since medical care is arguably a major component of any nursing home stay.
- A portion of long-term care insurance premiums.

Tax Credits Concerning Disability

A tax credit is available to folks 65 and older or those under 65 who are retired on permanent and total disability. The amount is 15% of the taxpayer's "section 22 amount" and its calculation defies easy description. Just be aware of it, discuss it with your accountant, or look for it on your 1040.

Interest Deductions

Interest you pay on your home mortgage (and home equity loan) is deductible. Other kinds of interest payments, such as on credit cards or store accounts, are generally not deductible.

Home Taxes

Many states give taxpayers over 65 a break on property taxes. In terms of federal taxes, if you are still paying for your house, that portion of your payment that represents interest payments continues to be deductible. The cost of home improvements is not deductible unless they were medically required (see the discussion of "medical expense deduction" above). However, keep records as to home improvements as their cost can be added to the amount you paid for your house to figure its basis. What this means is that if you sell your house for more than you paid for it, you can deduct from your gain the cost of home improvements. This is less important than it used to be in light of the next point.

Capital Gain Taxes from the Sale of Your Residence

Since 1998, you can sell your home and pay no federal taxes on the first $250,000 of profit ($500,000 for married couples). This exemption requires that you have lived in the home for at least two of the prior five years.

Reverse Mortgage Payments

In Chapter 9, we discussed how you might get cash out of your home's equity without selling it. The most popular way is the reverse mortgage. The monthly payments are not taxable as they are really loans to you.

Exempt Income

Money you receive from certain sources or for certain reasons need not be included in your gross income. Here we list some of the most common:

Inheritance and gifts. This means that if you make a gift to your children, they do not declare it as income (and you do not get any income

tax deduction). Income earned on the gift after it is made is taxed
to the recipient.

Compensation for physical injury or illness through insurance, judgments,
or Worker's Compensation.

Public assistance benefits.

Interest on some government bonds.

Veteran's benefits.

Social Security. Generally about 50% of your Social Security payments
may be subject to taxation. The exact percentage will turn on the
amount of other income you have.

Earnings on criminal activity are not exempt from income taxes. Al Capone
learned this the hard way. This puts criminals in something of a bind. Report
your income, the IRS turns you in and you get arrested. Don't report your income, the government need not show that you committed any specific crime,
only that you had a lot of income and didn't report it. The IRS allows individuals to file numbered returns. If they then get caught with large amounts
of cash, they can point out that they were at least paying taxes on it.

c. State and Local Taxes

Almost all states offer older citizens tax breaks in one or more areas: sales
tax, income tax, or property tax. States may adopt the federal approach to
some deductions, but not others. Because of the wide range of State approaches, we advise you to contact your accountant or the agency in your state
that is responsible for collecting taxes.

d. Taxes on Pensions, Annuities, and IRAs

"Dollars will be taxed just once, But once for sure!"

If the money you put into your retirement plan was tax deductible at the
time of contribution, your retirement benefits will be treated as regular income when you receive it. Money going into most pension plans is deductible, as is money going into traditional IRAs. When the money comes
out, it is taxed.

However, if the money that goes into the retirement plan was not tax deductible at the time, then when *that* money is returned to you, it is not taxed.
This is because you already paid taxes on those dollars before they went into

the retirement account. When you get the interest earned on those dollars, though, it is taxed as regular income.

To illustrate this, let's take the example of an annuity. Say you have $100,000 and don't want the trouble of investing it. You can buy an annuity. For your $100,000, a bank will promise to pay you a certain monthly amount over the next several years. Because it will have the use of your $100,000 from Day One, it will pay you interest. Assume that at the end of the annuity, it will have paid you $150,000. (Don't go to sleep!)

As to each payment, two-thirds will be return of capital (and not taxed), and one-third will be the interest earned (and taxable).

The new Roth IRA is a bright and shining exception to the rule "dollars will be taxed at least once." Money coming out of Roth IRAs that represents earnings on contributions is *not* taxed. See our discussion at Chapter 8-c.

PART 3

Trouble: Getting In and Getting Out

Introduction

"Baby isn't talking. I'm worried. Worried sick! It's been months. Not a single word. Not even 'Mama.' Something must be wrong! I'm calling Dr. Bronimman."
"But Dear, it's two in the morning"

When our children were small, we turned to Dr. Spock. With *Baby and Child Care* on the night stand, we slept better. It got us through the tough times. We looked into the future—"The First 12 Weeks," "Teething," "The Terrible Twos"—and took comfort knowing that others had gone before. We learned when to phone the doctor, and when to go back to sleep.

This part gives you a heads up on trouble you or your family might face.

Chapter 14 deals with the abuse and financial exploitation of elders, how to recognize it and how to deal with it. We even have some advice for where abusers can get help. Abuse and exploitation are very serious matters—you must realize that your family is not immune. Chapter 15 deals with a different kind of abuse—that inflicted on oneself, as in elders running off to Vegas or, depressed, committing suicide. In regard to that, we discuss the controversial issue of guns in the home.

The next two chapters discuss matters near and dear to us all, sex and driving. The news is not all good: we all must eventually give up driving. But the news is not all bad: not so sex.

If you have grandkids, take a look at Chapter 18. If you want to loan one of your children money, consult Chapter 19, which deals with this situation and the general support obligations owed between family member. We offer a few lines you can use as excuses for not making the loan. If you are getting divorced or remarried, slow down a tad: Chapter 21 is a critical read.

Finally we look at bad guys. First bigots who discriminate against you in employment and housing because of your age, disability or even your cat. That's Chapter 21. The last chapter of this part deals with crooks and bill collectors. Even if you are way ahead on your Master Card, a quick look at that chapter will give you hints on how to protect your identity.

Read the chapters that seem to apply to you now and be aware that they are there should the need arise at a later date. This is the same way you used Spock's book. Once you learned from it that babies learn to talk at different times, you could safely skip *Talking, late* and go to *Parental Rejection, early*.

A Note on the Limits of Law

Many of these chapters deal with family problems—raising grandchildren, financial dealings between family members, divorce and remarriage, and abuse and neglect.

Of course, there will be laws; there will always be laws.

We begin, however, with this short cautionary note, with a warning of the dangers of using lawyers and the law to solve family problems. Mediation and counseling often promise much better results for you and for your family.

Lawyers work best in a world of strangers, where they can snarl questions, point fingers, and stamp feet. When the dust settles, strangers pay up and walk away. Scars mend or are forgotten.

Kin *never* walk away; kin are for the long haul.

Lawyers are good in that small portion of the universe where people "start it"—where they run red lights, deliver defective widgets, and pull hair triggers. No one ever "starts it" in the family. Sure, Sis did hit us first, but in our hearts of hearts, we know we pushed her to it with our cruel taunts (which, of course, she richly deserved for what she said last week).

We are a society of *rights*. Individual rights are critical; without them, others would push us around and we would never be safe from bullies. *But a society based solely on rights is likely to fly apart.* Long ago there was a great legal reform movement in China: the laws should be written down so people could know them.

Who could argue with that? The followers of Confucius. If people know their rights, they argued, they will *insist upon them*. They will no longer compromise nor consider the interests and needs of others. The center will not hold. Happy societies, and happy families, need compromise and compassion.

In fights with family members, and indeed with neighbors, the question is not who is right according to the law. The question is how the fight can be resolved so as to restore peace. Counselors and mediators, trained in conflict resolution, can help you redirect focus from what happened in the past to what will happen in the future, from casting blame to sharing credit.

And the *earlier* you seek this kind of help, the more effective it can be.

To get counseling and mediation help, a good place to start is by calling your local Domestic Relations Court. Your Area Agency on Aging may have ideas as well.

CHAPTER 14

ABUSE, NEGLECT, AND FINANCIAL EXPLOITATION

Abuse gets <u>worse</u>, not better, more frequent, more severe. It does <u>not</u> self-correct—intervention is imperative.

Most think of abuse as being *inflicted* on the victim and this is the topic of this chapter. However, much abuse is self-inflicted: mom flies off to Vegas with her life savings or dad buys a gun and seems depressed. We will look at self-inflicted abuse in the next chapter.

We approach inflicted abuse from three perspectives: from that of a concerned relative, from that of the victim, and from that of the abuser. How can relatives recognize and deal with abuse? How can victims protect themselves? How can abusers stop their destructive and criminal ways?

a. Recognizing Abuse and Getting Victims Talking

Abuse comes in many forms: *physical abuse* (slapping, bruising, sexually molesting, restraining); *psychological abuse* (threatening, humiliating, ridiculing); *neglect* (abandonment, denial of food or health services); and *financial exploitation.*

Just because an elderly relative seems okay doesn't mean all is well. The signs of abuse are often hidden and those that do appear often go unnoticed. We're busy with our own lives. It is easy to accept cuts and bruises as being the result of falls; and it is easy to dismiss complaints as evidence of senility or the "natural grumpiness of old folks."

Abuse happens in the best families, abuse happens in the worst families; it happens on Boardwalk, and it happens on Baltic Avenue. Don't think your family is immune.

Most of the physical violence suffered by the elderly is inflicted by spouses, with husbands being the more frequent victims but wives the more severely injured. Frequently, the abuse is of *recent* origin. Retirement requires couples to work out whole new ways of living. Conflicts happen and old scores settled. Alcohol abuse becomes more common and frequently leads to physical abuse. If one spouse is disabled and the other becomes the care-giver, this adds extra strains. Caring for another is tough—see our suggestions in Chapter 32a.

Given the prevalence of elder abuse, if you have a fragile relative, unless you *know* all is well, *suspect abuse.*

Look for *isolation* and *changes.*

"Mildred's a little too tired to come to the phone just now." Abusers keep victims isolated so no one knows what is happening, and so the victim becomes more dependent on the abuser. There are always excuses why Mildred can't be seen or heard. Abusers then turn victims against their relatives. *"Mildred, isn't it a shame your son never calls?"* Now Mildred feels more isolated and, if her son ever gets through, she will be less likely confide in him.

Akin to isolation is the tactic of always speaking for the victim. *"Oh yes, Mildred has been doing much better on her new meds."*

Insist on visiting. Look for *changes.*

Unexpected or unexplained deterioration of health, bruises, burns, welts, cuts, punctures, sprains and broken bones; dehydration and weight loss; missing eyeglasses, hearing aids, or dentures. Abusers will explain these away as the results of falls or illnesses. Insist on details by asking them to explain exactly how and when things happened.

Insomnia, excessive sleep, and change in appetite may indicate depression and hopelessness due to *psychological abuse.* So too can tearfulness, paranoia, low self-esteem, excessive fears, ambivalence, confusion, resignation, or agitation.

As to financial exploitation, the sudden inability to pay bills, withdrawals of large amounts of cash, and living well below one's means, spell trouble. Children steal ("Well, I'll get the money later, anyway"); home-care workers steal. Others exploit the elderly in less criminal ways, often targeting those who live alone: home shopping channels offering companionship and political action committees offering protection from "gathering political storms."

Insist on looking at the checkbook. And even the checkbook is probably not enough—we have seen many, many cases of financial exploitation fueled by debit cards and cash withdrawal machines. If the senior doesn't know what an ATM is or where her card has gone, count it as a likely sign that something might be awry.

Other signs of abuse come, not from the victim, but from the care-giver. Is the care-giver drinking? Depressed? Resentful? Overworked? Or, alas, driving a new car? All of these may point to something amiss.

Why all this Sherlock Holmes stuff? Why not simply ask? Victims aren't likely to talk because they are scared or because they believe nothing can be done. Most often, the abuser has convinced the victim that they will be institutionalized if anyone acts to end the relationship, or that they will be physically injured by the abuser. To get the victim talking, first address those fears.

> *"I'm concerned that someone may be mistreating you. I know this is very hard for you to talk about. Before we get started, let me tell you a few things that might address some of your fears."*
>
> *"People who are abused often blame themselves, think it is somehow their fault, that they deserve it, or that it shows that they can no longer run their lives, that they are getting senile. Abuse is found in all kinds of families and it's not your fault. I won't think less of you no matter what you tell me."*
>
> *"Maybe you think I'll call the police and you don't want the person to go to jail. I promise not to call the police if you don't want me to."*

Usually you can keep this promise—though whether you really want to may be another matter altogether. There is generally no obligation to report crime. Some folks, however, are required to report, for example, the person's legal guardian, medical provider, or social worker. In many states, medical, legal, and mental health professionals must report physical abuse, not to police, but to a designated agency, most likely Adult Protective Services. Even if you report, unless the victim presses charges, police will not arrest the abuser, except in the case of extreme physical abuse. But you should feel a general obligation to the human community to not only punish abusers, but also to prevent them from acting again.

> *"Another fear is that the person abusing you is your care-giver. If you tell, what will happen to you?"*

This is the tough one. But there are solutions. Perhaps the abuser is just overworked and help can be found. Alternative living arrangements are possible.

> *"If you tell me, you might be afraid of getting beat up. There are ways to protect you."*

Short-term shelters are available, as well as the option of hospitalization. Many jurisdictions allow for easy-to-obtain domestic court orders of protection which will prohibit the abuser from coming to the victim's home. Locks can be changed.

Once you have addressed the victim's fear of talking, you still must convince the victim that it is in his or her interest to talk.

> *"Abuse gets worse, not better. Even if the person has promised never to do it again. There is help available for you and the person mistreating you. I want to help you. I can't, unless you tell me what's going on."*

There is one matter that is very difficult to raise, not only for you, but for us—we don't want you to throw this book across the room. Abuse is not always a one-way street, not always a black and white affair. Some victims trigger abuse by being too demanding, too sarcastic, too unappreciative. How can this be so? Because there may be payoffs for the victim, a sense of vindication when the abuser stumbles, falls, strikes out, and then, on bended knee and with flowers, seeks forgiveness. Such are humans.

As you work towards a possible solution with the victim, consider:

> *"Is there anything you might be doing that triggers the abuse? Sometimes victims stay in bad situations because they get something from them, like flowers and apologies. Anything like that going on with you?"*

Once the victim opens up and starts talking, you can begin working out a solution.

Often it will involve helping the person take steps themselves and we make some suggestions in the section "Self-help for Victims." But what if the person can't act for themselves due to mental impairment?

b. Helping Helpless Victims

If the victim is mentally impaired and hence unable to protect themselves, emergency *guardianships* can be sought to remove the victim from an abusive situation. Emergency *conservatorships* can be sought to freeze assets to protect against financial exploitation. The mechanics of these are discussed in Chapter 30.

If the individual is in a *nursing* home, the best way to prevent abuse is simply to stay involved. Visit often and at different times of day. Ask questions of nurses and doctors. Periodically ask to review the person's chart. Under the Nursing Home Bill of Rights, as the patient's representative, you have the right to examine current clinical records (within 24 hours after request) and to make copies of them. Discuss concerns with the staff and try to find solutions together. You are all working toward the same goal.

If problems continue or get worse, report them to the administration, and to any federal or state agency that oversees the home. Signs should be posted in the nursing home as to how to file a complaint and how to contact these agencies. See Chapter 33 for more on nursing homes.

c. Self-Help for Victims

If you are a victim of abuse and are like most other victims, you just take it. You are isolated, feel guilty, and do nothing. You feel both helpless and hopeless.

The abuser wants to keep you isolated, wants to keep you quiet. Your friends and relatives will be discouraged from visiting and you will be told that they don't visit because they don't care. Trips out become less frequent and those that occur are always with the abuser in attendance.

You'll need an ally. Someone outside. You need a plan.

But guilt may stay the effort. "Being abused is my fault. It shows how weak and senile I am. I deserve it." Fear of the future stays the effort. "If I say anything, things will go worse. Where will I live? Who will care for me?"

There are no easy answers and perhaps no happy endings, only improvements. Doing nothing means that the abuse will get worse, not better. That is the clinical history of abuse.

- Taking action to protect yourself does not mean that the person will be arrested. *Unless you file a criminal complaint,* only in extreme cases of abuse will the police arrest the person.
- The abuser may get help. Abuse may stem from overwork or lack of knowledge about community services that are available. These can be remedied. Counseling may address other problems.
- If you have no place to go, there are emergency shelters at secret locations. Friends and relatives can also offer shelter. To get help, call police, your Area Agency on Aging, or the Information and Referral Agency.

Where to find an ally? In emergencies, use 911. Talk to your doctor or lawyer. Call a relative. Information and Referral will have other sources of help. Most locales have Adult Protective Services which specializes in protecting the elderly. Again, the national clearing house: 1-800-677-1116.

Coping with Spouse Abuse: Protective orders

The law has been moving quickly to deal with spouse abuse. Local police are being trained to be more sensitive and are less likely to treat abuse lightly. In most jurisdictions, it is possible for a battered spouse (not always the wife) to go to court, fill out a simple form, and get a court order which will require the aggressor to stay away. There is no need to get a lawyer. You can get a protective order even if the person lives in the same house; he or she will have to move out. If the abuser shows up, they can be arrested for *violating* the order; they need not do anything more in terms of threats or abuse.

Abuse by Adult Children

It is very difficult to admit that your children are abusing you. Yet it happens. Physical is easier to recognize than financial. Most mental health hospitals have closed, and now many mentally ill live with their parents. Their continuing dependent relationship may fire violence and abuse.

It is easier *not* to let children move back in than it is getting them out. If they have moved in, you have the legal right to have them removed. Call police and change the locks. Protective orders, like those against spouses, are likely to be available.

Financial abuse is common as well. Children may seek a guardianship over you, not to protect you, but to protect their inheritance. Even if they don't have a formal guardianship, if they manage your finances, they may do so at your expense. It may be, for example, best for you to move into an assisted living facility, but your child will discourage that in order to save money. Again, the main block to doing something about this is making the painful realization that your child, the child you raised, is stealing from you.

Financial Exploitation

Dishonest children, friends, or nurses may simply forge your name to checks or, on their way to the bank to deposit your checks in your account, suddenly see a better alternative.

Get hold of your monthly bank statement. Check to see if all deposits were made and whether any of the returned checks have been forged. If you report a forgery within 30 days of receiving your statement, the bank *must* make it good; otherwise, probably not.

If your bank statement is missing, bells should go off. Dishonest relatives may have stolen it. If you suddenly stop getting your bank statement, check with the bank as to when it was sent. Duplicates can usually be sent, although it takes time.

If you are under guardianship, you have the right to demand an accounting of your financial affairs. Contact an attorney.

Nursing Home Abuse

Nursing homes that receive Medicare or Medicaid funds (and most do) must comply with the Nursing Home Bill of Rights. Your most important rights include:

- The right to be free of physical or drug restraints unless needed to protect you or other residents and only then upon the written order of a physician.
- The right to receive and send unopened and uncensored mail.
- The right to reasonable access to a phone and to make calls in private.
- Area Councils on Aging maintain an office of Ombudsman to take and investigate nursing home complaints.

d. Self-Help for Abusers

Abusers, like everyone, including Darth Vader, like to think highly of themselves and hence construct a world view that makes whatever they do, if not noble, at least justified; if not innocent, at most "guilty with an explanation." If you are a caregiver, ask yourself, "If I were the patient, would I like being treated the way I am treating them?"

If you are an abuser, the first step is to 'fess up. You're a criminal.

The following are *not* defenses to a criminal charge:

- the victim was hard to deal with;
- the victim abused you in the past; or
- the money, down the road, would have been yours, anyway.

Abuse is hard to self-correct; the natural course of abuse is downward, toward greater frequency and severity.

Confront the fact that you are abusing someone. It is easy to lie to yourself. Ask the cause and *seek help* dealing with it.

Read our discussion on caring for others (Chapter 32). It offers tips on how to cope with caring for the elderly. It is a very tough job. Frustrations and lack of sleep can lead to abuse. But there are several sources of help.

Alcoholism and Drug Abuse

A police officer friend, who has responded to over 300 cases of domestic violence, reports that all but one involved alcohol. All but one.

Alcohol gets more toxic as we age. Our bodies lose the ability to process it. We may slip into alcoholism or drug abuse and these conditions may trigger us to abuse others. Programs are available, such as Alcoholics Anonymous (AA). Many AA chapters are exclusively for seniors.

Psychological Resentments

Abusers are often financially dependent upon their victims and, resenting that dependency, resort to abuse. Sometimes spouses, over the years, begin to resent each other. Counseling may help. Separation, and even divorce, are possible solutions.

CHAPTER 15

SELF-ABUSE: VEGAS, BOOZE, AND THE QUESTION OF GUNS

Some of us don't age gracefully. Some begin to burn their candles at both ends, running through life savings, buying extravagant items, taking weird trips, falling victim to various charlatans. Others begin to abuse alcohol and still others contemplate suicide. The presence of handguns in the home no doubt contributes to the high suicide rate among seniors. We close this chapter discussing that issue.

We know you are alive, kicking, and aging gracefully. Reading this book is a sure sign. However, you may know someone who isn't: this chapter suggests what you might do to help.

a. Flying to Vegas

If a loved one suddenly begins to waste money, a conservatorship (in some states, "guardianship of the estate" or even, as in Louisiana, a "curatorship") can be sought on an emergency basis. The appointed conservator will take charge of the person's finances—bank accounts, property, stocks. See Chapter 30. Before that, banks, credit card companies, and financial institutions can be notified.

The rub: what looks like reckless to you may not look that way to the "victim:" it may look like sowing one's oats. Say your aunt is giving the gardener money and is taking him on weekend trips to Las Vegas. Unless she no longer has legal capacity or unless he is putting undue pressure on her, she is free to spend her money any way she wants—even if it means you won't be getting any.

My candle burns at both ends;
  It will not last the night;
But ah, my foes, and oh, my friends—
  It gives a lovely light!
    Enda St. Vincent Millay

You might want to read our chapter on deciding for others, which gives some ideas on how to filter out self-interest (Chapter 31).

b. Booze, Depression, and Suicide

Alcoholism is a serious problem and a lot of the drinking is of recent origin. Interventions are possible. A group of friends and relatives show up to confront the individual, not only with the harm drinking causes the person, but how it harms *them*. "You know, your grandchildren used to love coming over here; now I can't bring them." Interventions are intense and often effective. Local AA programs can offer advice.

Suicide is a problem. The elderly lead all age categories in suicides; white males lead the pack. In our discussion of Oregon's Death with Dignity Act (Chapter 35), (allowing physicians to prescribe lethal medicine), we indicated that sometimes suicide might be a rational choice. Our concern here is with the hasty choice, fired by depression and perhaps alcohol. Another concern is with self-neglect: not caring for one's basic needs.

Depression fuels both. Dealing with depression is very difficult. Begin by asking your physician. In extreme cases, consider *civil commitment*. Under most state laws, mentally ill individuals who present a danger to themselves (not eating, threatening suicide) or others (not careful with fire), can be taken into emergency custody and, after a hearing, committed to a mental hospital for treatment. The length of the commitment and the procedures vary according to state statute. Contact Adult Protective Services.

c. Guns

Handguns, not rifles, are the weapon of choice in elderly suicides. Guns don't require much planning: they are quick, easy, and the stuff of momentary despair. Further, guns in the house, at the time of a heated argument, often prove lethal. Murder/suicides are the stuff of daily newspapers. As we pointed out in our last chapter, much of physical violence committed on the elderly is committed by spouses; often that violence is of recent origin. The fact that a couple is quite happy today does not mean that there will not be violence tomorrow. The lurking threat of domestic violence suggests that the presence of weapons is a very bad idea.

But what about self-defense? The presence of guns, rather than affording protection, may make things worse. With guns drawn, stakes are definitely raised and home invaders may simply disarm, and then shoot, their victim.

Gun critics, however, overlook the peace of mind having a gun may bring. An elderly couple with a gun in their home may not be, in fact, safer and, in fact, statistically might be less safe. However, they *feel* safer and live less fearful lives. As home invasions and suicides are rare, the psychic benefits of gun ownership may outweigh the risks.

If you are going to have a gun, first don't advertise that you do with signs like "These Premises Protected by Smith and Wesson." This will just draw gun thieves. Second, realize the dangers guns present: suicide and family violence. These may not seem like possibilities now, not in your family, but they never do. Make it hard to use the gun in moments of blind rage or deep depression. Keeping the gun unloaded, keeping it locked up, and having trigger locks are possibilities.

If you have grandkids, keep the gun locked and know the state law on gun ownership. If the law permits you to carry a gun in your car, if you are stopped by police, with your hands on the wheel, immediately tell the officer that you have a gun in the car.

Learn how to use your gun. Take shooting lessons, to learn gun safety and to realize their lethal power. Some make shooting clubs a social focus.

Finally, consider a rifle, not a handgun. Rifles are less likely to be used in suicide or in domestic violence and they offer good protection. Possibly even better: shotguns. You don't have to be a good aim with a shotgun (as a Vice President once discovered). The buckshot spreads after leaving the barrel. And, we are told, nothing is quite as unnerving to a burglar as the sharp sound of a shotgun being cocked.

CHAPTER 16

SEX

"George is hot stuff here in the nursing home. The ladies love him, fight over him. He can dance.... and he has his teeth."

This sounds like something akin to a product placement, paid for by a maker of dental floss. It isn't. And it is more than a ploy to increase sales by appealing to your prurient interests. Sex is a serious topic.

When we first learned about "it," it was inconceivable that our parents did "it," at least more than once. As for our grandparents, not thinkable. But they did, probably frequently.

We report, you decide.

While looks and stamina fade, sex hangs in there. A study of healthy people, aged from 80 to 102, found that 88% of men and 72% of women have sexual fantasies. Furthermore, 72% of men and 40% of women engage in self-stimulation and 66% of men and 38% of women continue to have sexual intercourse. This last stat may puzzle the careful reader. It seems to suggest that many more men are having sexual intercourse than women. How can that be? Perhaps strange things happen as we age, women become floozies, men become gay. Probably not. Recall that at this age there are many more women than men; if the same number engage in intercourse, it would result in a lower percentage of women than of men. Do the math.

Sex is always more than sex. For the elderly it is a statement of continued involvement with life, a source of emotional support, and a validation of self-worth. It may not even result in orgasms. It can be simply caresses and gentle touching.

Self-help manuals abound, and many describe techniques and approaches to sex that are more elder-friendly. Rather than "adult diapers," consider such a manual as "No Serious Gifts" birthday gift. It would get as good a laugh and, who knows, maybe a whispered "thank you."

The law of sex is pretty straightforward. Competent adults, in privacy, can do what they want. Recently the Supreme Court underscored that right by striking down a Texas statute that criminalized gay sex, holding that it violated the Due Process Right of privacy.

On the other hand, forced sex is criminal. (We don't call it "rape" anymore; we call it "sexual assault.") "No" means "no" and sometimes "yes" means "no" as well. Consent obtained by threats, tricks, or force, is not consent. Nor is the "consent" given by someone legally unable to consent, children under the age of 16 or 18, and mentally impaired adults—but "impaired" for this purpose probably means something like "unable to understand the nature or consequence of the sexual act" rather than what their prudish adult children might prefer.

Forced sex, in addition to being a crime, is a tort. This means that the perpetrator can be sued for money damages. Not only can the perpetrator be sued, but so too anyone who had a duty to protect the victim but didn't.

All of this straightforward law pretty much means a headache for the administrators of George's nursing home. He and the ladies who fight over him have a right to do what they wish and a nursing home that attempts to prevent that is demeaning their personhood. (It would not be acting unconstitutionally as the Constitution limits only governmental actors, not private.) However, the picture changes if George is forcing himself on the ladies or if he is having sex with women who, due to dementia, do not have the legal capacity to consent, no matter what they say or do. In these two cases, George is guilty of sexual assault and the nursing home, under a duty to protect its residents, may be sued.

How nursing homes handle the situation varies a great deal. Many have no formal policies, handling the matters case-by-case. All will attempt to prevent non-consensual sex and some will tell family members if a resident is engaging in consensual sex. Some nursing homes, recognizing therapeutic goods flowing from relationships, openly discuss geriatric sex. If you are considering a nursing home, for you or your parents, you might want to inquire.

Sex is not just a concern of nursing homes. Fragile elders can be sexually abused by home-care providers and, as we discuss in our chapter on Elder Abuse, one should be sensitive to this possibility. Like its counterparts—teen sex, young adult sex, middle-age sex—elder sex can lead us into doing foolish and destructive things. In our chapter on Self Abuse, we discuss the "Vegas Fling Problem." Finally, there is the problem of sexually transmitted disease: Viagra has its costs.

Finally, knowing of our continued interest in sex, crooks will attempt to exploit it. One scam involves sending false bills to grieving widows, claiming that pornographic material was sent to their husbands. If you are male and frequent the internet, no doubt you get scads of daily emails offering Viagra and other sex aids. Best to talk to your doctor. Many of these medications will interact badly with your current meds; others will kill you outright. (These email spammers do not realize, however, that men our age will not spring for penis enhancement, having made our peace long ago.)

Have you ever told your parents a dirty joke? Despite the bravado of the Sixties, sex remains taboo. Get over it. Just as your parents once told you of the birds and bees, tell them now that *you* know that they continue to sing and buzz.

Buzz.

CHAPTER 17

DRIVING

"You might as well shoot me," said a nurse when told she could no longer drive. "It's like telling a patient they have terminal cancer."

Having to stop driving can be a horrible passage. Driving was the mark of adulthood; when we first got behind the wheel, we became the master of our own fate. Giving up driving signals a loss of independence, vitality, and control.

But it's not just symbolic. There are very practical issues at stake. Many of us live far from shopping and far from the center of our social lives: churches, movies, restaurants, friends' homes, social clubs. Public transport is often infrequent, scary, and difficult to access if you are in any way disabled. Even where local authorities offer special vans for the elderly, the picture is not bright. Often this transportation is only for the necessities (shopping and medical) and not for visiting, not for concerts. Even if your community has an efficient and adequately-funded public transportation system (and few do), the wait for a ride can seem interminable, the equipment shabby and even threatening, and the availability sporadic.

Loss of transportation has more than purely psychic effect. For the senior without wheels, life can become afternoon TV and a quick decline into depression and illness.

Driving entails danger to the driver and others. Drivers over 75 have more fatal accidents than any other age group save teenagers. Even younger senior drivers may be more dangerous—though they have fewer accidents than their younger peers, that statistic is skewed by the fact that they drive far fewer miles. Add a little dementia and elderly drivers are 7.5 times more likely to crash, exceeding the rate of even drunk drivers.

Why are the elderly bad drivers? First, a higher incident of sudden illness, strokes and heart attacks. Second, impaired vision, particularly night vision. Third, slower reaction time. Dementia adds two additional problems: forgetting one has those impairments and suddenly getting confused about where one is.

First, the legal issues: who is liable? If you negligently cause property damage, personal injury or death, you're stuck, perhaps for very big bucks. It is no defense that you never had a ticket before. It is no defense that you have bad night vision or slow reaction time due to a disability. (Driving with these conditions simply make you more negligent; however a sudden and unexpected medical emergency, such as a stroke, might be a defense.)

If a judgment against you exceeds your insurance coverage, the person you injured can come after your life savings. It is no defense that you need them to support yourself in your retirement: you're to go on welfare, not the person you injured.

You may be putting others at legal risk as well. For example, if you convince your daughter to loan you her car, a plaintiff might sue her on the theory that, knowing your condition, was negligent in doing so. If you are under guardianship, your guardian may be liable for not taking preventive steps.

But, no matter our relationship, we don't want the driver to be killed or to kill others. What to do? A family conversation, before the issue becomes pressing, helps. An agreement can be made and signed: "I agree that I will accept the decision of Dr. Kildare, my attending physician, or my younger sister, when either of them writes to me that they think I am no longer a safe driver."

Once bad driving becomes an issue, check for correctable causes. The AARP offers a refresher course ("55 Alive"). It stresses defensive driving. Commercial driving instruction companies do as well. While these courses certainly cannot hurt, and may help individual drivers, there is (sadly) little evidence that the functional driving abilities lost with normal aging can be compensated for by training, even specialized training.

Special equipment is also available, such as rear mirrors that provide a wider view of the road. Cars and vans can be outfitted to cope with many disabilities.

Certain medications can affect driving ability. Check with the doctor or pharmacist. Trip planning helps. Avoid rush hour, left turns, and frequent trips. Co-pilots help. If the driving doesn't improve:

> *"Mom, I'm worried about your driving. You don't want to get in an accident. I know you think you are fine. You are probably right. But I want you to take a driving test."*

Most State Departments of Motor Vehicles will conduct field driving tests to confirm or reject your fears. Private evaluators are also available, and the screening may even be covered by Medicare.

Talk to Mom's physician. If necessary, the physician can play the heavy (not you) and pull the plug on driving. Remember, though, that simply suspending the driver's license will not stop every driver.

If Mom is Irish—or for some other reason strong-headed—take off the plates, hide the keys, or disable the car by disconnecting the spark plugs. If your Mom's 100% Irish, she will call a mechanic to fix the disabling condition. Leave an explanation where the mechanic (but not Mom) will find it. Most often, redirection is the best approach—when Mom heads for the car you interrupt her train of thought, interpose a new and different task, and deflect both the threat of driving and the frustration and anger that will come from a failed attempt.

The good news about all of this is that there are a growing number of programs that provide stranded seniors transport. In some locales, there are programs where the family car is donated to the agency which in turn provides taxi services. There is a national movement fostering what is known as Supplemental Transportation Programs (STPs). They are run by local governments, churches and non-profits. The Area Agency should have information on them. A prime mover in the movement is the Beverly Foundation and information can be found at www.beverlyfoundation.org.

If you are retired, still a good driver, and still love it as much as you did as a teenager, these programs can always use volunteers. But no peeling out!

CHAPTER 18

GRANDCHILDREN

After all the years, after all the work, after all the bruises, after all the alarm clocks, after all our successes and failures, it has finally become our time, our time to be that quiet old lady, sitting with our grandchildren, whispering "Hush."

Well, maybe not.

Some grandparents not only put their grandkids to bed, they wake them in the morning, feed them, get them off to school, and help them with their homework. Usually this is because of divorce, unwed or too-young motherhood, parental incarceration or illness, and/or drug abuse. At the other end of the spectrum, some families are so fractured that grandparents are not allowed to visit. Tolstoy was right: every unhappy family is unhappy in its own way.

This chapter will look at the legal steps you can take in both situations, if you are raising your grandkids or if you are denied visitation rights. We also cover the situation where you are simply caring for the kids during the summer.

a. Raising Grandchildren: Legal Issues

You have joined a growing number. The AARP is on it! Its "Grandparent Information Center" (GIC) offers information on raising grandkids and step-grandparenting, message boards, and referrals. There is even a free newsletter, available in English and Spanish. Email: gic@aarp.org or phone 1-888-OUR-ARRP. Another source of help: Generations United: www.gu.org.

The legal issues usually revolve around housing, custody, financial support, and inheritance.

Housing. Some "adult" communities prohibit kids. It's best to try to work things out with whoever is in charge. Realize you have some bargaining chips: it costs money to evict and the house may remain vacant; further, no one (save some autocratic Homeowners Associations we know) wants to play the part of Darth Vader and throw kids out on the street. Some state statutes prohibit discrimination against children and, even where they don't, a good lawyer might be able to convince the court to adopt a common law rule to that effect.

Custody. Physical custody does not equal legal custody. Not having legal custody can lead to problems—doctors may insist on a parent's consent to a medical treatment, and school and welfare officials might also require it. If the child's stay with you is to be temporary, say over the summer or until the parents can relocate, then a *Parental Power of Attorney* should suffice in most states. Signed by the child's parent, it will give you power to act in the parent's stead in relation to medical and educational decisions. Even a letter, signed by one parent, is better than nothing:

> *To whom it may concern:*
>
> *I am the parent of _____ who will be staying with her grand-parents, _____, this summer. I give them the right to consent to any and all medical treatment for my child, and to exercise parental control on my behalf.*
> Signed (and better still, notarized)

Things become much more complicated if your grandchildren are living with you more or less permanently.

> *Sally, 22 and unwed, leaves her six-month-old baby with her parents "until she can work things out." She has an irregular work history, a minor drug problem, and a scuzzy boyfriend. Two weeks ago she went out for a pack of cigarettes; other than one collect phone call from Oklahoma, she hasn't been heard from since.*

Our advice: *consider adopting.*

Unless you have legal custody, Sally can suddenly reappear and pick up the child, insisting "This time I will make a go of it." Often, revolving doors. Young children need love and *permanence.* A general Power of Attorney does not guarantee permanence. It can always be revoked by the parent—or even by the *other* parent. Without legal custody, both you and the children will be hostage to the whims of the parents, and you already know how dysfunctional they are.

If you adopt your grandchild, it need not be forever. If the parent gets her act together, you can return physical custody to her. Without adoption, however, it is her choice; with adoption, it is yours.

Parents can agree to adoption. The father will have to be notified. If he is genuinely unknown, publication in the local newspapers will probably be required. Incidentally, when you tell the adoption lawyer "there is no father," please pause a few moments to allow her to chuckle knowingly, and to tell you how rare the reports of virgin birth really are. Once proceedings are begun, the father may intervene. If this is a real possibility, then you might wish to back off from the adoption since the father, married or not, responsible or not, probably has a stronger legal claim to his child than do grandparents. A good adoption lawyer can tell you what your state laws require to show abandonment by either parent; expect that it will be a higher standard than what you personally think constitutes abandonment.

If the parents do not consent, you have two, sometimes three, options. Some states allow for *permanent guardianships* which do not sever parental rights but which would protect you and the children. Otherwise, you may be able to secure a guardianship, but only so long as neither parent objects—the danger being that one or both might decide to object later, and terminate the guardianship despite what would be best for your grandchild. Another route is to have child welfare officials seek a court order declaring the children to be *dependent.* If a court determines a child to be neglected or abused by his parents, the legal custody of the child will be transferred to child protective services. The child will be placed in a home and, as grandparents, you're probably first in line. Meanwhile, the parents will have parenting and, most likely, drug counseling. If they eventually get their act together they can regain custody. If they do not, the court can sever parental rights and put the child up for adoption.

If you adopt, you have all the rights and obligations of a parent, including the legal duty to *support* the child until he or she reaches the age of 18 or is emancipated. In some states, for low income individuals and/or special-needs children, an adoption subsidy is available to help offset some of the expenses of raising your newly-adopted child.

Financial help. Adopted children are entitled to your Social Security benefits just like other children. That may mean that your under-18 adopted child receives a monthly check for a fraction of your Social Security (see Chapter 6). Even without adoption, however, your dependent grandchildren (over 18 if disabled) may be entitled to benefits. The rules are complicated, so call your Social Security Office and explain your situation to them. Adoption support payments may be available for low-income families. If the child is placed with you by the court as part of a dependency action, you will receive financial help. Special assistance programs may exist if your grandchild has a disability.

You might be able to run down other sources of financial help by contacting your local welfare office or Area Agency on Aging. Welfare and other programs may be available even if you do not have legal custody.

Check with the I.R.S. concerning whether you can claim a child as your dependent, and look into the *Earned Income Tax Credit* (EIC), which is a special benefit for low- and moderate-income people, including those raising grandchildren even if they don't have legal custody. This program provides a cash payment even if you don't owe taxes.

Note: If you are raising your grandchild under a court order as a foster parent, you may be entitled to federal payments for foster care under Title *IV-E* of the Social Security Act. These payments are substantially higher than welfare payments.

Inheritance. If you die without a will, your children, not your grandchildren, will get what you have. Even if you have adopted your grandchildren, they will split the goodies with your other children—their parents. If you don't want either to happen, you need a will and a lawyer. Since you now have adopted children who are too young to manage money, you might want to consider having a living trust (see Chapter 27).

b. Grandparent Visitation Rights

Lawyers are wonderful. On a TV call-in show, a lawyer is asked, "Do grandparents have any visitation rights?"
"No, absolutely none. Zilch. Nada."
They went to station break and another lawyer told the first, "Grandparents do have visitation rights. There is a state statute."
After the break, the first lawyer jumped before the camera. "In case anyone misinterpreted what I said before…." (Why don't you folks like us?)

Since the 1970s there has been a major change in grandparent visitation rights. The law previously allowed parents the absolute right to refuse visits; grandparents were at their whim. Now all 50 states allow grandparents to *petition* the court for visitation rights.

The right to petition doesn't mean you will win. Courts are reluctant to get involved in family disputes, and under the laws of most states, grandparents cannot obtain visitation rights if the nuclear family is intact—that is, if the biological parents are still together and both agree on denying visits.

The U.S. Supreme Court has even weighed in on this question. In its own inimitable way, it has confused the issue rather than clarified it. If you have a concern about visitation, you have probably heard of the case *Troxel v. Granville*, decided in 2000. Lawyers are still arguing about what it means, and state courts and legislatures continue to adjust their laws to comply with their best reading of the case. Suffice it to say that the state of the law is in flux: grandparents may have significant rights to visitation under state law, but it may be difficult to enforce those rights under Constitutional and common-law principles. Rather than starting with your legal rights, you might want to begin with practical ideas about how to cure your separation from your grandchildren.

If you are denied visitation, first try to figure out why. Maybe the parents think you are too critical or gossip too much. Perhaps there are old family issues that have not been resolved. Don't just assume that you are in the right and threaten lawsuits.

If you were the child's parent, why would you be denying visitation? Is there anything you can do to make things right?

Getting court-ordered visitation rights will be an uphill fight. State grandparent visitation laws differ, but usually require a showing of three things: that visitation is in the *best interests of the child;* that the family situation is *dysfunctional* in certain defined ways, such as a divorce or unreasonable refusal of visitation over several months; and that the prior relationship between the grandparent and grandchild was significant before the parents began limiting or denying visitation. Usually the refusal of visitation rights must be total, not partial. If both parents in an intact family refuse you visitation rights, it is much less likely that you would prevail.

If your grandchild is adopted by strangers, or by other family members with whom you do not get along well, what happens to your visitation rights? Courts struggle. There is a strong argument that there should be a clear break between the birth and adoptive families: grandparent visitation may undermine the authority of the adoptive parents. On the other hand, there is a strong argument that the significant relationships in a child's life should continue.

The general rule, however, favors the adoptive parents. This is clearest when the child is quite young, when neither the child nor the grandparents have formed strong emotional ties. This is less definite in the case of older children, where close ties with grandparents exist. Some courts, notably those in California and New York, have ordered grandparent visits even in the face of adoption by strangers. Given these exceptions, and a general movement away from secrecy and toward "open adoptions," if you are about to lose your grandchild in an adoption, talk with an attorney.

c. When to Seek Legal Help

• If you suspect your grandchild is being *abused* or *neglected*, contact Child Protective Services. They will investigate and all reports are confidential.

• If your grandkids will be *staying* an extended period with you, contact a lawyer to make sure you have the proper documents to seek medical and dental treatment for them or to enroll them in school. If their stay is triggered by their parent's involvement with crime or drugs, consider adoption.

• If either of your grandchild's parents should die.

When one parent dies, the survivor automatically assumes legal and physical custody of the child, even if there has been a prior divorce which gave custody to the other parent. (This is not necessarily so in the case of an unwed father who has not been determined legally to be the father, and especially if he has not contributed support.) If the *second* parent dies, the Probate Court will probably appoint a guardian for the child (otherwise there will be no guardian). Usually, but not always, the court will follow the wishes of the second parent to die as described in his or her Will.

Encourage your children to nominate guardians in the event of their death. This will likely avoid fights between sets of grandparents or others.

• Pending divorce of the parents.

If your child is likely to lose custody, your visitation rights may be threatened. Whether or not you can intervene at this stage will depend upon state law.

• Dysfunction in the Family.

Dysfunction comes in many forms: an arrest of a parent or child; drug abuse and alcoholism in the family; the filing of a dependency petition filed against the parents alleging neglect or abuse; or the placement of the child for adoption. To what degree you have the legal right to intervene in such situations will vary: the point is that because so much is riding on the outcome of these situations, find out.

All of these situations involve heartache, anger, and fights. Consider, every now and then, in the heat of battle, whispering "Hush."

CHAPTER 19

FAMILY FINANCIAL DEALINGS

A smoky saloon; cowboys playing poker. One throws his cards on the table, stands, and is about to draw his pistol. "What did you call me?" he snarls.
"I called you a liar," responds the man across the table.
"A liar? Well that's fair," resuming his seat. "I thought you were calling me a lawyer."

In this chapter we validate *all* of the jokes and prove, beyond reasonable doubt, that lawyers are heartless.

- Don't co-sign notes with your children or parents.
- Don't bail them out of jail.
- Don't loan them money.
- As for your spouse, pay the bills, but only reluctantly.

Our heartless advice: be heartless. While no man is an island, try to be!

You are not legally obligated to support your kids once they turn 18 and you are not obligated to support your parents (with very few exceptions on both scores). This means, unless you have co-signed, the creditors of your adult children and of your parents cannot sue you for their debts. As to husbands and wives, they are *generally* responsible for supporting each other, and for paying family debts. Let's flesh out the implications of all of this.

a. Loans, Gifts and Bail

If you co-sign a promissory note or contract with your children, you are responsible no matter their age and no matter the purchase. Co-sign for your 45-year-old son on his purchase of a Corvette, and you are legally stuck if he doesn't pay.

But what if we're talking, not Corvettes, but getting out of jail?

If your adult child is arrested, the judge will set bail. If the bail is posted, your child gets out pending trial. Bailbondsmen will post the bond for you for a fee, usually 10%. If the bail is $30,000, the non-refundable fee would be $3,000. In addition, they will require that you give them security in the full amount of the bail: stocks, bonds, savings, and/or real property worth at least $30,000. If your child splits, you lose your security—your stocks, bonds, home.

We don't want to make light of this heartbreaking situation. It is very hard to say no to a child sitting in jail. You will hear a compelling story and heart-felt pledges of the straight and narrow. And perhaps even subtle suggestions as to why it is all your fault.

Don't do it! We know too many parents who have lost their homes and savings. We know too many parents who have posted bail only to have their child, while on bail, commit another and more serious crime. The concept of tough-love comes to mind.

As to lending your kids money, don't. *Give* it to them. If you lend it and they don't repay, you won't sue. It may just ruin your relationship.

If you give (or lend) money to one child but not to another, realize that money is a funny thing—it is more than purchasing power; it seems like love. *"Mom loves Sis more than me because she's always giving her money."* Better to explain to all what's going on.

If you have made substantial gifts to one child but not to the others, at the time of your death there will be a question of whether the gifts were advances on that child's share of your estate, or whether they were simply separate gifts. Say your Will provides that your estate is to be divided among your three children. During your lifetime you make a $10,000 gift to one. At the time of your death, does that child get an equal share or does the $10,000 come off the top? This question *may* lead to litigation and *will* lead to hard feelings. You can avoid this by expressing your intent in your Will: "Because I have given Sis $10,000 in my lifetime, this is to be considered an advance of her share of my estate" or "I give all my estate to my three children in equal shares, without any adjustment for gifts I may have made during life." Short of, and less effective than, something in your Will, tell folks what you have in mind.

> *"I gave Sis $10,000 as an advance on her inheritance, because she is starting her own business. If you other kids do, I'll try to do the same."*

or

> *"I gave Sis $10,000 as a separate gift, not as part of her inheritance, because well, frankly, I love her more."*

b. Responsibilities for Minors: College

You are responsible for supporting your minor children (usually until the age of 18), unless they have been emancipated. This obligation goes only to the necessaries of life, such as housing, food, health, and education. (When lawyers think of what is necessary in life, we think of hamburgers and tennis shoes, not of poetry, love or community. Whether this is a matter of nature or nurture is beyond our scope.)

So kids are on their own when it comes to Corvettes. If a creditor provides your minor child with a necessity, they can look to you for reimbursement. But if your kid goes out and buys a Rolex, you are *not* obligated to pay for it. Your kid is probably off the hook as well. Children under 18 generally do not have contractual capacity, and hence cannot be sued on contracts they sign— great news if your children are being threatened by CD Clubs or Book Clubs.

"Dear Record Club: When I signed your offer, I was under 18 and hence had no contractual capacity. Please stop writing me. Thanks for sharing."

If your minor children are living on their own and are running up bills for which you may be responsible, you may be able to file an action to have the court declare them *emancipated*. This means you will no longer be financially responsible. Of course, once they are emancipated, you no longer have the legal right to supervise them, either (but it doesn't sound like they were paying much attention to you, anyway). In most states, when a minor marries he or she automatically and immediately becomes emancipated—but we think that's a lousy reason to let your children marry young.

Some states (but not many) have expanded the parents' common law obligation to support their children beyond the age of 18. A statute in California, for example, provides:

The father and mother have an equal responsibility to maintain, to the extent of their ability, a child of whatever age who is incapacitated from earning a living and without sufficient means.

This expresses a nice sentiment. However, there are sufficient loopholes if a creditor of your adult child presents you with a bill. First, generally the child must have become incapacitated before age 18. Second, the bill will have to be for a necessity (as your duty is only to maintain the child). Finally, your liability extends only to your ability to pay.

A common question concerns college education. Although you are not responsible for paying for your child's college education (note to divorced parents: your divorce settlement may change this answer), colleges will consider family income in determining the amount of scholarship or financial aid that will be available for your child. Using complicated formulas, colleges will look at the family's income and assets and then determine how much the family can afford to pay toward the child's education. It then decides how much it costs to attend the particular college and, after deducting the amount it deems the family should pay, makes up the difference in loans and grants to the student. In theory this means that the family will spend the same amount no matter how expensive the college attended. How much the student must *borrow* is an entirely different matter.

c. Support Obligations between Spouses

Your spouse is home from the hospital and you receive a bill for $20,000. You don't have any joint savings or checking accounts that could pay this. But you have stock in your name that could. Should you pay the bill?

As to daily bills, the family assets are liable for either spouse's expenses.

The issue "who is responsible for what" really only arises if one spouse has incurred large medical bills or has received public assistance. Unless you are a co-signer on the bills, we advise against paying them without first seeking legal advice:

1. If your spouse has died, the bills should be paid first from his or her estate. Only if the estate is exhausted can the creditor go after you.
2. Under the common law necessities rule, a husband would be liable for his wife's medical care and support. However, some states have thrown out this rule as it denies equal protection (treating men differently from women) while others have leveled the playing field by imposing a similar obligation on the wife. Some states have family expense statutes which make one spouse liable for the debts of the other.

Even though you might eventually be held liable for the bills, our advice remains the same—don't pay them without first seeking legal advice. Most courts, even if they impose spousal obligations, do so only to the extent that it will not leave you broke. A lawyer can probably cut a good deal for you. Further, in the face of large unpaid bills, you should discuss the possibility of bankruptcy. See Chapter 22f.

If you live in one of the states that recognize "community property" principles (Arizona, California, Idaho, Louisiana, Nevada, New Mexico, Texas, Washington or Wisconsin), the results may be slightly different. Still, the basic concepts apply: your individual assets (those you brought into the marriage, or gifts or bequests to you alone) will not generally be reachable for even the "community" debts incurred by your spouse—like medical care, or necessities.

d. Your Kids' Obligation to Support You

Generally, the ungrateful brats are *not* liable for any of your debts or expenses, again, unless they are co-signers. If your children are in fact supporting you, they may be entitled to claim you as a dependent on their federal tax return.

Some states attempt to impose liability on your children if you are likely to become a public charge. These laws are generally called "poor laws" or "general assistance laws." Some may even carry a criminal penalty. However, usually they are used to "attribute" some portion of your child's income to you for the purpose of determining eligibility for public assistance, or in seeking reimbursement for public benefits supplied to you.

e. Nursing Home Expenses

We began this chapter by advising you not to bail your child out of jail. Well, we can be heartless both ways. Your children should never sign to be responsible for your nursing home expenses.

Under a 1989 Federal law, most nursing homes are prohibited from *requiring* relatives to co-sign for their charges. In some states, however, relatives can agree to pay for extra services.

Even though they cannot require co-signing for expenses, nursing homes can *request* it—and they often do request it, usually in sneaky ways that play on the family dynamics at a time of personal emergency and confusion (like when admitting a parent to a nursing home). Some may ask a son or daughter to sign as "the responsible party." This sounds like you are signing as the person to contact concerning emergencies; what it means, according to the small print, is that you are responsible for the bills.

Tell your kids not to sign. But after *you* left them sitting in jail, they probably won't, anyway.

CHAPTER 20

DIVORCE AND REMARRIAGE

Second marriages represent the triumph of hope over experience.

Samuel Johnson

a. Divorce: Property, Alimony, and Health Insurance; Alternatives to Divorce

Divorce will be a financial disaster. Both of you will have a lower standard of living. You will likely lose half of your accumulated property and much of your income. Expenses will increase; and then there are hefty lawyers' bills, his *and* hers.

Divorce will be an emotional disaster. There is less opportunity for "new beginnings" (look in the mirror). Divorce doesn't make you younger.

We'll look at alternatives to divorce after we look at the financial implications of divorce: property settlements, alimony or spousal maintenance, and health insurance.

Dividing the stuff. State divorce laws differ as to distribution of property. Some follow the old Spanish tradition of *community property,* while most follow the English tradition of *Dower.* While there are nice theoretical distinctions between the two, as a practical matter most judges will try to split the property acquired during a long-term marriage. Let this sink in for a moment. *If you divorce now, likely you will lose half of what you accumulated over your married life.*

Half of it.

Unless there is a lot of cash lying around for buy-outs, you will have to sell the family home. That may be just as well if neither of you has enough resources to pay the mortgage and upkeep costs alone.

Assume your mortgage is paid off and your house is valued at $200,000. Dividing its value, each of you is entitled to $100,000. If you have $200,000 in savings, one of you could take your $100,000 share of those savings, and "buy out" the other's share in the house. Of course, one of you is now broke and the other homeless—but you're the ones who couldn't get along. If you don't have savings of $200,000, most likely the house will have to be sold and the cash divided.

Pension plans present unique problems of evaluation. Assume the wage earner is 55. How much is his or her pension plan worth now, given the fact that it will pay, at 65, an amount based on earnings during the last three years before age 65, earnings which won't be earned for another seven years?

We have to project what the pension would pay at 65 and then figure out how much such a plan would cost. That might be the easy calculation. Let's say we figure it out and come up with the figure of $400,000. Fine. But what's the *current* value of a benefit which will be worth $400,000 in ten years? How much would you have to invest now in order to have $400,000 in ten years? This calculation is contentious since it rests upon assumptions as to rates of interest and inflation.

Expert economists love long, leisurely discussions concerning the future worth of pensions, with color charts and computer printouts. And, if both partners have retirement plans, both must be evaluated and then compared. Expert economists, of course, bill in *current* dollars.

To solve these difficult evaluation and current value problems, some states allow the judge to simply order that the wife receive, at the time of her husband's retirement, a percentage of that retirement. Federal law allows this to be done for Military benefits as well.

Social Security solves these problems this way. After a divorce, at the age of 62, the non-wage earner can collect on her ex-husband's Social Security account if:

1. They were married at least ten years, and
2. She has not remarried. (If she remarried after the age of 60, she does not lose eligibility.)

Note: If you are divorcing and have been married less than ten years, it might be smart to swallow your pride and wait a while in order to create Social Security eligibility. Conversely, you might want to curb your enthusiasm and wait until you're 60 to remarry.

Alimony. You can't go back to Constantinople; you can't go back to alimony. As we rush toward our brave new world, we discard old sexist traditions such as "alimony." We now call it "spousal maintenance." The basic notion is to "maintain" the non-working (or less-earning) spouse at relatively the same standard of living, while she (it is almost always she) can bring her skills up to speed to allow her to make her own way at a comparable level. While *alimony* might be permanent and thus "demeaning," *spousal maintenance* is to be temporary and thus "empowering."

This philosophy makes no sense at all in the case of elderly women. Their chances of entering the labor force and earning enough money to support themselves at comparable levels is almost nil. Recognizing this, many judges are now ordering permanent spousal maintenance. In setting the amount of that maintenance, the court will consider the assets that the spouse receives at divorce, as they may produce significance amounts of income.

If your spouse is not only elderly but also spending significant amounts of money on care (medical bills, household support, nursing home payments, etc.), the amount of spousal maintenance you are required to pay may increase accordingly.

Health Insurance. Many married people have health insurance only under their spouse's work policy. When both work, the couple will decide whose health policy is best and go with it. Upon divorce, one will lose coverage. However, a federal law, called *COBRA*, gives ex-spouses the right to maintain that insurance for three years. They must pay the premium, thus *increasing* their expenses. If they do not become eligible for Medicare within this three-year period, they will be severely disadvantaged, as it will be difficult and expensive to obtain other insurance. These expenses should be reflected in the amount of support ordered.

Alternatives to Divorce. Counseling is a good place to start. Often, the problems really aren't with each other. They are with the pressures of aging and retirement. Divorce won't make you dashing, nor will it give you things to do. Divorce doesn't solve problems; counseling might.

You can try living together but separately. Separate bedrooms, with occasional angry glares over the kitchen table, solve most of the legal problems we have been discussing in this chapter. There is no need to divide property, to obtain additional health insurance, or to pay lawyers. And just maybe if you fell out of love, you might fall back in.

Note: this is not living in sin. Rather it combines the worse of both worlds.

Another alternative is a *legal separation*. It can provide for a formal settlement of economic issues, while allowing for the continuation of health and death benefits. Under a legal separation, the parties are still married.

If you don't want a divorce and your spouse does, contact a lawyer. Don't let the matter go by default. Even in no-fault divorce states, marriage dissolutions can be delayed and sometimes counseling ordered.

There are two situations where elderly divorce does make sense:

1. If one plans to get remarried; or
2. As a device to save the family assets from Medicaid nursing home expenses.

Nursing home expenses can bankrupt families. Medicaid will pay them but only after the family has "spent down" to a certain level. In addition to other exemptions, such as the family home, the law allows for the non-institution-alized spouse to keep $75,000 of other assets. Say the couple has a large estate, say $300,000 in nonexempt assets. If they divorce, the non-institutionalized spouse will be able to keep his or her share, probably $150,000, rather than only the $75,000 which would be allowed under Medicaid rules.

b. Marriage: Prenuptials and Wills

First, our enthusiasm: Congratulations on your marrige!
Second, our wisdom: Get a prenuptial and change your Will.

A new marriage requires a new estate plan. Do you want your new spouse to inherit all of your property? Perhaps, given his or her financial situation and the length of your relationship, you want to bypass your new spouse and leave everything to your children. If you do not rewrite your Will, things will be messy when you die.

There is a special problem if both of you have children from prior mar-riages. You will probably want to provide for your new spouse after your death, but at the time of his or her death, you would like to see your assets revert to some or all of the children. You both agree and draft new Wills, leaving every-thing to one another, remainder divided among all the children. You die first. How can you be sure your new spouse will keep his or her end of the bargain? Betrayal! The stuff of Shakespearean tragedy.

Double, double, toil and trouble;
Fire, burn; and caldron, bubble.
Eye of newt, and toe of frog,
Wool of bat, and tongue of dog,
Tear my Will, a thousand pieces,
Leave it all to my portly nieces!

A *living trust* is a good solution. (See Chapter 27.) The assets of both spouses are placed in trust for their use during their lives. Upon the death of one, the spouses have agreed that the trust will become irrevocable and pro-vide that income will go to maintain the survivor (with liberal principal inva-sion terms to cover such things as medical emergencies). At the death of the survivor, the assets can be distributed as provided by the original trust in-strument; i.e., divided among the couple's children from prior marriages. This approach is an improvement over relying on fidelity continuing for years after your death, but it is not perfect. Who will be trustee of the trust, and therefore decide whether the surviving spouse really needs that cruise, or sundeck on the house, or nursing home payment? The surviving spouse? The deceased spouse's oldest son, who is both an accountant and a lawyer and has a heart of coal? And what will happen to the trust if the surviving spouse remarries, or moves out of the house (and in with the massage therapist)?

If a living trust is not for you, a lawyer can help you set up other devices to accomplish your goals. You might want to discuss signing reciprocal Wills, and maybe even agree that neither of you will change your Wills after the death of the other spouse. Lawyers love these arrangements, as they get to charge more when you sign, and much more when your heirs fight over what the agreement meant and whether the survivor breached it. More valuably (for you), a lawyer can draft a "prenup."

> *A cartoon shows two young boys standing next to a swimming hole. There is a rope tied to a tree limb that was obviously used to support a tire used as a swing over the pond. The rope is broken. The tire is floating in the water. One boy is saying: "I'll go get another tire, you go tell Tommie's mother."*

The hardest part about prenuptial agreements is broaching the subject. Blame us. Copy this chapter and leave it on the pillow, anonymously.

A "prenuptial" is simply a written agreement between the happy couple. Sometimes, in an effort to convince clients that they actually speak Latin, lawyers use the term "antenuptial"—it just means "before the marriage," not "against the marriage". It can cover such things as:

1. Who is responsible for the debts brought into the marriage?
2. In the event of divorce, what happens to the property brought into the marriage *and* to property acquired during it? What of support obligations?
3. Who is to inherit what?
4. Who takes out the garbage?

Number four is not a joke (at least not much of one). We all tend to get a tad set in our ways. Marriages require adjustments. It might be well to hammer some things out—such as vacations, hobbies, relationships with ex's, and things of that ilk. These concerns may seem petty, but they are the stuff of life.

A prenuptial (even without number four) is a good idea in and of itself. It will help you focus on issues that may otherwise be ignored, issues that can create real friction later.

However, the potential for overreaching and misunderstanding is great. *Each of you should be represented by separate lawyers.* Given the potential conflicts between you, one lawyer should not represent you both. Both lawyers should sign the agreement—don't just recite in the agreement that each person consulted with their own lawyer before signing. Recitals may not stand up in the event of a challenge.

Full disclosure of assets, debts, and other matters that might bear upon the agreement, must be made under most states' laws governing prenuptial agreements. Otherwise, a court will most likely throw it out.

If you are currently married and don't have a prenuptial agreement, *post-nuptial* agreements are possible, as are contracts to make Wills.

Without a prenuptial agreement, your new spouse may be entitled to half the property earned during the marriage and, in some cases, some of the property brought into the marriage. More importantly for many newlywed couples at or near retirement age, the children of your new spouse may have a claim to a share of what you think of as "your" property in the event your new spouse dies before you. Support may also be ordered in the event of divorce; you can agree in advance to limit or eliminate support payments. In other words, prenuptials can hammer out the respective rights of the parties while they still agree on most things, and still have a good feeling for what is fair and reasonable.

Of course, if a lot of money is involved, expect a fight as to the validity of the prenuptial agreement. Unlike death and taxes, prenuptials ain't certain.

But planning to remarry at your age, you are obviously not averse to taking chances. Good for you. We always applaud the triumph of hope over experience. (In an over-cautious world, there would be little joy and, still worse, little need for lawyers.)

CHAPTER 21

AGE AND DISABILITY DISCRIMINATION

Supervisor: *Henry, don't bother signing up for training on the new computer program. Old dogs can't learn new tricks and, besides, you would just forget it, anyway.*

Boss: *Mary, we have this great new early retirement program, but you must sign up by the end of next week or face layoff.*

Recruiter: *You are just too qualified for this job.*

Boss: *Real sorry about your disability, but we have to let you go because you can no longer do the job.*

Supervisor: *Come on over and give me a big hug.*

Co-worker: *Hey babe, look at hot pictures.*

Bank: *Sorry, no credit.*

Boss: *Sorry, old goat.*

Landlord: *Sorry, no goat.*

Discrimination comes in many forms: triggered by the victim's age, disability, race or sex. We have two main topics:

1. A discussion of the various laws that prohibit discrimination; and
2. Tips on how to recognize discrimination.

a. An Overview of Anti-Discrimination Law

The law is pretty good in prohibiting discrimination.

Age and Disability Discrimination in Employment. Age discrimination, beginning at age 40 (yes, 40) is illegal. This applies in hiring, termination, and job treatment, such as promotions or job reclassifications. Similarly, you cannot be discriminated against merely because you become disabled and have a more difficult time doing the job (assuming that your employer, or prospective employer, has at least 15 employees). The employer must work with you, trying to find "reasonable accommodations" which would allow you to go on working.

Age and Sex Discrimination in Credit. Legislation prohibits age and sex discrimination in the credit industry. Widows, who may be forced to apply for credit after the death of their husbands, should *suspect* discrimination if they are denied.

Disability Discrimination. While *age* discrimination, at least at the federal level, is prohibited only in employment and credit, protection for the *disabled* is far more extensive. Disability discrimination is generally prohibited in the following areas:

Housing
Public accommodations
Government services
Employment

Racial and Sexual Discrimination. These kinds of discriminations are outlawed in employment and in many other areas as well. The "hot" area is *sexual discrimination in employment.* The law recognizes two forms of sexual discrimination: direct (supervisors demanding sexual favors) and indirect (employers allowing a "hostile work environment" to exist, such as where co-workers are allowed to post explicit sexual pictures or to make crude remarks). The law also prohibits same-sex harassment (male on male or female on female).

The protective legislation we will look at had its genesis in the Civil Rights Movement. The root notion is that the law should act to protect citizens against irrational discrimination, whether based on race, national origin, religion, sex, age, or disability. There are a few other general comments we can make:

- While we focus on federal law, many states have parallel anti-discrimination laws. State laws may provide for broader judicial relief (a polite way of saying "more money").
- Most Civil Rights laws provide that, if you win your lawsuit, the defendant must pay your lawyer. Thus you *can* afford a lawyer.
- Most Civil Rights laws are enforced by governmental agencies. It is easy to report discrimination and let them investigate and take appropriate action. These agencies will contact the other side, hear their side of the story, and then try to conciliate the matter without going to court.

- In all cases of discrimination, it is important to act quickly. If you wait too long, your complaint may be barred by the Statute of Limitations. Further, much of your evidence might be lost. People move and forget.

We begin our discussion with pet discrimination.

b. Cat Discrimination

No, this is not a clever gambit to catch your interest. Well, not entirely. Discrimination against pets can have devastating impact. Pets provide substantial physical and mental benefits to their owners, particularly older people who live alone. Recognizing this, Congress passed a law in 1983 prohibiting owners of *federally assisted housing*, designated for the elderly or disabled, from having flat rules against pets, including cats, dogs, and fish. Thus you can keep your cat unless the landlord shows that it is a nuisance or a threat to the health or safety of others. (Lions, crocodiles, and T Rex, all have to go; old goats fall in the grey area.)

Although this law has a narrow application, if you are renting from a private landlord, you might point to it if you want to keep a pet. A creative lawyer might be able to convince a judge that it would be against public policy to allow a private landlord to evict an elderly tenant because the tenant kept a cat. A good landlord might see that the basis of the federal law makes sense, even if it doesn't really apply to his or her apartment complex.

c. Credit Discrimination

The Equal Credit Opportunity Act prohibits creditors (stores, credit card companies, and banks) from discriminating against any applicant on the "basis of race, color, religion, national origin, sex, marital status, or age," or because the applicant is receiving public assistance.

Creditors can turn you down if you are not credit-worthy—if you have a history of late payments or if your income and assets do not justify the amount of money you wish to borrow.

Thirty days after you apply for credit, you must get a decision. If you are turned down, the creditor must tell you why. Don't be satisfied with explanations such as "Bad credit risk" or "Bad credit record." Insist on details, and if the creditor remains vague, call the local office of the Federal Trade Commission, which enforces the Equal Credit Opportunity Act. Again, widows and older persons should suspect discrimination.

d. Housing: Disability Discrimination

In the area of housing, it is illegal to refuse to rent or sell to a person because he or she is disabled, while it is legal (at least to Uncle Sam who, despite his appearance, is apparently younger than you thought) to discriminate on the basis of age. Federal law does not outlaw age discrimination (as opposed to disability discrimination) in the sale or rental of housing. If you have been turned down because of your age, the only recourse you may have is state law; check with your State Attorney General's Office to see if your state prohibits age discrimination in housing.

On the other hand, federal law does outlaw housing discrimination against the disabled. This protection is afforded by the *"ADA"—Americans With Disabilities Act*.

A disabled individual is a person who has a "physical or mental impairment that substantially limits" one of the major life activities, such as walking.

A covered owner or landlord cannot *refuse to sell or rent* to an individual simply because the person is disabled, unless the handicap is such as to threaten the health and safety of others or would lead to substantial property destruction. The only housing exempted from the ADA is single dwelling residences rented or sold without a Realtor; small housing complexes of four or fewer units where the owner occupies one; and housing run by religious organizations and private clubs.

Incidentally, it is also a violation of federal law to refuse to rent or sell to a tenant because of race, color, religion, sex or national origin. Those protections are provided by the Civil Rights Act of 1964.

An Important Note to Disabled Renters. You have a right, at your expense, to make *reasonable modifications* (for example, put in ramps or grab bars, or lower or raise counters) to your rental to accommodate your handicap. Your landlord cannot refuse to allow you to do so, although the landlord can insist that you agree to restore the place to its original condition when you leave.

Disabled victims of housing discrimination can either file their own lawsuit or contact the federal Department of Housing and Urban Development (HUD), or a state or local housing enforcement agency. The State Attorney General's Office can point you in the right direction.

e. Employment: Disability Discrimination

The Americans with Disabilities Act of 1990 (ADA) also protects disabled individuals in employment. The first reported case under the ADA concerning employment discrimination involved a 56-year-old executive who was discharged after being diagnosed with terminal brain cancer. He sued and won $250,000.

If a physical or mental disability prevents you from doing your job, you have no recourse against an employer. However, your employer cannot *assume* that you cannot do the job simply because you are disabled. If you become disabled, your employer must allow you to try to do your job and cannot simply assume you can't.

Further, your employer must work with you in figuring out how to change the job so you can do it. An employer must make "reasonable accommodations for known physical or mental limitations of an otherwise qualified individual." If a disability is interfering with your performance, are there things you or your employer can do to remedy the problem? Changing the height of desks, getting additional training, or taking more frequent rest breaks may help. How far employers must go in making "reasonable accommodations" is unclear. On the one hand, they must make good faith efforts and not just go through the motions; on the other hand, they need not incur unreasonable expenses.

The requirement of reasonable accommodations throws new light on an old dilemma: *If you are having a hard time doing your job because of a disability, should you tell your boss?* The fear is that, if you do tell, you will be fired. However, if the employer doesn't know of your disability, he or she is under no obligation to offer reasonable accommodation and, if you are fired for bad job performance caused by your disability, you will not be able to claim the ADA's protection.

Only small employers are exempt from the ADA: those with fewer than 15 regular workers. However even small employers may be covered by state or local statutes, and may even be motivated to do the right thing when the law has clearly defined "right thing."

Disabled individuals may also face discrimination in government programs (no programs for the deaf in school) and public accommodations and facilities (no ramps in retail stores). These aspects of the ADA are beyond our scope, but if you feel that you have suffered because of your disability at the hands a government agency or private business, you should contact the federal Equal Employment Opportunities Commission (EEOC), which enforces the ADA, or your state's Attorney General's Office. You can also seek private counsel.

f. Employment: Age Discrimination and an Aside on Common Law

Before we give you the details of employment law, let's take a brief look at "common law" and one of history's very first cases—*Barney Rubble v. Fred Flintstone.*

Common law is judge-made law. This is opposed to *statutory law,* which is made by the insurance industry. In the early days of our country, we followed the law of England (despite the fact that we didn't think much of the King). The law of England at the time was mostly judge-made. Here is an example of how the common law works:

Let's take the first employment case, long, long ago. There are no records but we are convinced that it involved Fred and Barney. Fred had hired Barney to help him fix up the cave, but, after a couple of days, fired him. Barney went to court and complained, "Fred fired me without any good reason. I was doing a real good job."

The *factual question,* to be decided by the jury if there were a trial, would be "Was Barney doing a good job?" But, before the matter could get to this point, a *legal* question would have to be answered by the judge, "Does an employer need good cause to fire someone?" If the judge held "Yes," then there would be a trial as to whether Fred had good cause; if the judge held "No," there would not be a trial because, as a matter of law, employers could fire for any reason they chose.

Some are critical of the judiciary, arguing that judges should not "make law." But note that to decide the case, the judge had to decide the question—the judge would be making law either way.

The first judge, perhaps a secret admirer of Wilma, said "Sorry. Barney, I hold that an employer can fire anyone for any reason or for no reason." Thereafter, other judges, wishing to "treat like cases alike," followed the ruling of the first judge. Over time, it became "law," the *common law.*

This is the concept of following *precedent,* also known as *stare decisis,* and it, at least in theory, creates predictability. Employers and employees will know the rules and will be able to plan their lives. Important decisions will not turn on the whim (or politics) of individual judges. When, centuries later, Cosmo Spacely is thinking of firing George Jetson, he needs to have some reliable standards to apply in making his decision. But then, having seen Cosmo's work, you know he will act on whim rather than applying the law, anyway.

Some have argued that the doctrine of precedent cannot hold, cannot keep its promise that like cases will be treated alike. This is because judges can "distinguish" prior cases. Assume a judge is dealing with a case involving a ranch-hand fired from a dinosaur ranch. She can write: "The rule laid down in the case of *Fred v. Barney* only applies in cases of individuals working in caves; the case before me involves employment at a dinosaur ranch, and I will adopt a different rule to govern this kind of case."

The more flexible the law, the more judges can fine-tune it for unique situations. Maybe there are important differences between cave work and ranch work that would justify a different employment rule. However, the more flexible the law is, the less predictable it becomes. If it is flexible enough to deal with every unique situation, the law may collapse into the individual whim of the judge.

We could neatly solve this timeless jurisprudential dilemma for you. But if we did, the price of this book would skyrocket, so let's return to employment law.

Common law starts with the notion that an employer can fire you for any reason at all. Even if you are doing a great job, you can be fired to make room for the employer's third cousin from Toledo.

Rather than call this "The Third Cousin from Toledo" rule, lawyers labeled it the "at will" doctrine. It left employees quite vulnerable. Unless you have a contract or your employer has an employment policy to the contrary, the employer is not even obligated to tell you why you are fired. Many are told by their lawyers not to. "The less they know, the harder it will be for them to sue," the lawyers say, as the audience hisses, and throws popcorn.

So where can employees find protection? Perhaps in employment contracts and, if not, in various kinds of legislation modifying the common law "at will" doctrine.

Contract Rights. If you are one of those rare individuals with an employment contract, the "at will" doctrine does not apply to you. The contract has to be for a specified period of time such as a year. The contract can be oral—but then, of course, it is much more difficult to show what it provided. With a contract, an employee can be fired only according to the contract's terms, which typically require "good cause"—that may include sleeping on the job, but not making room for the boss's distant relatives.

Even if you don't have an employment contract, you may have contract rights you don't know about, and they are the first place to look if you have problems at work.

Labor Union Contract. Labor unions enter into collective-bargaining agreements with the employer. These spell out a worker's rights concerning termination and conditions of employment. *Unions have a duty to represent you* if your job is covered by a collective bargaining agreement, even if you are not a member of the union and even if your shop foreman has lost a major bet with you on the Super Bowl. Further, labor unions cannot discriminate on the basis of age.

Employee Manuals as Contracts. Some employers have an employee manual or a set of work policies which may describe the circumstances in which an employee can be fired or laid off, and what kind of notice must be given. Creative lawyers have argued that these policies in effect become part of the employment contract and hence are legally binding on the employer.

Legislation: The Age Discrimination in Employment Act (ADEA). If you have no recourse to contract rights, turn next to legislation. It has made major inroads into the "at will" doctrine by prohibiting discrimination based on race, sex, and age. Our concern is with age discrimination, so we turn to the provisions of the Age Discrimination in Employment Act (ADEA) which was passed by Congress in 1967.

A major aspect of this legislation is to outlaw mandatory retirement. The narrow exceptions deal with matters of public safety; for example, airline pilots must retire at age 60. Another exception, approved by the Justices of the U.S. Supreme Court: state law can require retirement of state court judges, but federal judges are immune.

The other major aspect of this legislation is that it protects people 40 and older from discrimination in terms of hiring, firing, promotion, and pay. This applies to both part-time and temporary workers as well. What employers cannot do is to treat people over 40 differently because they assume that, because of their age, they cannot do as good a job as younger individuals. Employers can, however, fire individuals for bad job performances, even if those poor performances are due to the aging process, and can also reduce the work force, as long as they do not single out the elderly.

This law applies to almost all employers (private and public, profit and non-profit) but only if the employer has 20 or more employees. Certain high-ranking employees aren't covered, nor are top managers.

g. Proving Discrimination and Why Employers Discriminate

Occasionally there may be direct evidence of age discrimination. In one case, the defendant fired the plaintiff, calling him an "old goat." The old goat sued and won big bucks; with a nod to Winston Churchill,"*Some goat!*"

Our lawyers did not get the Churchill reference. Fearing that it is somehow actionable, they demand that we explain it. At the beginning of

World War II, Hitler bragged that Germany was about to grab Eng-
land like a chicken and break its neck. Churchill, in one of his great
speeches, repeated Hitler's threat, and then paused...."Some chicken!"
he roared.
Thunderous applause. After several minutes, the audience fell silent. An-
other pause....
"Some neck!"

Most employers are too cagey to call you an old goat. (This awkward construction in no way suggests that *we* are calling you an old goat.) Not all employers are so closed-mouth, however; in one notable case the 76-year-old employer turned down a 74-year-old applicant, saying "people our age are considered dinosaurs."

Employers are likely to claim they just love older folks but that you, alas, cannot do the job. How can you prove that they are in fact discriminating against you because of your age? To win an age discrimination suit, you don't have to prove that age was the *only* factor in an adverse employment decision, only that it was a factor. How? We recommend three basic steps:

1. Ask yourself: Does my employer have a reason to discriminate against me?
2. Demand explanations of conduct you believe might constitute discrimination.
3. Sit down and write out why you think you have been victimized.

Why do employers discriminate against older folks?

1. To cut insurance costs.

Seniors get sick more and hence have higher bills. To avoid higher premiums, a company might refuse to hire or might fire (or force into retirement, or make life hell so that they quit) older workers. This is against the law.

Employers cannot discriminate against seniors on the basis that they trigger higher benefit-plan costs. Employers can, however, insist on spending the same amount on all employees. This may result in lesser coverage for older workers; the same premium will get more coverage for a younger worker than for an older one.

2. To cut payroll and to weasel out of retirement commitments.

New hires are paid less than folks with experience. Some employers are tempted to cut costs by replacing more senior workers.

As to weaseling out of retirement commitments, federal law provides that, once you have worked for a company for five years, you have a vested right to be in the company's retirement plan (if they have one). This means that the employer cannot get back its contributions to your account. Be very suspicious if you are fired as you approach the five-year mark.

3. To let stereotypes do their thinking (it is easier that way).

Some employers simply assume that over a certain age people won't be able to do the job. *Most of us can.* Studies suggest mental function remains high well into the seventies.

Civil rights legislation protecting minorities, women, the disabled, and the elderly can be thought of as anti-stereotype legislation. Employers cannot simply assume that, for example, no elders can do a job simply because some elders cannot. Individual decisions must be made. Further, these laws force employers to think through job qualifications. Employers may simply assume that people need to have certain skills to do a certain job when they really don't. It is a violation of law to have a job requirement that is not really needed if it acts to discriminate against the elderly. For example, if a job requires no heavy lifting, employers cannot insist employees pass strength tests that would discriminate irrationally against the elderly.

After thinking about whether there was a motive to discriminate against you, the next step is to *demand an explanation.* If you weren't hired because you "aren't qualified" or are "too qualified," ask "In what respects?"

University professors, for example, are not over-qualified for repetitious, boring and mind-numbing jobs. Just look at their publications!

If you were fired because you "can no longer do the job" or "no longer get along with customers," demand specifics. Be suspicious of vague answers and the refusal to respond.

If you are going to talk your employer, take someone with you. You might need a witness later.

Writing down why you think you have been victimized should prove worthwhile. Writing is simply a great way to slow your mind to allow you to sort things out. Things will come to you that you would overlook if you just thought about it.

Now some tips for specific situations:

If you weren't hired, consider:
- Was there anything the interviewer said or asked that indicated age bias? Did the interviewer tell you the job qualifications and did you meet them? Vague qualifications coupled with "You aren't qualified" are suspicious.
- Did the interviewer tell you why you weren't being hired? If they were to "get back to you later" and later you were simply told "Nope," write a letter: "Why didn't I get the job? In what ways wasn't I qualified?" A failure to respond to this inquiry increases suspicions.
- Was the job kept open? You could have a friend call or even apply. If the employer is hiring a lot of folks, are any of them your age?

If you think that your employer is setting you up to be fired:
- Watch the paper trail of bad evaluations. Respond to them in writing.
- Talk with co-workers your age and see if the same thing is happening to them.
- Record the incidents that you feel are suspicious.
- Seek legal advice early on, *before* the axe falls.

h. What to Do

Typically, if someone runs you over, you can go directly to court (at least after you get out of the hospital). Not so with most civil rights legislation or with age discrimination legislation. The law requires that you first file a complaint with the governmental agency whose job it is to enforce that particular law. The idea is that the agency will investigate your complaint and try to resolve the dispute. If it cannot, and it believes you are right, it *might* go to court on your behalf. Even if the agency finds you are wrong, you still can go to court after you have given the agency time to investigate.

If your state has an age discrimination law, you must first file a complaint with the agency that enforces it. If your state does not, then you have to file with the local office of the Federal EEOC (Equal Employment Opportunities Commission). Things can get complicated and these offices will guide you through the ropes.

What you need to know now is that you need to *act quickly*. If you wait too long to file a complaint, it may be barred by the Statute of Limitations. (The length of Statutes of Limitations varies from state to state.)

Your possible remedies under federal law include payment for lost pay, reinstatement, front pay (if reinstatement isn't appropriate) and injunctive relief (a stern judicial warning not to do it again). Awards for pain and suffering are not allowed. However, if there was a *willful* violation, your recovery can be doubled. Punitive damages are not allowed under the federal law although they may be if you pursue other theories of recovery.

i. A Concluding Note on Early Retirement

If an employer has a pension plan, it will provide full benefits when a worker retires, usually at the age of 65. (It cannot *require* retirement because, again, mandatory retirement is almost always illegal.) Employers can, however, offer workers the opportunity to retire early and offer such incentives as

- paying full retirement benefits now; and
- supplementing payments with additional cash ("bridge payments") to help out until the worker becomes 65 and thus eligible for Social Security and Medicare.

If offered early retirement, *you don't have to take it.* While early retirement plans can be good things (we're waiting by the phone), don't be pressured into agreeing. Think long and hard about retirement and the loss of income, daily direction and status it may entail. Consult a financial adviser. And, if you are interested, there may be room to negotiate better terms. One big item will be health insurance and who is to pay the premium.

Some chapter!

CHAPTER 22

TROUBLE WITH THE
BILL COLLECTOR

A British Lord had a horrible nightmare. He dreamt that he was in the House of Lords, giving a long and boring speech, and everyone was nodding off. He awoke in a sweat, only to find that he was in the House of Lords, that he was giving that long and boring speech and that, indeed, everyone was nodding off.

This story comes to mind as we begin this chapter on consumer law. We're not promising the *Poseidon Adventure*. Not even the remake.

If you are living on Easy Street, skip this chapter. It's for folks who, probably for the first time in their lives, are having a hard time paying their bills on time. You're not alone.

First, *what not to do*. Don't dig yourself in deeper by borrowing more money. At the other extreme, don't stick your head in the sand and hope your creditors will forget about you. Second, *what to do*. Get debt counseling, consider bankruptcy, keep in touch with all your creditors, and buy your meds!

Debt counseling agencies can help you with a budget and can contact creditors. Some are free. Contact your Area Agency on Aging or your local Information and Referral.

We'll look at what creditors and collection agencies can do: things are much improved since Dickens' time. Then we will look at why you shouldn't get a "bill payer" loan and why you should *not* allow creditors to repossess furniture or your car. Next we discuss which bills to pay first. Finally: what happens if you get sued and a brief look at bankruptcy.

a. Bill Collectors: Barks and Bites

- Don't panic! *Creditor barks are worse than their bites.*
- There is no imprisonment for debt—you won't go to jail.
- Social Security checks are safe, so you won't starve.
- You won't get thrown out in the street (only the bank which holds your mortgage or, if you rent, your landlord, can throw you out).
- Your car and most of your personal property (TV, furniture, kitchen appliances) are safe *except* from creditors with security interest in them. You *may* have given a security interest to the nice lender with the storefront office across the street from your bank, or to the appliance dealer who sold you the washer and dryer on credit, but otherwise it is not very likely that anyone will have the ability to take your personal property from you. In many states, you are at least guaranteed the right to keep a shotgun, a Bible and a mule—all the necessities for starting over, at least in the 19th century, the last time many state legislatures considered the problems of consumers.
- Collection agencies cannot tell your neighbors or employers that you are a "deadbeat."
- Creditors cannot sue your children (unless they co-signed).
- You are not liable for the debts of your adult children (unless you co-signed).

Most creditors are willing to deal. Most will give you more time and perhaps cut the bill *if* they are convinced that you are in good faith and are willing to work with them. It costs them money to sue you or turn the matter over to a collection agency. Plus you have the bankruptcy card. Thus there is room to negotiate.

Work with your creditor *before* the matter is turned over to a collection agency. When this happens, the creditor loses between 30% and 50% off the top. This means, if you pay *most* of your bill, the creditor comes out ahead by not turning it over to an agency.

Collection Agencies. The Federal Fair Debt Collection Practices Act protects you.

- Collection agencies *cannot* contact other people (except to learn where you are) and cannot tell them that you owe any money.
- Collection agencies *cannot* call late at night, use obscene or threatening language, or threaten to publish your name as a deadbeat.
- If you tell the agency you are not going to pay the bill or that you don't want further contact with it, it must stop contacting you, ex-

cept to advise you that it is filing suit. If you get a lawyer, then the agency can only communicate with your lawyer.

If you dispute the debt, write the collection agency. It must then obtain verification of the debt and communicate that verification to you before taking further steps to collect it.

If you have been mistreated, contact a lawyer; a federal act gives you the right to sue. Or you can file a complaint with the Federal Trade Commission. Check with your local U.S. Attorney's Office.

b. Avoid "Bill Payer Loans" Like the Plague

Actually plagues are very hard to avoid; otherwise they would never be plagues, only a few dead rats in the harbor. (Oops. Wrong book, wrong century, hopefully.) Bill Payer Loans seem too good to be true—pay off all of your bills at once and still have *lower* monthly payments. Where's the catch?

Longer repayment schedules. Most credit card bills treat the loan as a loan for 36 months: your minimum monthly payment is 1/36 of the outstanding balance. Most small loan company loans are for 72 months: your minimum payment is only 1/72 of the outstanding balance. Because the payback period is much longer, monthly payments go down *even if the interest charged is significantly higher.*

Pre-payment penalties. Unlike credit cards, you can't pay them off all at once to avoid further interest payments.

Security interests. Debts owed credit cards, doctors, and hospitals are *unsecured.* That means that if you default, these creditors will have to go to court before they can take any of your property and, even then, they will be limited in what they can take. Bill Payer Loans are generally *secured* which means that you have put at risk your home, car or furniture. Often these lenders aren't so much interested in getting your property if you default as they are in having the *threat* of taking your property to force you to pay them rather than, say, buying your meds.

c. Never Agree to a Repossession

Some sellers and loan companies take a security interest in some of your stuff, most likely your car or household furniture. If you fail to pay on time, they may come to repossess the item. Don't let them. Although they have a contractual right to repossess (you gave it to them in the small print), *they cannot commit a breach of the peace in doing so.*

The problem is that once they take your car or your furniture, you still might owe them money. They will sell the item and deduct what they get from what you owe. You may *still* end up in debt. Lock the door and get a lawyer's advice. It may be best to call their bluff. Yes, they can go to court and get a court order (which the Sheriff may enforce), but will they? It will cost them money—sure, you may be liable to pay those costs, but can they be sure of collecting it from you?

d. Which Bills to Pay First

In George Orwell's parody of the Russian Revolution, *Animal Farm*, the animals rose up, took over the farm, and created Animal Paradise. Their Constitution spoke to their idealism: "All Animals are Equal."

Alas, this utopia was not to last. Soon the pigs took over and grabbed the good stuff. They were, after all, pigs. Noting the apparent contradiction between their behavior and their Constitution, the pigs realized one would have to change. They opted to amend their Constitution:

Some Animals Are More Equal than Others. Some creditors are more equal than others in the sense that they can hurt you worse. While paying something on all your bills, give priority to some. Priorities are based on how badly the creditor can hurt you. Of course, you should also consider paying off higher interest debts before others.

Court Ordered and Government Creditors. Child support and alimony are *top* priorities. If you don't pay them, *you can go to jail*; not for debt, but for contempt of court.

Debts owed to the IRS are *not* dischargeable in bankruptcy, and interest and penalties on IRS debts can be substantial. Don't ask what your government can do *for* you; ask what it can do *to* you.

Creditors Who Can Cut Off Services. Don't pay your car insurance, your health insurance, or your fire insurance, you lose your coverage; don't pay your electric bill, you lose your lights.

If you are renting, your landlord can *evict* you for non-payment of rent. To do so, however, the landlord must first go to court and serve you with papers. Depending on the market, your landlord may have less of a hair trigger than other creditors. If you are evicted, the landlord must find a new tenant or the place stands vacant, bringing in nothing.

Secured Creditors: Acceleration Clauses, Repossession and Deficiency Judgments.

We've already talked about the problem of *repossession*. Another small-print term in many contracts is an *acceleration clause*. It provides that if you miss one or more payments, the creditor can declare all the rest of the payments due now. The *entire* amount you owe becomes due. If a creditor tells you that you are in default because of late payments and demands that you now pay the entire outstanding balance or he will repossess the secured item, see a lawyer. There are defenses to a creditor's use of acceleration clauses.

Finally, there is the matter of *deficiency judgments*. Let's use the example of Smilin' Sam, Used Car Dealer. If you miss a few payments, Sam can *repossess* your car *without* going to court; then he can sell the car and apply that amount to your unpaid balance. If you still owe more than they received from the sale of your car (a likely situation), Sam can come after you for the remainder *plus* the attorney fees you agreed to pay in the small print. This is known as a *deficiency judgment.*

Say you purchased a car for $10,000. You put $500 down and made another $1,500 in payments, leaving a balance owed of $8,000. You miss a few payments and the finance company declares a forfeiture and has someone pick up your car. They then sell the car for $6,000. As you still owed $8,000, there is a $2,000 deficiency. The company can sue you for it, plus their attorney fees, say an additional $500. Things could actually be a little worse. But note the bottom line: you have paid $2,000, still owe $2,500, and are taking the bus!

One is reminded of a scene in Dickens' *Oliver Twist*. A man is told that he is responsible for the criminal acts of his wife, as the law presumes that the husband controls his wife. "If the law presumes that," he responds, "the law is a ass, a idiot."

It seems, thus far, that all of your creditors can inflict great harm. There is a final category of creditors, however, that do not have the same teeth and, thankfully, many of your bills are no doubt owed to them. These are your unsecured creditors.

Unsecured Creditors. Unsecured creditors include credit card companies, hospitals, other medical providers, and service providers such as lawyers and accountants. While the most virtuous, these folks have the lowest priority. Before they can reach any of your property, they must go to court and get a judgment. Further they are most vulnerable to losing part of their claims in bankruptcy. While it seems like these should be your lowest priority, realize that in with some you are paying a high rate of interest and this might put them near the top.

e. If You Get Sued

If a creditor sues you, it will serve you with an official looking document known as the Complaint. Service, with rare exceptions, must be by hand; the creditor cannot simply mail you the Complaint. Usually a process server will show up at your house or your place of employment and ask you your name and then hand you the papers. It is not a great experience.

The Complaint will state why the creditor (known now as the "Plaintiff") thinks you owe it money. The Complaint will then pray for judgment and state how much it claims you owe. This will include the amount owed on the debt and, most likely, attorney fees and court costs. These can run up quickly.

It is important to read the Complaint to see if the Plaintiff got things right. Often they don't. Common consumer defenses include:

- Fraud or misrepresentation on the part of the seller.
- Failure of consideration: what was purchased broke.

If you get served, you gotta see a lawyer *quickly*. Legal Aid offers help to low income defendants. Most local Bar Associations have referral programs which allow you to talk to a lawyer for a minimal payment, say $25 for a 30-minute consultation.

If you and your lawyer decide to fight the Complaint, your lawyer will write an Answer which will be filed with the court. Thereafter, the lawyers will negotiate a deal. Often, even at this late stage, creditors are willing to compromise. If a deal cannot be made, the matter will be set for trial, often far in the future.

If you ignore the Complaint, hoping it will go away or waiting for a better time to deal with it, after about 30 or so days, the creditor will get a *default* judgment against you in the amount asked for. Once this happens, it can get court orders allowing it to attach your property.

Once a creditor gets a judgment against you (either by default or after a trial), it becomes a "judgment creditor" and can:

- Attach your wages—up to 25%. ("Attachment" is a Court Order directing your employer to pay up to 25% of your salary to the creditor rather than to you. It can continue until the judgment is paid in full.)
- Attach, by court order, your stocks, bonds, vacation homes, and bank accounts. Once an asset is attached, it can be sold and the proceeds applied to the judgment. Monies left over go to you.

The good news is that a judgment creditor cannot get any of your exempt assets. Exemptions are generally governed by state law, but let's take a look at the common ones

Your Home. Most states allow you to file a "Homestead Exemption" which will protect your home from execution. Homestead laws protect homes only of a certain value; check with your County Clerk for more information.

Your Furnishings and Car. Most states make most home furnishings and one car, below a certain value, exempt from execution. In addition, your tools needed for work are exempt.

Social Security Checks. These cannot be attached (executed upon). Bank accounts can be. So once Social Security payments are placed in bank accounts with other funds, they may lose their exempt status. *Keep them in separate accounts* or use cash.

For a lot of people, most of what they own is exempt from execution. Lawyers call this "judgment proof." If you are living on Social Security, have homesteaded your modest home, and have no stocks and bonds or large bank accounts, there is nothing your unsecured creditors can go after. If you are in this situation, consider writing your creditor: "Stop bothering me. I will pay when I can. But I am judgment-proof."

f. Bankruptcy

Law schools offer courses in bankruptcy law; lawyers specialize in the area; there is even a special court that hears nothing but bankruptcy cases: bankruptcy is not for beginners, and is not for "Do Your Own" books.

Before 2005 bankruptcy law was pretty complicated, but not complicated enough for the credit card industry. Sure, the industry pushed its product to anyone with a mailbox. However, it became very upset when some folks acted "irresponsibly" by running up large debts on their numerous credit cards (Duh!) and then, when they were hopelessly over their heads, had the gall to seek bankruptcy protection. In 2005, Congress "reformed" the law: it is now much more difficult to seek bankruptcy shelter. (The good news is that it is even easier to get credit cards.)

But enough political commentary. Suffice it to say, going bankrupt is a perfectly respectable thing to do, that you can do so and still keep most of your belongings, and that you should go to a lawyer, not a bookstore.

PART 4

In Case "Something Happens"

Introduction: On the Pitfalls of Self-Help Books

Yogi Berra, on the way to a friend's funeral, remarked, "If you don't go to theirs, they won't come to yours."

This section deals with "estate planning". We begin with documents you can sign now that will allow you to appoint a trusted friend or relative to make your medical and financial decisions if you become unable to do so. We then look at ways to pass your property on: the main courses (Wills, trusts, and living trusts), and the condiments (life insurance, joint ownership, and IRA accounts). We will discuss how to avoid probate and whether you should. We will even tell you what probate is. We end describing estate and gift taxes.

If you don't have an estate plan, this section is a *must*. You will learn of all the marvelous things you can accomplish. Even if you have an estate plan, this section may give you some new ideas.

Our topics here are the stuff of self-help books: *Write Your Own Will, Create Your Own Trust, Commit Your Own Malpractice*. Our book is *not* a self-help book. Self-help books have inherent problems that, because we didn't write one, we are happy to share:

- *State laws differ.* What works famously in California may violate Oklahoma statute or Vermont common law (and folks in Oklahoma and Vermont may be thankful).

155

- *Law changes.* Probate used to be horrible, something to avoid at all costs. Not so today. Estate taxes used to be extremely high. Not so today.
- *One size doesn't fit all.* You did it your way. Self-help books compress life's complexity into three or four choices.
- *Self-help authors don't tell bad jokes.*

This section will give you a general understanding of the law in this area, one we know you find fascinating: how the law deal with life's really tough problems. We will also give you a basic understanding of the numerous options you have; meeting with your lawyer will be all the more productive.

CHAPTER 23

KEEPING CONTROL: LIVING WILLS, HEALTH CARE POWER OF ATTORNEY, JOINT ACCOUNTS, AND POWERS OF ATTORNEY

Death is scary. Disability is scary. Dementia is terrifying. Waking up in a place we do not know, surrounded by strangers busy with other things. Nancy Mairs in *Waist-High in the World* describes it as the *"manic terror that things are slipping from our grasp."* Every time we lose the keys, "Is this the beginning?"

Dementia is not a certainty but it is a possibility. Take steps now to assure that if your medical and financial decisions slip from your grasp, they will be made by people you trust in accord with your wishes. You'll need some documents:

> *A Living Will.*
> *A Health Care Power of Attorney* (sometimes called a *Proxy Designation*).
> *A Durable Financial Power of Attorney.*
> *A Living Trust* (For some, but not all.)

All of these items will be included when your lawyer prepares your Estate Plan. Here we provide background information. We'll discuss Living Trusts in their own chapter as these Shmoo-like devices can accomplish wondrous things in addition to financial management in the event of disability.

a. Medical Decisions: Living Wills, Health Care Powers of Attorney, DNRs

Living Wills state what kind of medical treatment you want, or don't want, if you are dying and are no longer mentally competent. We have already discussed our take on them and urge you to forego forms and write your own (Chapter 2). Be that as it may. Your lawyer may disagree.

All elder law lawyers would agree that you need a *Health Care Power of Attorney*. They are actually more important and more effective than Living Wills which are often ignored. Basically you appoint someone to make your medical decisions *anytime* you are unable to do so, due to unconsciousness or mental incompetence. There is no need for you to be in a terminal state as there is with Living Wills.

What if you don't have a Health Care Power of Attorney? Two possibilities, neither of them good. Say you are in the hospital, unable to make or communicate your wishes, and an immediate decision must be made whether to amputate an arm. One possibility is that your family and doctor simply agree. However, if the treatment is major or if there is disagreement, then your family will have to go to court to get a formal guardianship, a time-consuming, expensive, and often heartbreaking process.

To avoid the hassle and expense of guardianships, some states have passed *Family Agency Acts* (some states refer to the family members as "surrogates"). These list those who can make medical decisions when you can't, usually your spouse first, then your adult children, and thereafter other relatives and, in some states, domestic partners.

Even if your state has a Family Agency Act, you should still have a Health Care Power of Attorney.

- You might not like the person the statute selects: families fight and spouses may be too sick or too depressed to take on this added burden.
- In some cases, the most significant person in your life may not be "officially approved." This has been painfully illustrated during the AIDS crisis where longtime companions have been refused entry into hospital rooms.
- State laws may restrict the decisions that can be made by family members, or may give them much more authority than you are comfortable conveying.
- Finally, the person designated by the Act *may not make the decisions you would want made*. Their power may come as a total surprise, at the worst possible time.

Have your lawyer draft a Health Care Power of Attorney. Give the matter some thought before you get there. *First, who do you want it to be?*

Don't necessarily appoint your spouse. He or she may be sick at the time decisions must be made or may be too depressed or confused to do so. Usually children or long-time friends are better choices. If you select one child but not another, wisdom would dictate explaining your choice to both of them. Appoint a back-up.

Second, what powers do you want the agent to have? Unless the document says otherwise, your agent may not have the power to move you to a nursing home or to take you from the hospital against doctors' advice. And, unless the document says otherwise, your agent may not have the power to remove you from life supports. That's where the Living Will comes in.

Before leaving the topic of health care directives, a few words on *DNR* (Do Not Resuscitate). These are serious documents. They direct hospital personnel not to do the "Stand back, Clear, Zap" routine made so popular by shows like *ER* and *House*. Depending on your age and condition, you may be asked to sign one when you enter the hospital. Sounds heartless, but it may be a very good choice. Usually emergency procedures, often quite painful, don't work, except, of course, on television where they succeed close to 90% of the time. In real life, in *your* life, less than 20% survive and, of them, over 80% of them were dead within one year.

Elderly folks who do not want to be "rescued" by paramedics fill out specialized directives that they not be resuscitated in the emergency room, at home, or at the mall. State laws and procedures vary widely on DNR designations and advance directives prohibiting resuscitation; be sure you know whether your planned approach will be legal and effective.

b. Financial Decisions: Joint Accounts, Powers of Attorney, Trusts

If you suddenly become unable to handle your own finances, who's going to pay your bills? Make your investments? Give your gifts?

If you do nothing now, your family will be forced to go to court to get formal guardianship or conservatorship of your estate. Not only is this a complicated, time-consuming and possibly expensive choice, the person appointed to make your financial decisions may not have the legal authority to do what you wish, such as give money to a favorite charity or to a grandchild who has cut his hair, removed his nose ring, and has gone to law school.

To keep control of your finances, you have three choices: *Joint Accounts, Powers of Attorney,* and *Trusts*. If your estate is large, clearly the way to go is to create a trust. However, as trusts are viewed primarily as a method of passing property at the time of death, we will defer our discussion of them until later in the book. Joint accounts (often touted by self-help books) and Powers of Attorney, both present legal complications and probably should be generally avoided. That said, some specifics.

Joint Accounts

If your income consists mostly of Social Security checks, pension checks, and dividends, joint accounts are fine. It is fairly easy to set up a joint checking account (arranging to have the checks deposited directly into it). The co-owner can now simply write checks to pay your bills.

Most joint accounts also come with the right of survivorship. That means the co-owner owns the account at your death. In Chapter 25-e, we discuss joint ownership as a method of avoiding probate and point to better ways.

Joint accounts are easy. But life never is. The dangers of joint accounts:

1. Without putting too fine a point on it, the other person may use the money for their own expenses. (They *always* intend to put it back.)
2. Further, their creditors might come after the money. Creditors can include persons who sue for such things as automobile wrecks, as well as divorcing spouses.

A *designated signer account* avoids the problem of the other person's creditors getting the money. Trusts and powers of attorney also avoid the creditor problem.

Some use joint accounts as ways of passing money at time of death. Say you want to leave a small amount to each of your grandchildren. You can set up joint accounts with the right of survivorship. The problem is that the joint owner can take the money at any time. If you want to prevent this possibility, set up a *payable on death (POD) account*. The beneficiary you list will be able to close the account by showing the bank your death certificate, but, before that, neither he nor his creditors can reach it. A variation of this is used for brokerage accounts: these are called *transfer on death (TOD) accounts.*

If there are a lot of assets involved, setting up joint accounts and joint ownership to cover them all will prove too cumbersome. You will need to give someone a more general power over the assets. A Living Trust, discussed in Chapter 27, is one solution. Here we discuss the other—Powers of Attorney.

Powers of Attorney

With a properly executed Power of Attorney, the person designated can manage your bank accounts, stocks, and other assets. A Power of Attorney is simply a specially prepared piece of paper that allows one person (called the agent) to act as a deputy and make legally binding decisions (buying and selling real estate, for example) for the principal (that's you).

Powers of Attorney can help in many situations; for example, you will be out of town and it is necessary for your daughter to sell your car. However, it is a very bad idea just to give anyone a *general* power of attorney. They can use it to get everything you own. Yes, we know you trust the person, that a general power shows trust and love, and that it will "avoid complications down the road". We also know that some of our closest friends and relatives may be compulsive gamblers or drug abusers or, deep down, simply jerks.

How can you protect yourself? Have a Special Power of Attorney which limits the power of the agent to doing certain things, such as "Sell my Ford Explorer" or "Withdraw money from Savings Account 1234 at People's Savings." You could also limit the time frame: "Good only to August 1 of this year."

If you are thinking of using a Power of Attorney to cope with your possible legal incapacity, think again. A traditional Power of Attorney is valid only as long as you are competent. To prepare for incapacity, you must create a *durable* power, one that remains effective even if you are incapacitated.

You probably don't want to give that power unless and until you are incapacitated. To accomplish this, use a *Springing Durable Power*. It "springs" to life when you become incapacitated. Your lawyer can draft triggering devices, such as certification by your attending physician. Or your lawyer can simply keep the Power and not give it to your agent unless and until you become incapacitated.

A downside to springing powers is that third parties might be more reluctant to honor them, insisting on documentation that the spring has sprung. Because of this, some lawyers recommend against using springing powers.

A lawyer can draft the needed document. Some issues to consider.

1. Who do you want your agent to be?

Name a back-up. Tell that person of your decision, as well as folks who might be upset because they weren't chosen (other children, for example). You can name two people as agents. Must they agree, or can they act separately? A lawyer can draft a document that allows separate decisions for minor matters, joint decisions for major ones.

Try to avoid putting your agent in a *conflict* position. If your agent will inherit your estate, he or she will have an interest in keeping as much money in your estate as possible. If you end up in a nursing home, for example, your agent may resist spending your money for things you really want or need.

2. What powers do you want your agent to have?

State law will determine the agent's powers under a general power. It is best to discuss with your lawyer what precise powers you want your agent or agents to have. Consider giving the agent the power to sign IRS and state returns; open bank accounts and safe deposit boxes, and have the safe deposit box drilled if need be; change beneficiaries of pensions and life insurance; make loans and gifts to others (this power may make you nervous, and with good reason); pay herself for work as your agent.

A few words are in order about the power to make gifts. If your estate is large, it may be appropriate for you to be making regular gifts to your children, grandchildren and other beneficiaries of your estate. In that case, it is a good idea to give your agent the power to continue (or initiate, if you know you should be making gifts but just haven't gotten around to it) your pattern of gift-giving. Conversely, if your estate is more modest, it may be appropriate to give your agent the power to make gifts to help you qualify for Medicaid or other public benefits at some future time. However, the value of this planning technique has been substantially reduced by recent changes in the law. Finally, you may just want your agent to be able to do what you might do—to help out family members who need some assistance to go to college, or buy a first house, or pay for medical emergencies.

If your agent will be making investment decisions for you, you may wish to write out general directions as to aggressiveness or security. ("Buy low, sell high" won't do.) We discuss this issue further in our chapter on Living Trusts, as the trustee will also have broad powers over your assets. There are some limits to an agent's powers. They can't divorce your spouse nor can they write—or revoke—your Will.

c. Durable Powers of Attorney Compared to Living Trusts

Compared to a Living Trust, a Durable Power of Attorney is cheaper and quicker. There is no need, as there is in the case of a living trust, to take the necessary legal steps to transfer your assets; the Durable Power covers whatever you list.

However, a Living Trust is more certain. Whereas some banks and businesses may refuse to honor a Durable Power, most will honor the directions

of the trustee of a living trust. Further, a Durable Power is not an estate planning tool: at your death, the power of attorney ends, and your property simply remains in your estate. So what happens to your stuff when you die? (Ed-
itor's note: Nice segue.)

CHAPTER 24

WILLS AND ESTATE PLANNING

Lawyers have pretty much given up on the meaning of life. Instead they focus on what to do with the decedent's stuff.

In the last chapter we mentioned that your lawyer would include a living will and a health care power of attorney as part of your estate plan. No doubt you squirmed: "Lawyer? Estate plan? Nobody said anything about that. Isn't it enough I bought this lousy book?" A quick look at your excuses.

I don't even want to think about it.

What this gains in honesty, it loses in insight. Of course you think about death. In fact, like the rest of us, you spend great amounts of energy pretending you don't. Face facts, make plans, and move on.

I can't do anything until I get my records in order.

Nope. You can create a trust and put "everything I own" into it or you can write a Will which provides "My three kids each get $20,000 and the remainder goes to the Denial of Death Foundation" or even "I don't care what happens as long as Uncle Joe doesn't get anything."

I'm not sure what I want to do with my property.

Unless you start writing, you will never be sure. Writing things focuses the mind. Nothing is in stone. You can always change your Will (rather than call them "changes" or "Second Thoughts", lawyers call them "codicils"—we are, after all, a learned profession).

I don't have time to meet with a lawyer.

Nope. You can write out your own Will. *Right now.* But what if you stay in denial and on the couch?

a. Intestacy and Its Discontents

If you die without a Will or Trust, your property will pass by intestacy. Worse things have happened. State intestacy laws represent the legislature's best guess as to how most people would want their property distributed, generally first to their spouse, then to their children, and then to more distant relatives. There are problems:

- Your property may not go to whom you would want it to. Many states provide that at the death of one spouse, only half of his or her property goes to the surviving spouse, the rest to the children. You may want all of your assets to go to your spouse, or all to go to your children. We have seen very few folks who wanted to split their estates equally between spouse and children.
- Intestacy laws treat everyone the same: children take in equal shares even though some may be younger, some may have special problems, some may have already gotten a college education or a shiny red convertible at your expense, and some may be brats.
- Under intestacy, none of your friends, distant relatives, or favorite charities receive anything.
- You won't be able to nominate guardians for your minor children. It will be up to a judge to decide, and the decision might not be the best.
- If you die without an estate plan, you won't be able to use trusts to avoid the problems of outright gifts to minor children and disabled relatives.
- If you die without an estate plan, you can't pick the person who will administer your estate. This may lead to family fights about who that person should be.
- If you have a business, it will be shipwrecked.
- All of your assets will be tied up in probate for awhile; family members who rely on them may have a rough go of it.
- Estate taxes may take a large portion of what you leave.
- You won't avoid probate.

A good estate plan can avoid all of these problems. We will show you how as we discuss the various estate planning devices in this chapter and those that follow.

b. Holographic Wills

Holographic Wills are the first choice of nervous flyers everywhere.

If I die before I land,
This is my stuff, I do hand:
. . . .
. . . .

OK, fine. Take your best shot. But Shakespeare wasn't about to take a small plane to Duluth, on a dark and stormy night.

You must write this Will entirely in your own handwriting (no typing, no Word Perfect, and no just signing what someone else wrote for you). *Not* a substitute for a formal Will, a Holographic Will can fill the void until you get back home — depending, that is, on where "home" might be. Holographic wills are not valid in most states, and may face other restrictions in a few of the states where they are recognized.

There's no set form:

Holographic wills don't have to rhyme,
Just be sure to date and sign.

Here's an example:

Date. . . . .

I intend this to be my Will to be effective upon my death. I have no other Wills. I am of sound mind and am writing this of my own free will. Upon my death, I want the following:

a. That my sister, Sherina Cadnum, of Albany, California, become the guardian of my two minor children.

b. That $2,000 of my estate go to the Humane Society.

c. That my children get the rest of my estate when they turn 22 but before that time my sister will keep the money for them to pay the reasonable and necessary expenses for their care, comfort, maintenance, and support, including education.

Signed. . . .

No witnesses or notaries are necessary (but they can help). The problem with Holographic Wills, and it is a big one, is that they are recognized only in certain states. Even where they are recognized, it is best to use them only as a stop-gap measure. Formal Wills are preferable to get things right.

c. Signed, Handwritten Wills

You can turn that holographic will into a perfectly valid, effective will even in states that don't recognize the genre. Just write it out, or type it, or prepare it on your word processor, sign it in front of two witnesses and have them sign indicating they watched you sign. That should work. Probably.

d. Formal Wills

Next to the funny birthday cards at the drugstore, you'll find the Will forms. There will be blanks to be filled in, boxes to be checked, and language designed to impress—"per stirpes", "aforementioned clause III (b) (2)", and, of course, "being of sound mind" (the latter is known as a "Sanity Clause" and, in the case of a Will contest, it is of doubtful efficacy, although few have gone as far as Chico in *Duck Soup* in totally dismissing their effectiveness: "I don't believe in no Sanity Clause.")

If you buy a form Will, fine. But be sure to pick up a condolence card as well.

> *Granddad wanted to leave me some money but he was too cheap to get a lawyer to do it right so all he left me was this Stupid Card!*

An estate plan won't cost you much. Lawyers don't make their money writing wills; they make their money upsetting wills. (Actually they make their money in administering estates at the time of your death.)

To speed things up, before you talk to your lawyer, give some thought to the following:

Do you wish to give money to minors or relatives with special needs?

If you have minor children or mentally disabled relatives you probably don't want to make outright gifts to them. Trusts are the answer. They allow you to delay and condition gifts, to be paid out over a span of years. Such trusts, when properly drafted, allow the individual to continue to receive public benefits while the trust assets can be used to meet supplemental needs. See Chapter 26-e.

Who do you want to administer your estate?

When your Will is probated (bills paid and gifts distributed), the person in charge is known as the executor or personal representative. You can name that person in your Will. It's important. There will be discretionary calls; pick someone your family will trust. In the case of remarriage, where two families will be involved, fights over probate can be bitter. Consider joint executors— one Hatfield, one McCoy—but if you are going to take that approach, choose the nicest of the Hatfields and the most accommodating of the McCoys. These two are going to have to work together, and if they have to go see the Judge every time they try to pay the electric bill, the cost of handling your estate will quickly become exorbitant.

What special gifts do you want to make?

"My wedding ring to my niece, Jessica" and "$2,000 to Public Radio." What is left of your estate is the Residual Bequest and it is usually the largest. It can go to specific individuals or into a Trust. Bills are paid out of this Bequest— if the bills are large, the residual beneficiary might not get anything. This might mean you should cut back on your specific bequests.

Many people think they need to list all their assets and identify the recipient of each. That's fine if you really feel that way, but if not, you might try dividing at least the cash (maybe not the family heirlooms, but that's another story) by percentages. Then you don't have to worry that if you pay for your nursing home care from the lowest-interest-rate bank account, you're going to effectively disinherit your daughter.

What if someone dies first?

Assume you have three adult children and want to divide what you have into three equal shares. What happens if one of the three dies before you? Should the other two now divide your estate or should the children of the deceased child divide the one-third? Or should they take a share equal to your two surviving children (one fourth for each)? Your lawyer, who spent three of his or her span of years on such fascinating quandaries, can draft language to accomplish what you wish. Here's where *per stirpes* comes in.

Do you want to keep your house in the family?

Should you give your house to the children now, or as part of your Will? This is tricky, but your lawyer can walk you through the options.

Do you want your family business to continue?

This is extremely tricky. You may have to consult a specialist, and not just a qualified estate planner. Family business succession planning is a special skill, and the odds of success do not start out in your favor.

Will how you divide your property cause family friction?

Sometimes you might not wish to treat your children equally. One might have special needs or maybe you have already given one money or property. To avoid bitterness (there is nothing worse for a child than to think their parent loved a sibling more), consider putting in your Will why you are treating your children unequally.

There are certain dangers in reciting in your Will why you are doing what you are doing. While that might make it easier for your heirs to understand your choices (and hence resent them less), you make your Will more vulnerable to attack. "Dad said in the Will that he was cutting me out because I smoked dope and that's not true—or at least I never inhaled—and putting that in shows that he was incompetent at the time he signed the Will." We have even known defamation suits arising out of Will recitals.

Another way, probably a better way, of explaining your choices is a family meeting. Maybe he wasn't smoking dope after all and this will allow him a chance to defend himself. Another good idea: write your loved ones a letter, not part of your will, telling them why you are doing what you have done.

e. Taking Arms Against a Sea of Troubles (Disgruntled Heirs)

It is curious that, even if you inherited everything you have from your parents, you can turn around and cut out your kids (their grandkids), leaving everything to, say, a Playboy bunny. Not so in Shakespeare's time; Falstaff's wenches were out of luck. English wealth was land and English lawyers figured out ways to keep the land in the family for generations. Each generation, actually the first-born son, would inherit only a life estate; at his death, it would automatically go to his first born and so on. The system was hard on second-born sons and on all daughters, but it did fill the ranks of the ministry and of the military, and it gave us *Pride and Prejudice*. Although we digress, our point is that our view of wealth, that it is individual and not family, is not inherent in the nature of the universe.

Today the only one you can't cut out (in most states) is your current spouse who will take one-third or one-half of your property, or perhaps half of what you acquired during your marriage. You can cut out a spouse only if you have been abandoned or if the spouse signed a prenuptial giving up all claims. (Playboy bunnies, recall the famous warning: the price of inheritance is constant vigilance!)

Your Will can be contested by disgruntled heirs—individuals who would take some or all of your estate under intestacy laws-or by those who are named as beneficiaries in an earlier Will. (If you leave your money to a trust and its ultimate distribution cuts these folks out, they can contest it as well; thus accompany the trust with a Will that reflects the cautionary steps we advise here.) If your Will is thrown out, your estate will be distributed under intestacy laws or, in some circumstances, pursuant to your earlier Will.

How can you protect yourself from sore losers? (Of course, as lawyers, we work both sides of the street. We'll have some advice for disgruntled heirs in Chapter 37.

Will contests are usually based on one of three theories:

1. You didn't realize you were signing a Will at all—perhaps someone asked you to sign the grocery list, and then slipped the Will under your pen;
2. You were subject to undue influence by one of the Big Winners; or
3. You were incompetent, and therefore legally incapable of executing your Will.

Protect your Will from these attacks.

- Name all of your children (legitimate or not), and spouses (current or not), even if you don't want to leave anything to them. If you don't, the claim will be that you forgot all about them, thus indicating that you were incompetent.
- No one who will inherit should sign as a witness to your Will (that doesn't automatically invalidate the Will, but it makes the challenge easier). Better yet, don't even have the person in the room or even in the lawyer's waiting room.
- As to legal capacity, first make sure you have it. This is a good reason for not putting off doing a Will. You could be in an accident tomorrow which would leave you mentally unable to execute a Will.
- To show you had capacity, consider videotaping your signing. (One of our colleagues suggests getting Leading Citizens to be witnesses. They are found under "L" in the Yellow Pages.)

- Finally include a *No contest clause:* "If you contest this Will, you are a worse loser than I thought and now you will get nothing!" If they are successful in contesting the Will, it, including the clause, will be thrown out. If the person gets nothing under your Will, there will be nothing to lose by the contest. Leave them something, enough to make them think twice about losing it if their contest fails.

Of course, most people do not need to worry about these precautions very much. If you intend to leave your entire estate to your spouse and children, they are the same folks who would receive everything if the Will was successfully challenged. So why would they challenge it? They wouldn't, and won't—and no one else has any standing to do so.

Again, family conversations can help reduce misunderstandings and hurt feelings. If your family knows why you did what you did, there will be less chance of challenge. More importantly, it will prevent family members resenting other members who seemed to get more.

Neither family conversations nor crafty lawyer drafting will prevent all Will contests. There have been some famous ones. In our own time, *Playboy Bunny v. Billionaire's Son.* As it has only sex and money, it is not the stuff of a novel, but of cable news and, at best, a made-for-TV movie.

Compare the case of *Jarndyce and Jarndyce* in Dickens' *Bleak House.* It showed the human toll of litigation. Families become obsessed and fly apart; individuals, awaiting their inheritance, are ruined. Lawyers and litigants should think past their clever quibbles, nitpicks, hurt feelings, and blood oaths; they should pause where now they rush.

CHAPTER 25

AVOIDING PROBATE

In the movie Ghostbusters, *Bill Murray removed ghosts from haunted houses. This often brought him into close contact with ghosts. He had one rule—"Never have romantic relations with a ghost." This worked well enough until he met a very seductive ghost. "Well, it really isn't a rule," he mused, "it's more of a guideline."*

a. Avoiding Probate

Despite the hype of self-help books, which have turned "probate" into "plague," avoiding it shouldn't even be a guideline. The devices we describe in this chapter will help you avoid probate, but don't choose them because of that; choose them only if they make sense for you and your situation. But first, what is probate?

"Probate" comes from the Latin "to prove." (Lawyers love butchering Latin. It makes us look, well, educated.) Originally "probate" just meant the process of proving the validity of a Will. Now it means much more. It includes determining the heirs in cases where there is no Will, and paying the decedent's debts, and taking care of taxes, and much more.

If you have a Will, at the time of your death your heirs present it to the Probate Court. An executor (in many states called a Personal Representative) will be appointed (usually the person you named in your Will), who will gather your assets, pay your bills, and distribute what's left according to your Will. If you die intestate (without a Will), the same process will occur, but the executor (now often called "administrator" or, once again, Personal Representative) will be chosen by the court (don't worry about strangers—it will probably be one of your children, your spouse or another relative, and may even be the person your family all agrees upon) and your property will be distributed according to the state's intestacy law.

Note that we just described how your Will gets admitted to the Probate Court. One of the most enduring myths about estate planning is that a signing a Will helps you avoid the probate process. It doesn't. It does tell the Probate Judge what you wanted to happen, and it will be followed, but it does NOT avoid probate.

So what's wrong with the probate process? Until it is complete, and it can be lengthy, your heirs will be out there hanging: until the court changes title, they cannot sell or borrow on the property, stocks, or saving accounts that you are leaving to them. Your family may be short of cash.

One way to avoid the problem of short-term cash problems is to deposit sufficient cash in either a joint account (with survivorship) or in a *payable at death account.*

In any event, probate is much improved today. Most states provide for "family allowances" which allow for immediate distributions to families to meet their short-term needs. Further, many states have informal, inexpensive, and fairly quick probate processes. With smaller estates, surviving heirs simply file a document with the proper court and the clerk will walk them through the steps. No lawyers! In these states, the costs and hassles of avoiding probate can be worse than probate itself.

In some states, however, probate remains expensive and/or lengthy. New York, California, Illinois and Florida are often cited as states where probate is less attractive for one reason or another. In an effort to streamline the probate process, a national group of lawyer activists developed the Uniform Probate Code thirty years ago; it has now been adopted in almost half the states (particularly in western and midwest states). The Uniform law introduced what was then a radical new idea: let the heirs figure out what needs to be done, and keep the Probate Court out of the picture unless and until an actual conflict arises. That approach has been followed in a handful of other states which have not adopted the actual law. You can ask your lawyer how complicated and expensive probate is in your state, but note that lawyers tend to minimize the difficulty (hey—it doesn't seem all that hard to us!) and most clients think probate is much more complicated than their lawyers believe.

Another important principle: don't confuse *avoiding probate* with *avoiding taxes.* Uncle Sam wasn't born yesterday. As we will see, much of the money you get out of your estate as a method of avoiding probate may still be counted as part of your estate for tax purposes. However, as we will see in a later chapter, estate taxes are not a concern for most of us (unfortunately, you gotta be rich).

Most estate plans consist of a Will and some form of trust, often a living trust. We describe trusts in the following chapters. Here we take a quick look at some of the other devices you can use to pass on your property:

- Lifetime Gifts
- Gifts to Minors and Disabled Individuals
- Life Insurance
- Joint Ownership
- Retirement Annuities, Roth IRA's and traditional IRA's

b. Lifetime Gifts

Don't be too shrewd.

Two friends from grade school remained close. One became rich and the other did not. The rich man, wanting to acknowledge his deep love for an old friend, decided to pay for a cruise for him and his family. His lawyer advised, "Wait until next year; it will make better sense from a tax point of view." The rich man waited; next year, his friend was dead.

Pay attention to the tax implications, but make your decisions about gifts based on how much the recipient needs, how much the gift might help them, and how much you can afford.

Gifts to children can cause resentments. Money is often confused with love. Mom must love Sis more. Let the others know why you are doing what you are doing.

"I am giving Sis a $10,000 advance on her share of my estate."
"I am giving Sis $10,000 to help her start her own business."
"I am giving Sis $10,000 because I love her more."

Gifts also present a tricky tax problem. In the case of *appreciated assets,* such as property and stocks, it is often best to pass them as part of your estate rather than by lifetime gifts. Why? Because if you pass them at death, the beneficiary gets a *stepped-up basis.* In the case of gifts, the beneficiary takes your basis. Say what?

Assume you paid $100,000 for a hot new internet stock and it is now worth $200,000. If you give it to your daughter as a lifetime gift (don't sons get anything in this book?), she will keep your basis of $100,000. If she sells it for $200,000, she will have a taxable capital gain of $100,000. On the other hand, if you pass the stock to her under your Will, she will get a stepped-up basis when she takes it at your death. The stepped-up basis is the worth of the asset at the time of death, here $200,000. If she now sells it for $200,000 she will have no capital gain. (Maybe she'll take her brother to dinner.)

Some good tax news: the gift you give to your daughter will not be taxable to her as income. Of course, you don't get any income tax deduction. There may be *gift tax* implications. If you give away more than $12,000 per person per year (double that if you and your spouse are making the gift jointly), you must file a gift tax return. However, you need not pay any gift tax until the total of all such excess gifts in your lifetime exceeds $1,000,000. The $12,000 figure, incidentally, will probably increase to $13,000 in about 2009.

c. Gifts to Minors and to the Mentally Disabled

Outright gifts to minors and mentally impaired adults create a host of problems. If you give stock to your 12-year-old granddaughter, it will now be in her name. Although she is the owner, she can't sell it, even to pay for emergencies (minors do not have contractual capacity). Most likely, her parents will not be able to sell the stock either. A guardian (of the estate) or conservator will have to be appointed for the child and this will require a court proceeding.

There are problems at the other end as well. When the child turns 18, the child is outright owner of the stock and she can squander it.

Many grandparents want to leave money to their grandchildren to be used for medical emergencies while they are minors and for their college education thereafter. With estate planning, this goal can easily be achieved; without planning, it cannot be.

Consider *Uniform Gifts to Minors* or *Uniform Transfers to Minors:* laws which allow you to appoint a parent or other responsible adult (of your choice) to be the child's financial guardian for the gift. One downside of this approach is that the income on the gift will be taxed at the parent's rate until the child is 14. Another is that the gift will be considered entirely available to the child when he or she gets around to applying for college financial aid and this will mean less college aid. Yet another: though the automatic transfer to the child may (depending on your state's law) be delayed until 21, in our experience most 21-year-olds are little better than 18-year-olds at handling money. Neither, in our jaundiced view, really, really need new, fast, brightly-colored cars.

Special trusts are now available for educational expenses as well. The most popular (and with good reason) are known as "Section 529 plans" after the section of the Internal Revenue Code providing favorable tax treatment. Check with your bank or broker; they will happily take your money. Also look online for the leading authority on Section 529 plans, www.savingforcollege.com.

The same kinds of problems arise with gifts to mentally disabled individuals, but worse: a minor will eventually grow up, but a disabled adult (or child) may never be able to manage money. As with minors, mentally disabled adults do not have contractual capacity to manage their affairs and may squander money if they get the cash. Again, trusts are a solution.

A further note on the mentally disabled recipient. If the person is receiving some form of public assistance, money received from a gift or trust may make the person ineligible or at least reduce their benefit. Carefully drafted trusts (usually called "Special Needs Trusts") can avoid this problem. Legal help is required.

d. Life Insurance

Beneficiaries of your life insurance policies collect upon your death by simply presenting your death certificate to the insurance company. This feature makes life insurance an attractive estate planning tool if the concern is to get some money to your heirs quickly. Probate, even in the best of cases, takes time—and proceeds from life insurance policies may come in handy.

The proceeds from your life insurance do not pass through your estate and are not subject to creditors of your estate. Life insurance can be a good method of avoiding probate. You take money from your estate *now*, using it to pay the premiums, to have it paid out on the other side, so to speak. However, because life insurance proceeds likely will be figured as part of your taxable estate, it should not be used as a device to avoid estate taxes unless special steps are taken. Sorry, you'll need the advice of a tax lawyer.

On the other hand, some advise folks to cancel their life insurance policies because their kids are most likely grown and do not need life-insurance protection. Indeed, if we recall correctly, *we* advised that elsewhere in the book. We recommended that you consider long-term care insurance instead.

e. Joint Ownership

Some tout joint ownership of property and stocks as the best way of avoiding probate. We disagree. The basic idea is that when you die, the joint owner simply files the right piece of paper and the title will be rewritten in that person's name alone. No need to go to Probate Court.

But except for smaller items, such as a car and relatively small bank accounts and stock holdings, we recommend against joint ownership. We have our reasons:

- There are several forms of joint ownership; only some have a "right of survivorship" which vests title in one joint owner at the time the other dies. *Without* such a survivorship aspect, joint ownership does not avoid probate: at the death of one joint owner, his or her share stays in his or her estate.
- Even with survivorship, joint ownership doesn't avoid probate, it only postpones it. When the surviving owner dies, the property will be in his or her estate. Trusts can avoid this.
- Joint ownership presents problems if both owners die at the same time, and may have adverse income, gift, and estate tax consequences.
- Joint ownership means you give up control over the asset; while it is easy to add someone to a title, it is hard to get them off.
  Many married couples hold title to their house as joint tenants with right of survivorship, and that usually (but not always) works out just fine. Assume a couple has been separated for several years, with the wife living in the house. In her Will she leaves everything to her daughter. When she dies, however, the daughter may not get the mother's interest in the house: it passes, without probate, to the surviving husband. The husband is now free to sell the house or leave it to anyone he wishes.
- As long as property is in joint ownership, the creditors of the other person can attempt to reach it. And, of course, joint owners can always cash in and run off to Brazil.
- In some states, joint ownership won't even speed transfer of assets upon death, and some states automatically freeze these accounts until tax officials can check things out. (Banks assign employees to read the obits.)
- Joint tenancy assets are still included in your estate for purposes of calculating your estate tax, at least to the extent that you were the one who put the money into the asset.
- If you put one child on as joint owner, trusting that they will follow your wishes, you are relying on their goodwill and their perfect knowledge of what those wishes might be. If your distributive scheme is the least bit complicated, joint ownership will probably foul it up.

f. Retirement Annuities, Roth IRAs and IRAs

Don't overlook the possibility of using your retirement nest eggs as a method of providing for your loved ones after your death. For example, if you had a pension plan and have decided to take an annuity, consider appointing a loved one as your beneficiary. Your monthly check will be reduced but, if you can afford it, your beneficiary will continue to receive a monthly check for years or for life, depending on how it is set up. (See Chapter 7-c.)

The new *Roth IRA* is definitely worth a look. A major advantage the Roth IRA has over a traditional IRA is that you need not begin drawing on it after age 70. This means the entire amount, with its earnings, will be available to your beneficiaries. It will create a lifetime stream of tax-free income for them. They will have to begin drawing on it at the time of your death.

It is possible to convert any IRA you currently have to a Roth IRA. You will have to pay any taxes due on it at the time of conversion, but this might be well worth it. You should talk to your accountant.

Finally, you can pass money to a loved one by designating him or her as your beneficiary under traditional IRAs.

g. Living Trusts

A very popular device to avoid probate is the *living trust*. One advantage it has over the other estate planning devices (such as Wills and various forms of joint ownership), is that a living trust also solves the problem of having someone else deal with your financial affairs if you become incapable of doing so. That is, a living trust has many of the advantages of a Durable Power of Attorney which we discussed in Chapter 23-b.

But before we turn to living trusts (and decide, once and for all, whether to capitalize them), we will describe the most wonderful legal device of all—the Trust!

CHAPTER 26

Trusts: Legal Shmoos

Remember the "Funnies"? In Li'l Abner, the Shmoos were unique beings that did just about everything—shopped, cleaned, set the table—and then cooked themselves for dinner.

Trusts are like that. They do about everything. In basic form, trusts are quite simple. They are written agreements between the trustor and the trustee, providing that the trustee will use the money or property the trustor puts into the trust for the benefit of a third party, the beneficiary. Say what?

You (the *trustor, grantor* or *settlor*) give money or property to a *trustee* (a bank, a friend, or, as we will see, *yourself*) to be managed and used in trust for the benefit of the *beneficiary* (a minor child, a disabled relative, or, as we will see, *yourself*). The money or property is to be used as directed by the *trust instrument* ("for the college education of my grandchildren" or "for the medical care of my niece Joanna").

Trusts cannot live forever, although they can hang in there a very long time. When their time is up, the trustee distributes the remaining assets to the individuals named in the trust instrument. Thus, trusts are like Wills in this regard; they are a way of passing money and other assets after death. Many people use trusts as part of their estate plans.

a. The Marvelous Trust

The basic virtue of trusts is that they allow you to delay and structure your gifts. You can provide money for your grandchildren's education without fear they will drink it all up, and you can provide lifetime support for a disabled nephew. Trusts are quite flexible and can be tailored almost any way you want:

> *"The trustee shall accumulate interest until my grandchild enrolls in college and then the trustee will pay for tuition, room and board, and necessary books for four years of college and any graduate education there-*

*after. After my grandchild finishes his education, the trustee shall pay
him the interest on the trust until he turns 40 years old, and then the
principal shall be distributed, one-half to him and one-half to the Denial of Death Foundation."*

You can create trusts during your life (called *inter vivos trusts*) or you can
create them as part of your Will (*testamentary trusts*). Or you can create one
now, but fund it with a nominal amount (say, $10 or, in some states, noth-
ing at all), and then have other assets pour over into it from your estate at the
time of your death (let's call these *standby trusts).*

Why can't you keep your property in trust forever? English landowners tried.

*My beloved country estate, Blackacre, I leave in trust for my first-born
son, for his use during his lifetime, and thereafter for the use of his first-
born son and thereafter for the use of his first-born son, etc., etc., etc.*

English judges, who gave us much of our common law, were not fools. If
these trusts stood up, neither they (nor *their* first-born sons) were likely to get
very much of anything. (It was, by the way, *always* the first-born *son*.) So these
judges, clever old codgers that they were, came up with the *Rule Against Perpetuities.* It is so complicated that it drives law students batty. The California
Supreme Court went so far as to hold that lawyers don't even have to understand it. (We kid you not!)

Basically, the Rule means that at some point you will have to let your incompetent heirs finally get their grubby hands on the property. Trusts can last
only for *a life in being plus 21 years*, which is much easier to say than figure
out. Before you go trying to figure it out, you should know that several state
legislatures have been tinkering with it for decades. Unsuccessfully. Now no
one is completely sure which rule the lawyers don't have to understand.

If you are considering using a trust, the first thing to do is to ask your
lawyer to explain the Rule Against Perpetuities. Like hitting a home run your
first time at bat, this will signal that you are not to be trifled with. You probably won't gather useful information this way, but you will have a pleasant afternoon's entertainment.

b. Trusts for the Disabled

If you want to provide for a relative who is mentally disabled, you can create a trust for their benefit, to pay out income during the course of their life,

with the ability of the trustee to invade the principal for emergencies. One problem to avoid: the income may make the individual ineligible for welfare assistance. Your lawyer can draft around this problem by creating what is known as a "Special Needs Trust." With such a trust, the beneficiary can receive some benefits (travel, for example, or entertainment, education, extra therapy, furniture, paid companionship, or almost anything but cash, food or shelter) without any effect on welfare services. In some cases it might even be both possible and advisable for the Special Needs Trust to provide food and shelter. This rapidly developing area of the law really calls for involvement of a lawyer with expertise in the field.

c. Revocable or Irrevocable?

If you create a trust during your lifetime, the basic choice is whether you want to make it revocable or irrevocable. A revocable trust allows you to change your mind and tell the trustee to return your property. Times change and you may need your property back to make ends meet. Or you may change your mind as to whom you want to get your property. (You move to Los Angeles and now, rather than give anything to the Denial of Death Foundation, you want to give everything to some weird cult, the Denial of Good-taste Foundation.)

One *disadvantage* of revocable trusts is that the law treats the money in them as yours; just as you can get your money back, so, too, your creditors. The other is that the transfer of assets to a revocable living trust is not a "transfer" for tax purposes. Income it earns is reported on *your* individual tax return. A transfer to an irrevocable trust is a taxable event since you are forever giving the stuff away. It may be subject to the Gift Tax. (See Chapter 28.)

The pros and cons of the *irrevocable* trust are the mirror image of those of the revocable. You can't change your mind but it usually (not always—and that can actually be a good thing) pays its own taxes. Further gifts to them may help reduce estate taxes.

The most common use of irrevocable trusts: to own life insurance policies on the life of the person who established the trust. This technique helps get the life insurance out of the insured's estate for tax purposes, without giving the premiums outright to the kids (maybe they can't be relied on to keep the insurance current). The second most common irrevocable trust: the Special Needs Trust described above. Most, but not all, of the other trusts we deal with are revocable.

d. Administering the Trust

English novels teach us that trustees tend to be conservative (at least when they're not falling in love with their shy, beautiful ward, who is, in turn, madly in love with a poor but struggling—and destined for greatness—doctor).

Trustees are in something of a bind. They have obligations both to the current beneficiary and to those who will take the remainder of the trust when it ends. The law calls these folks the "remainder men"—better than "left-over men." If the trustee is too free and easy giving the current beneficiary money, or invests the trust's assets only for the benefit of the income recipient, he may be sued by the remainder men.

Help him out.

> *I intend that the provisions of this trust be liberally construed and that the term "education" include trade and art schools, educational travel and all necessary expenses related thereto, including the purchase of a car.*
>
> *＊ ＊ ＊*
>
> *I intend reasonable medical care to include the costs of non-traditional pain relief, such as hypnotism, bio-feedback, and massage, and I authorize medical treatment at home even if it costs more than institutional care.*
>
> *＊ ＊ ＊*
>
> *In making discretionary distributions and investments, the trustee is to consider first the interests of the income beneficiary; the trustee has express authority to distribute trust principal even to the exhaustion of the trust estate if she, in her sole discretion, deems it appropriate to do so.*

e. Powers of the Trustee

What your trustee can and cannot do with your money will be a matter of state law. Best to have your lawyer draft what you want.

- No power to buy speculative stocks, or options? No power to buy "sin" stocks?
- Authority to invade principal to handle emergencies?
- Power to make gifts?
- Power to settle claims?
- Power to hire accountants and others to help administer the trust?

f. Choosing the Trustee

Banks and other financial concerns will not get involved unless the trust is large, in the range of $150,000 to $500,000 in discretionary assets in most communities.

For smaller trusts, relatives are often used. First you should check with them to make sure they are agreeable. Should they receive a fee for their services? Honesty is important—a trustee can run off with the money. Also consider the trustee's:

- Relation to the beneficiaries;
- Financial skills and stability;
- Age in relation to beneficiaries;
- Geographical proximity.

Co-trustees are possible, perhaps a bank for wisdom and a relative for compassion.

We know of a case where a dying woman named her manicurist as her trustee. She really liked the manicurist, and she secured a solemn promise that the trust would be carefully administered. The problem was that the manicurist simply had no conception of what a $1,000,000 trust meant. The beneficiary lost out, the manicurist had a big judgment levied against her, the lawyers got more of the estate than they should have. You can read this story broadly, competence trumps well-meaning and agreeable; or narrowly, don't appoint your manicurist.

Always name an alternative or successor trustee, just in case.

g. Funding the Trust

There is no need to *create* and *fund* a trust at the same time. When you actually put your money or other assets into the trust will turn on tax issues and inertia.

If future emergencies are a concern, you can create an irrevocable trust but simply not put that much money in it. For maximum flexibility, you can make the trust revocable or make it a testamentary trust, one funded at the time of your death.

There is one form of trust that is very popular, the so-called Living Trust. It deserves its own chapter and its own Movie Moment.

CHAPTER 27

LIVING TRUSTS

In the movie comedy Raising Arizona, *a baby is kidnapped and the father is approached by one mean-looking bounty-hunter who offers to find the baby for him.*
"Why should I hire you?" the father asks. "I have the police working on it."
"If you want to find your baby, ask me. If you want to find Dunkin Donuts, ask the police."

Nice story but how does it fit?

"If you want a Living Trust, ask a lawyer. If you want a free donut, go to a Living Trust Seminar."

Today's hot item is the Living Trust, sold by traveling salesman at free breakfasts, lunches, dinners, and seminars. The price ranges from $900 to $1,500 but that comes last. First, all the marvelous things these shmoos can do:

- They'll be there if you become incapable of managing your finances, thus replacing the need for a durable power of attorney;
- They'll distribute your property when you die, thus replacing the need for a Will;
- They'll allow you to avoid probate and defer, and perhaps reduce or eliminate, estate taxes;
- They'll allow you to manage your own money as you are today and to easily change your mind about the whole thing without messy "codicils."
- "Wow. All that, and free donuts too. Where do we sign up?"
- "Fine. That will be $1,200."

Save your money. In our experience, nine out of ten people who purchase living trusts *don't need them.* There are many other devices to accomplish the same goals. If you are considering one, see a lawyer who knows the law in your state, who knows current tax law, and who knows other devices that may suit your needs more closely. There is more to it than signing the papers. You must transfer your property to your trust and legal advice will be needed as to how.

a. An Example of a Living Trust—Parsed

The Living Trust of Teddy and Larry Durbin

The assets of this trust shall be used for the benefit of Teddy and Larry Durbin, husband and wife, and shall be administered by them. In the event that they become incapable of administering this trust, it shall be administered by their son, Matthew, or, if he cannot, by the First National Bank. At the death of either Teddy or Larry, this Trust shall become irrevocable. Thereafter, the assets of the trust will be used for the benefit of the survivor. At the death of the survivor, the assets remaining in the trust shall be distributed in equal parts to the then surviving children of Teddy and Larry (or, for example, "shall be held in trust for the then surviving children, with the income to be distributed to them yearly, with the remaining assets distributed to them when the youngest turns 25").

With a few more bells and whistles, that's about it! That's it? $1,200? Sure, they were *glazed* donuts, but still!

To make matters a tad worse, in all likelihood *you'll still need a Will*. Before getting to that, what have you accomplished? Let's, as we do in law school, parse the language.

> *"for the benefit of Teddy and Larry Durbin, husband and wife, and shall be administered by them.*

You continue to manage your financial affairs as before, but now must sign as "trustee."

> *At the death of either Teddy or Larry, this Trust shall become irrevocable.*

This is a fancy way of saying *until* the death of either of them, the trust is revocable. This means a couple of things. First, you can change your mind and take everything out of the trust. Second, it means that the trust is not a separate tax entity. Income it earns will go on your individual return. Once a trust becomes irrevocable, then it becomes a separate tax entity, will have to get its own tax number, and will have to pay its own taxes. Third, when the trust becomes irrevocable, the surviving spouse *cannot* change who gets the remainder when the trust ends.

At the death of the survivor, the assets remaining in the trust shall be dis-
tributed in equal parts to the then surviving children of Teddy and Larry.

Here the Living Trust is acting like a Will. Fair enough, but don't skim. The major thing law students learn (hopefully) is how to read closely. The assets go to the "then surviving children." Pause and consider the implications of that.

Assume the Durbins have two kids, one of whom has children but dies before his surviving parent. The grandchildren would get nothing. What if both kids predecease their surviving parent? Then the assets will be distributed as if the surviving spouse died without a Will, meaning that the relatives of the survivor, but not those of the first spouse, get it all.

These nice points underscore the need for a lawyer, not a salesman, to do the drafting.

The assets shall be held in trust for the then surviving children, with the
income to be distributed to them yearly, with the remaining assets dis-
tributed to them when the youngest turns 25.

The trust continues but defers distribution until the kids grow up (again, hopefully).

In the event that Teddy and Larry become incapable of administering
this trust, it shall be administered by their son, Matthew or, if he can-
not, by the First National Bank.

Here the Living Trust is acting like a Durable Power of Attorney. Note that there is a potential conflict of interest in having Matthew act as guardian. As he will share in what is left in the trust, he may be tempted to skimp.

A further advantage of a Living Trust is that the assets do not go through probate. As a practical matter this means that the survivor has immediate access to them. If they were in a Will and had to go through Probate, as we mentioned earlier, the survivor might have to wait until that process ran its course.

Why is it, after all of that, that you will still need a Will?

Probably not everything you own will be in the trust. Most people move their major assets into the trust (stock accounts and real property). It is too much of a hassle to change your checking account, re-register your car, that sort of thing. You'll need a Will to dispose of your incidental stuff. If you wish, that Will can provide that everything you have pour over into the Trust. (This is known by the more literate of the legal tribe as a "pour-over" trust.)

Finally, you will need a Will if you are cutting your kids out of the final distribution. A trust can be attacked by disgruntled heirs, saying that you forgot them, saying that you were incompetent when you signed the documents (sugar high?) or that you were under the evil influence of the Denial of Death Foundation. In our chapter on Wills, we suggested ways to defeat these folks and, if we recall correctly, made some poignant literary references. Contesting a trust is much like contesting a Will, with this difference: a Will has to be submitted to the Probate Court, and all the potentially disgruntled heirs given notice of their opportunity to make a fuss. A Trust, on the other hand, ordinarily does not see the inside of a Probate Court, and the disgruntled heirs have to initiate the legal proceedings.

Two final matters, in praise of Living Trusts, and then a Cautionary Note.

b. Property in Other States; Blended Families

Living trusts handle quite nicely two problems that Wills struggle with: the problem of real property in different states, and the problem of "blended families."

If you have real property (land or houses) in other states, it may be necessary for your heirs to open probate proceedings in each of those states. Courts in California, for example, have no jurisdiction over land in Colorado (otherwise California would have stolen all the water). However, if your trust owns the property, the trustee can simply sign the deed and give the property to your heirs.

As to "blended families," say Larry had three kids from a prior marriage when he married Teddy and she had two. Both agree that when either Larry or Teddy dies, the other should have all their assets and, at the time of the survivor's death, what remains be divided among the five children. Now they could draft their Wills to accomplish this:

> When I die, I want everything I have to go to Teddy. However, if she predeceases me, then everything should be divided equally among my children from a previous marriage, Manny, Mo, Jack, and Teddy's two kids, whose names escape me; but like, I mean, you know, the ones with the tattoos and nose rings.

If we can trust Larry (and we can't, he is an old high school friend), there is nothing to stop him from rewriting his Will when Teddy dies, cutting out her kids. Some states will enforce mutual agreements not to change one's Will. However, Living Trusts are easier: when Teddy dies, the Trust, including its ultimate distribution, become irrevocable.

c. A Caution: Praising Formality

Compared to Wills, Living Trusts are quite informal. There is no need, for example, for the ponderous language:

Being of sound mind, this is my Last Will and Testament.

These are serious matters. What you decide will affect your life, your spouse's, and your family's. Ponderous language, indeed pomposity, reminds one of the momentous decisions you are making. Don't be distracted and louse up your family's future by the hope that they will bring out more donuts. And, finally, don't sign the contract unless they are going wild with least apple fritters.

CHAPTER 28

ESTATE AND GIFT TAXES

Two things are certain in life: death and taxes. At this writing, the Republicans are working on the latter, advocating repeal of the estate tax. Had they reversed their priorities, they would have gotten our votes for sure.

If you have a large estate, get competent legal help. You will save much more money in estate taxes than you will pay in lawyer fees. Here are some basics.

Unless you're rich, be happy. Congress rewrote the estate and gift tax rules a few years ago, and the tinkering continues. At the moment, only estates larger than $2,000,000 face any estate tax liability at all, though the limit is scheduled to drop back to $1,000,000 in 2011 unless Congress takes some further steps. (No one believes that the estate tax will return to the lower figure.) Gift taxes are imposed on lifetime gifts of more than $1,000,000, though there is an exemption for gifts of up to $12,000 per year per recipient (double that if a husband and wife join in making the gifts). The bottom line here: unless your net worth puts you in the top 1% or so of all citizens, you simply don't have to worry about estate or gift taxes.

For those who do need to worry about estate and gift taxes, the worrying can be profound. Tax rates are capped at 46% of the excess over the amounts listed above (45% in 2007 and 2008), so the stakes are high.

Gifts. If you give away enough money or property during your life, you will eat into the $2,000,000 estate tax exemption. In other words, if you make a $500,000 gift to your doting nephew this year, you will have to file a gift tax return and report a $488,000 gift (remember that the first $12,000 was free). That means that your estate will pay an estate tax on everything over $1,512,000 because you have used up part of your $2,000,000 exemption. And just when that starts making sense to you, the numbers will change.

You can give away $12,000 per year to as many individuals as you want without it counting against your Lifetime Exemption. You can get a lot of money out of your estate (and away from the taxman) by this device. Each year, a husband and wife can EACH give each of their children $12,000, each of their children's spouses $12,000, each grandchild $12,000 and each of the authors of this book $12,000.

There's even more good news. Gifts for educational and medical purposes don't count at all, provided that they are given directly to the educational institution or medical provider. Don't hand your grandson a check for $50,000 and tell him to spend it at Harvard, your alma mater; write that check directly to the Harvard bursar.

Don't worry about having to stay healthy for three years after your gifts—that's the old rule, and there's really only one artifact from those days. If you make a gift of a life insurance policy (changing the owner, not just the beneficiary), you have to stay alive for three years before the policy has gotten out of your estate.

Most people have never even heard of the "*Generation Skipping Tax*" (the GST). It kicks in if bequests to grandchildren or other young recipients exceed $2,000,000 total. That's the same level as the estate tax itself, but with an additional kick: the GST rate is another 46%. In other words, Congress continues to strongly discourage efforts to put large estates out of circulation for multiple generations.

Bequests to your spouse are not taxable. You can leave as much as you like to your spouse without triggering tax liability. However, when your spouse dies, there could still be taxes (assuming that the total of your estate, your spouse's and any accumulation after your death exceeds the $2,000,000 figure—or whatever the exemption is in the year your spouse dies), unless you have consulted a good tax lawyer.

Give to charity. Any gifts that you make to charities by will or by trust distribution are not included in your estate for purposes of calculating estate taxes. Such gifts allow you to determine how your money will be spent after your death. But there are some additional benefits available by charitable gifting. It is possible during your lifetime to transfer assets to a charity and get the benefit of the charitable donation on your income taxes while having the charity agree to pay you a lifetime income from the earnings it receives on the gift. This gets complex, but a gift of appreciated assets (such as that IBM stock that you bought for $10 that is now worth $100) can give you a deduction for nearly the full value, while giving you an income from the charity for life based on the value at the time of your gift.

These are called *Charitable Remainder Trusts* and they come in many flavors and are well understood by experienced estate planning attorneys. The point is, if you have charitable intent, get advice—it may be far better for you to be donating assets than it would be for you to write a check.

Retirement accounts (401k's, IRAs, TSAs and the like) are special cases.

As retirement accumulations have grown over the past few decades, the problems with passing those types of assets to later generations have become more sharply defined. In general terms, you probably do not want to name your trust as beneficiary of your IRA or qualified retirement plan (except when you do want to name the trust as beneficiary—the legal principles are just about as confusing as that sounds). You may not want to name a collection of individuals as beneficiaries, either, as there may be significant benefits (for them, not for you) in separating the accounts and naming one beneficiary for each of the new, smaller products. Plus, if you have charitable inclinations, your retirement account may be the perfect vehicle to utilize; the charity will pay no estate tax and no income tax, and your retirement money will go further for the charity than it would for your children. Put another way, you will get more mileage out of using the retirement account to satisfy your charitable leanings than you can get out of any other asset.

Estate tax planning is very complicated and the more you have, the more complicated it gets. Estate tax planning is not for amateurs and requires professional help. Those who have substantial amounts of land or a big interest in a family business have lots of options that only the specialist in the mysteries of the Internal Revenue Code can implement and sometimes explain. If you have ever heard of Family Limited Partnerships, Discounts for Marketability, etc., get thee to an estate planning attorney, a specialist.

PART 5

DISABILITY IN THE FAMILY

Introduction:
Confronting the Manic Terror

When you begin to notice that a loved one, perhaps a parent, perhaps a spouse, is slipping into physical or mental disability, you are not the only one. They notice, too.

> *"What I wanted was to maintain a sense of control. Even more than the dread of becoming a burden, helplessness triggers in us a manic terror that things are slipping from our grasp ..."*

So Nancy Mairs writes of her slide into the physical disability of multiple sclerosis. Her inspiring book is *Waist-High in the World*.

Severe disability will put heavy strains on you and your family. In the chapters that follow we will discuss how to cope with physical disability (making a home senior-friendly, home care versus nursing home care), and how to cope with mental disability (short term solutions and legal guardianships). We will also offer advice on caring for yourself and, as you will often be making decisions for others, what the law says on how you should go about it.

It's easy to get caught up in all these details. As difficult as they may be, we are on fairly safe emotional ground. To step back, to come to grips with how it is for your parent, for your spouse, can be emotionally trying and scary. Your number one job, however, is not helping them find hearing aids or even a good nursing home; your number one job is to be with them facing the "manic terror" as things slip from their grasp.

For a tangle of reasons we are reluctant to sit with someone suffering and honestly confront their future and, indeed, ours. Like J. Alfred Prufrock, we "come and go, talking of Michelangelo."

"You're looking good."

"Are the nurses treating you right?"

"How about them Bulls?"

Who are we kidding? Our lives are changing and current events are not our most pressing problem.

"Dad, I know things are rough on you now. Don't worry about being a burden—not only am I happy to shoulder it, I insist on the privilege. We'll get by. And I'll be here to help you keep on top of things. What's your biggest fear?"

Now, the safe stuff.

CHAPTER 29

SLINGS AND ARROWS

We will all suffer the slings and arrows of outrageous fortune. We described some them in Chapter 3, Growing Old. In this chapter we will look at four common and disabling conditions of advancing old age: depression, memory loss, hearing loss, and financial confusion. While taking arms against them may not end them, there are things we can do that will help. Our next chapter deals with severe mental incapacity and the last two of this section deal with home care and nursing homes.

Let's begin with a typical problem.

Your loved one is becoming more difficult. They seem to have lost interest in living and are becoming more forgetful and less helpful in caring for themselves. And they are getting grouchy. What should you do?

First, what *not* to do. Don't assume that this is an inevitable part of aging and that nothing can be done. Conversely, don't assume that the behavior is within the person's control and that shouting at them will improve things. Sitting by doing nothing, or making things worse by losing your temper, are preludes to elder abuse and lousy lives for everyone involved.

Most conditions can be improved, or at least accommodated.

The easiest conditions to correct are those caused by bad meds or hearing loss. More difficult are those caused by depression and dementia. Finally, we will look at the situation where the person only needs help in paying their bills.

a. Bad Meds

Improper medications can lead to depression, physical ailments, and memory loss. *One in five* seniors is taking either the wrong dosage or the wrong drugs. Dosages that were fine before may become toxic as one ages. Drugs from different doctors, for different conditions, may interact badly. Don't assume that each doctor knows what the others have prescribed, and while pharmacists are good and getting better at catching drug interactions, don't assume that all the problems have been noted.

Additionally, many medications the elderly take can make depression worse. They can include steroids, anti-cancer drugs, tranquilizers, anti-anxiety drugs, and drugs for Parkinson's, high blood pressure, heart disease, rheumatoid arthritis, and pain.

If your loved one starts to sink, check the meds *first*. Take all the prescription bottles to the pharmacist. As a general matter, this should be a yearly routine.

b. Hearing Loss

We should have stayed with Sinatra.

Is your irritable, listless loved one going deaf but too vain to admit it? Some signs: complaints that you mumble; that voices get lost in background noise; turning up the TV; blasting talk radio as teens blast hip-hop. (Their turn will come.)

Presbycusis (age-related hearing loss), can be devastating. It isolates and distracts from family and social life. And once one gets used to partial deafness, it may be harder to correct later.

Don't blithely accept your father's repeated assurances that he hears well enough. Refusal to acknowledge hearing limitations is commonplace, and also unhelpful. Insist on a hearing test and point out (loudly?) that there have been vast improvements in hearing aids—they are no longer bulky and ugly and they no longer distort sound. Some are even digital and more snappy than teens' iPods.

Hearing Aids can be expensive. They are not covered by Medicare or by most insurance policies. In selecting a Medicare HMO, coverage in this area may important. You can get information on state and federal help from the Better Hearing Institute (1-800-Ear-Well). Hear Now (1-800-648-HEAR or 303-695-7797 hearing impaired) may help those in financial need.

c. Depression

Depression, when it doesn't lead to suicide, destroys life's pleasures, both for the victims and their families. About one in seven over 65 suffers depression and, of that number, 70% to 90% go untreated. This is tragic: more than *80%* of elders will respond well or completely to treatment.

Why this dismal record? Symptoms are often overlooked. Many elders, and their families, *expect* them to be depressed, what with deaths of friends, or unsatisfying retirement, or moves to a new home. *Depression is not a disease of circumstance; it is a disease of chemicals.* While depressing events can trigger episodes of depression, if they do not lift within, say, six months, you are dealing with brain chemistry gone amuck. And some clinical depression simply happens without being triggered by external events.

Depression may also be masked because the victim may not feel sad and the usual signs of depression—sadness, poor appetite, bad sleep, and quitting activities once enjoyed—may not be present. Instead the depression may present itself as memory problems, irritability, anxiety, loss of energy. and vague aches and pains.

Treatment is often resisted. First, there is the stigma of depression; and second, not only electric shock, but many of the other treatments suffer from bad raps. But side effects have been greatly reduced. There are many new drugs. A patient will be put on one and, if that doesn't work, after 6 to 12 weeks, another is tried.

Ken Kesey's book, and Jack Nicholson's movie, *One Flew Over the Cuckoo's Nest,* gave electric shock something of a bad name. But, like many of the victims of the 60's (soldiers, cops, Sinatra), it is making something of a comeback as a last-ditch treatment for severe depression. The treatment itself has undergone dramatic changes, resulting in dramatic reductions in harmful side effects.

Women are much more likely to become depressed and a vitamin B12 deficiency has been linked to it.

Two bottom-line points:

1. Depression is an illness of the mind, caused by chemical imbalances; it is not a moral failure or a self-willed choice. Like any other disease, it should be treated.

2. Treatment is promising, not only to improve mood and enjoyment of life, but also to reduce physical infirmities, prolong life, and occasionally reduce the symptoms of dementia.

Alcoholism is a frequent flyer with depression. Look for hidden bottles; remember vodka is "breathless."

d. Memory Loss and Alzheimer's

Memory loss is *not* the same thing as dementia and does *not* necessarily lead to it. Although dementia usually entails memory loss, it is much more:

it is the inability to think things through, the inability to recognize options and choices and the inability to make sound decisions—what the psychologists sometimes call "executive function."

Expect some memory loss. The first to go is short-term memory, "What did you have for breakfast yesterday?" And names tend to escape one's grasp. Names fade because they are arbitrary—our dentist could have been named Sally instead of Carol. We may forget her name but not that she is a dentist, and certainly not those long, pointed, curled, threatening silver things she handles so deftly.

Memory loss is irksome and frightening: is this the first sign? Reassure the elders in your life that memory loss does not inevitably lead to dementia or senility. It does not necessarily get worse. Few become senile. Being fearful is a good sign. Geriatric physicians will ask patients, "Are you worried about memory loss?" and if the answer is, "yes," they are relieved. The answer that troubles them is, "No, my memory is fine."

We don't want to make light of dementia. The National Institute on Aging estimates that 5% of those 65 to 74 suffer from dementia of the Alzheimer's type, and the percentage grows quickly after that, reaching 50% for folks over 85.

If you are concerned about a relative, you might want to test their "executive function" by asking questions like, "If you wanted to take a trip to Europe, how would you go about it?" If the answer touches upon travel agents and airline tickets, fine. Be concerned with "I don't know" or "I would ask my daughter to take care of things." Consider a medical checkup.

If a relative is suffering from any form of dementia, you will need a lot of emotional support and a lot of physical help. Sources of help can be found at Area Council and on the Web. Buy a copy of "The 36-Hour Day" by Nancy L. Mace and Dr. Peter V. Rabins—it contains invaluable advice, information and comfort for anyone with a family member suffering from dementia. Then buy another copy for each of your siblings, adult children and friends from church.

One constant fear is that the person may wander off. When this happens and police must be called, some, out of respect for the person's privacy and dignity, will not report to the police that the person has dementia. Don't do this. Police have thousands of missing folks to find: if they know the person suffers from dementia, they will give it the same high priority as a missing child. Otherwise, perhaps not.

There is a "Safe Return Program" that can help. For a one-time $40 registration fee, a bracelet and clothing tags will be provided. The items have a toll free number on them: if someone finds the person, they call the number and the operator will then contact the caregiver listed in the database. This service is 24 hours a day. For more information, call the Alzheimer's Association at 1-800-272-3900 (hearing impaired 312-335-8882).

Many fear that Alzheimer's is genetic. Autopsies disclose that close to half of those who were thought to have Alzheimer's actually did not. This is one good reason for an autopsy.

e. Paying the Bills: Social Security Checks and Durable Powers of Attorney

One task you will likely have to assume is helping your relative with their finances. Don't be tempted by your little voice that whispers, "The money will soon be yours, anyway, buy that new car." It is still theft.

One problem is with checks coming in. *Representative payee* status can be established for Social Security checks, Veteran's benefits and most pensions. No court involvement is required, and the level of accounting and oversight mandated by Social Security is manageable. Establishing representative payee status requires that the benefits recipient be found (by the agency) to be unable to manage their own funds; this usually means that a letter from his or her physician must be provided to Social Security.

Another possibility is a *convenience signer account* (really just the bank's version of a power of attorney) offered by many banks. Social Security can send the checks directly to the bank, and a relative, good friend, or neighbor can be added to the account to pay monthly bills. These accounts are better than joint accounts because the convenience signer does not have an ownership interest in the account; their creditors cannot get the cash. On the other hand, at time of death, the convenience signer cannot simply take what's left in the account. In other words, it cannot be used to pass money at the time of death.

If the financial situation is more complicated—because of ownership of cars, houses, stocks, real proper—then you should consider joint ownership or, more generally, a *Durable Financial Power of Attorney*. These choices are described in Chapter 23. If the disabled person becomes unable to make medical decisions, a *Durable Health Care Power of Attorney* will be required. (See Chapter 23.) These documents *must* be signed while the person is still competent. Once a loved one starts to slip, feel time's winged chariot hurrying near. If the needed documents are not signed, then you will have to seek something more formal. Which leads nicely into a discussion of Guardianships. Turn the page.

CHAPTER 30

MENTAL INCAPACITY

The only purpose for which power can be rightfully exercised over any member of a civilized community, against his will, is to prevent harm to others. His own good, either physical or moral, is not sufficient warrant.

John Stuart Mill, On Liberty

Sometimes it is necessary to seek a guardianship or conservatorship for a relative. It is, and should be, a painful experience. These legal arrangements allow power to be exercised over the person against his will, not to prevent harm to others, but for his own good, physical or moral.

The right to make our own decisions, even foolish ones, defines adulthood. It is premised, however, on our capacity to make responsible decisions. Obviously, we need not actually *make* responsible decisions. Making bad decisions is part of adulthood, too. (Alas.)

a. The Concept of Legal Capacity

Legal capacity involves the ability to recognize alternatives, to weigh pros and cons, and to project into the future. We don't, for example, give much credence (nor did John Stuart Mill) to a five-year-old's adamant:

> "I'm running away and I'm taking Puppy with me, and this time I'm really serious!"

Grown-ups make decisions for children because children do not have the mental capacity to always know their best interests, or those of their puppies. Sometimes, in fact, the puppies can be better at this skill.

A good way to check on someone's capacity is to engage them in a conversation concerning recognition of alternatives, judging pros and cons, and projecting into the future.

> "What else might you do other than running away?"
> "What's going to happen when you get there?"

"Why is running away better than locking yourself in the bathroom and screaming?"

Some use the "planning a trip" question. "Mom, if you were going to take a trip back to your hometown, how would you go about it?" "Ask you" is not a passing-grade answer.

Most of the elderly, even in old, old age (defined as "older than us"), retain mental ability. Mental functions do not necessarily diminish. But some elderly do lose legal capacity. Accidents, strokes, disease, and acute depression happen. Then relatives or friends must step in.

b. Formal Interventions: Guardianship and Conservatorship

First, a word about terms. We use "guardianship" to describe both the authority obtained over the physical person, and the similar-but-different authority over their finances. Sometimes we use "conservatorship" to mean only a proceeding over finances. We refer to the subject of a guardianship (or conservatorship) proceeding as a "ward." We have adopted those conventions because they are the most common usage in state laws, but they are far from the exclusive meanings. In some states "conservatorship" can be both person and finances, or "guardianship" can be "of the person" and conservatorship "of the estate". Some states use completely different terms ("tutors," "committees" and our favorite, "interdicts", for example). Before applying the principles we write about here to your local legal language, be sure you know what the terms mean in your state.

A majority of the elderly never need a guardianship because they never become incompetent. Even then, most guardianships are sought at the insistence of third parties:

1. Financial institutions may require appointment of a guardian or conservator to allow access to funds;
2. Hospitals may require appointment of a guardian for certain medical treatments; and
3. Nursing homes may require guardianship for admittance (under the laws of some states, formal guardianship is required).

Routine formal guardianships are quick and relatively inexpensive. A short court hearing will be held and usually the ward (the disabled person) will not be present. The person seeking the guardianship, his lawyer, and the lawyer for the ward (usually court appointed) will meet in an informal hearing to see if all is in order.

Contested guardianships are more like trials. When are guardianships contested?

1. When relatives seek to prevent an individual from squandering his money, and the individual wants to go on doing it. (you say "Vegas Fling" and I say "It sure doesn't feel like squandering to me!")
2. When relatives squabble as to who should be in charge of the ward's affairs.
   Note: Even after a guardianship has been granted, another relative or friend can petition the court to remove that guardian if the guardian is cheating the ward, or otherwise not doing a good job.
3. When there is a family fight over discontinuing life-sustaining treatment in the face of terminal illness. (Living Wills help, see Chapter 2).

What Will Happen in Court? State laws govern guardianships and they vary a great deal. Here we will give an overview.

The Probate Court where the disabled person resides or is located usually has jurisdiction to grant a guardianship or conservatorship. A petition may be filed by almost anyone, including neighbors. In almost all cases, a lawyer will be needed by the petitioner and thus the costs may be substantial (in the neighborhood of $500 to $3,000). In many states (but not all), a separate lawyer for the ward and/or a court investigator will also be appointed, incurring an additional cost. Pre-disability planning (Living Wills and Durable Powers of Attorney) saves these costs. (See Chapters 2 and 23.) If physicians testify, or if the matter is contested, the bills could be much higher. These charges will usually be paid by the ward's estate. All interested parties must be notified of the hearing, which they can attend.

What is required in the petition will vary by state. It will include allegations of why the guardianship is needed and often what plan the proposed guardian has for the ward. A listing of the ward's income, expenses, and assets may also be required. Some states require that the petitioner also explain why there is no less restrictive alternative to guardianship.

The legal concept of least restrictive alternative *holds that, when the law is forced to interfere with a citizen's rights, it must accomplish its goal in the most narrow and unobtrusive possible way. For example, in the area of Free Speech, assume the mayor is concerned that a protest parade will disrupt traffic. She cannot simply bar the parade, but she can insist that it take a certain route. In the context of guardianships, there may be al-*

ternative steps that can be taken to protect the elderly person short of guardianship: trusts, durable powers of attorney, or simply sitting down and getting the person's consent to what you recommend.

The court hearing comes quickly, usually in a few weeks (and emergency situations can make the system respond even more quickly). The proposed ward usually will not be present unless the matter is contested, though he or she has the right to attend. Some judges will even go to the person's home to conduct the hearing. The individual has a right to an attorney (to resist the guardianship or to object to a particular person as guardian) and, in some states, if the individual has not selected a lawyer, one will be appointed. In some states, before the hearing, the court will appoint a Court Visitor (sometimes formally called an Investigator).

A Court Visitor, someone with a background in social work or medicine, may visit the ward before the hearing to make recommendations. Court Visitors may also visit the ward thereafter to see how things are going.

At the hearing, the judge (in some states, the jury, if requested by the ward) first decides whether the individual is incompetent or not. If the person is found competent, everyone goes home to the puppy. If the decision goes against the individual, two questions remain: what kind of guardian should be appointed, and who should be the guardian?

There are three kinds of guardianships:

Guardians of the Estate. These may be known as Conservators and provide for *management* of the ward's finances.

Guardians of the Person. Provide management of living arrangements and medical decisions.

Plenary Guardians. These have both powers and are appropriate only if the individual is incapacitated in both areas.

Guardianship is a sharp and broad sword. The ward loses the legal capacity to act in the areas of the guardianship. For example, if you are under guardianship, Smilin' Sam will not sell you the car because your promise to pay for it is not binding. ("But what if Smilin' Sam doesn't know about the guardianship?" Good question. Come to law school! Sit next to Smilin' Sam's daughter!)

Given the drastic nature of guardianships, some states allow for limited guardianships which allow the ward to make certain decisions. For example, if a ward cannot make medical decisions, a guardian can be given powers in that area while leaving the ward free to decide all other life decisions, such as where to live.

The final question the court will have to decide is, "Who should be the guardian?" Usually it will be the petitioner, who is often a family member or close friend. However:

- In the case of large or complicated financial estates, it might be a bank or trust company.
- If no family member can or wishes to serve, the guardian can be a social service agency or other institution which will charge a fee. Public Guardians are available in some states for individuals who cannot afford a fee or have no one else who is willing and qualified to act for them. If relatives are bitterly divided, a Public Guardian may be appointed as the default choice.
- Private fiduciaries are also available in most communities. For information, you can contact the National Guardianship Association, 526 Brittany Drive, State College, PA 16803 (814-238-3126 or www.guaardianship.org) or the National Association of Professional Geriatric Care Managers, 1604 N. Country Club, Tucson, AZ 85716 (520-881-8008 or www.caremanager.org).

Typically, family members serve without charge. Expenses (lawyers, accountants, travel) can be charged against the ward's estate. Institutional guardians charge for their services, usually on an hourly-fee basis or for a percentage of the estate assets.

c. Disabled Parents in Distant Cities

If your parents live far away, you won't be there if they become disabled. Urge them to have Durable Financial Powers of Attorney and Durable Health Care Powers of Attorney. These will authorize old friends to act in the case of their disability. As to a personal guardian, one option might be a local social service agency or a private care manager. See above. If your parent lives out of state and you wish to be appointed guardian, you will have to go to that state to do so. Further, some states, but not most, require that the guardian reside in the same state as the ward.

d. Individuals Who Are a Danger to Themselves or Others

Guardianships are for mental incapacity, not for insanity. If an elder, or anyone for that matter, is suffering from mental illness that makes the person dangerous to themselves or others, then civil commitment should be considered. States have procedures that can be used to commit dangerously mentally ill people to state or local hospitals for treatment of their condition. Some states, but not all, allow for civil commitment of individuals who are in need of treatment—such as individuals who refuse to take needed medical treatment.

For further information about such care, contact a local mental health screening agency, which you can locate by calling a nearby hospital or law enforcement agency.

CHAPTER 31

DECIDING FOR OTHERS

You've called the hospital. Your mother has been in a bad auto accident and is unconscious. Her chances aren't great but the doctors tell you that they would be much improved if they amputated her arm. If it were you lying there, you would agree in a heartbeat. Further, you believe that amputation is in your mom's best interests. However, you recall her telling you that she would rather be dead than to lose an arm. What do you decide?

Dealing with elderly relatives we may be called upon to make decisions for them, often informally (as someone helping with their finances), and sometimes formally (as a court-appointed guardian). While the law doesn't tell us what to decide, it gives us some guidance to help us think through how we should approach the decision.

a. The Legal Standards

Our grisly and no doubt unrealistic hypothetical (please, no nitpicking doctors writing in; some of these folks are worse than lawyers), illustrates three decision-making approaches:

1. Do what you would do if you were the one;
2. Do what is in the "best interests" of the other person;
3. Do what they would do for themselves. This is known as *substituted judgment.*

State laws that address this issue, in the context of guardianships, are fairly uniform in rejecting the first approach. The reason for this is simple: we want to preserve as much of the disabled individual's autonomy as possible. Just because someone cannot make their own decision doesn't mean we should ignore their personhood. As a surrogate decision-maker, the cardinal principal is that you are deciding for the other person, not for yourself.

The choice is between "best interests" and "substituted judgment," and state laws vary on the proper standard to follow. Academic journals that spill a lot of ink on such issues usually favor "substituted judgment," as it best protects individual autonomy. Being the captain of one's own ship means the right to make your own decisions, even if they are not in your "best interests."

However, on the street, things get muddier. Seldom does the real world present sharp distinctions between "best interests" and "substituted judgment" and, when it does, it probably doesn't matter too much because clever boys and girls can manipulate them.

As to *substituted judgment*: "Sure, Mom said she would rather die than have an amputation, but she said that when she wasn't actually facing the decision. Who knows what she would say now?" As to *best interests*: "Sure, it seems like increasing the chances of recovery are in her best interests, but knowing how she feels about amputation, maybe not."

If you are making decisions for others, just remember to do your best in figuring out what they would decide, not what you would decide in a similar situation. Even that ain't easy.

b. The Problem of Self-Interest

Your uncle is making a fool of himself, chasing windmills, running through his money, and causing you and the rest of his family great embarrassment. You can stand by and do nothing or you can have him restricted to his estate, where he will be out of physical danger, have all the comforts of home, and live the life of all good uncles. What do you decide?

Your uncle is none other than Don Quixote, Fighter of Dragons, Dreamer of Impossible Dreams, Reacher of Unreachable Stars. If you are like his niece, you lock him up, while in song assuring the audience, and yourself:

In my body, it's well known
There is not one selfish bone ...
I'm only thinking and worrying about him.

Closer to our own time and situation, in Wallace Stegner's *Angle of Repose,* the children want their crippled and aged father to move from his cabin in the woods to a place in town where he will be nearer to them and no doubt safer.

"They keep thinking of my good, in their terms. I don't blame them, I only resist them."

Usually, it's money.

Say you are managing your parents' finances. As you or your children will inherit, you will want the estate to be as large as possible. This perfectly normal desire may distort your investment and health care decisions.

You will be tempted to invest in growth stocks rather than in stocks paying the highest income, when higher income may be in the best interests of your parents. You will be tempted to skimp on nursing home amenities that would improve your parents' lives.

Of course, things are never simple. Your parents have an interest not only in their own well being but also in making sure you receive a large inheritance. It might very well be that they would choose to have their money go to the college education of their grandchildren (or a vacation for you) rather than a plasma TV set at the nursing home.

There are no easy answers. Perhaps the most important way to cope with the problem of self-interest is to admit that you have it. Repeat, after us:

"I have at least one selfish bone!"
"I have at least one selfish bone!"

Knowing temptation is the first step in resisting it. Philosophers have offered other solutions. Kant recommended that we universalize our decision as a way of factoring out our own interests.

"How would you have all nieces decide the issue?" In an interesting aside, note that the judicial doctrine of precedent operates in much the same way as does Kant's approach. As a judge's decision will become precedent and thus followed by future judges, the judge must think in terms of choosing the best rule of law for all similarly situated persons, not just the parties before him. It forces the judge to universalize.

Others recommend that when you are faced with a difficult decision, think of a wise person you know and ask, "How would he or she decide?" At first blush, that struck us as not very helpful but, having tried it, there is more there than you might think. Of course, we can always cheat by picking someone we think will come out where we want to: "How would the folks at Enron come out on this one?"

Conversations can be more helpful than philosophy. Talk to the person affected, even if they don't seem "all there."

"If you move into a nursing home, should I go first class or keep an eye on the grandchildren's college education?"

One more quote, this one from someone you've never heard of, a legal historian by the name of A.V. Dicey.

A man's interest far oftener distorts his judgment than it corrupts his heart.

This is the crux of the matter. Sure, Quixote's niece knew what she was up to, knew she was acting selfishly, knew her heart was corrupt. When we are in such situations, more often it is our judgment that is distorted, and we really believe that we are acting in our relatives' best interests and doing what they would do themselves.

c. Court-Appointed Guardians: Powers and Duties

No more quotes. Dry stuff. State laws vary as to the specific powers and obligations of guardians, those individuals appointed by a court to make personal decisions for their ward. If you are appointed guardian, the judge will review your responsibilities and powers. Here's a likely list.

- You have the powers and responsibilities of a parent of a minor except that you do not have a support obligation. You are responsible for seeing that the ward's personal needs, such as food, clothing, and shelter are met. But you do not have to pay for these things from your own pocket. You do not need to live with the ward.
- You are responsible for the ward's medical decisions, often even over his or her protest. Generally, you have the power to place the ward in a nursing home but not, without court approval, a mental health institution.
- You must take reasonable steps to protect the ward's personal effects.
- *Never, ever, not once, co-mingle funds.* It is simply too easy to forget that you put some of the ward's money in your checking account. People go to prison for things like this. Always have separate accounts.
- You are entitled to be paid a reasonable fee if the court approves.
- You cannot simply walk away from your responsibilities. You must go back to court to be relieved of them.
- You will be given an official court document to show to banks, doctors, and others.
- You will probably be asked to report back to the court yearly or even more frequently.

- *Never, ever, not once, co-mingle funds.* It is worth repeating.

Keep records. Even if you are not court-appointed, records are a very good idea. Indicate what you spent, why, and, hopefully, the ward's involvement in the decision.

> *After extended discussions with Uncle, in the presence of his good friend Sancho, we used $4,000 to visit the windmill region of Spain. By the way, Uncle did reach the Unreachable Star and has inspired me, now it is I who dream impossible dreams.*

CHAPTER 32

HOME CARE

"In the unlikely event we lose cabin pressure....

If you're a nervous flyer, you froze, only to hear the cheerful flight atten-
dant warble something about oxygen masks dropping on your head, and then
advising, as the plane careens downward (will flip over?), that you should put
on your mask first (are they serious?) and then put one on your screaming
child. (Thankfully there is reassuring news: the seats can be used as floatation
devices, even on flights across Arizona.)

The advice of flight attendants, while not welcome, is sound: As a caregiver,
take care of yourself first; otherwise you won't do a good job caring for others. After some suggestions on this score, we will discuss how to make your
house safe and elder-friendly.

In almost one in four homes, someone is caring for an older relative or
friend. This is a sharp increase, over threefold in only ten years. People are
living longer; those over 85 are members of the fastest-growing age group in
the country. Hospitals, to cut costs in the face of government limitations, now
release people much sooner. Medicare is effectively saving money by throw-
ing the expense to families.

We have observed before how often the care of our seniors looks like the
care we not-so-long-ago (and maybe even now) provide to our minor children. Here's a change that might startle you. In 1950, there were more than
five times as many dependent children in households as dependent seniors. In
2050, the projection is that the ratio will be very nearly 1:1. We're all getting
older, but you knew that already.

What you may not have known—or appreciated unless you have been
doing it—is that a typical caregiver for a senior spends 18 hours a week providing care: doctor visits, managing finances, and providing hands-on help.
Two-thirds of the caregivers also work outside the home and, of these, more
than half have to make workplace adjustments: coming in late, going part-
time, giving up promotions.

These folks, mostly women, need help.

a. Oxygen Masks for Caregivers

Caring for others is hard work. Expect resentment. Expect exhaustion. And expect guilt.

> *"I'm not doing enough. My dad did so much for me. And I just want to go the movies."*

Support groups help you deal with the emotional side of care giving. Many are formed around specific illnesses such as cancer, diabetes, heart disease, arthritis, or Alzheimer's.

Time out is your oxygen mask.

- Adult Day Care programs are available.
- *Respite care* is available to give you a break. Some is offered in the home; some as temporary stays in a nursing home. Insurance and Medicare may cover the costs.
- If you work, your employer might be agreeable to flex time. Many corporations now have eldercare programs to help employees find resources they need.
- Under the Family and Medical Leave Act, companies with more than 50 employees must allow *unpaid* leave to care for sick family members.
- You can hire part-time or full-time help. Be cautious. Be sure that the person is qualified and be sure, as sure as you can, that the person is honest. Theft is a worry; so too, abuse.
- Local programs offer things like Meals on Wheels and transport for doctor visits. Your Area Agency on Aging is a good place to start. Or call Eldercare Locator Service, 800-677-1116.

b. Making Your House Safe and Elder Friendly

What makes your house unsafe? We don't know; you haven't even had us over for dinner. As far as we know, you have a Pit Bull. Or killer bees. (A cartoon shows a small beehive with the sign, "Lawyers." "Those are the lawyer bees," someone is explaining, "They represent the killer bees.") If you are caring for an elder in your home, take a safety walk. Put yourself in their shoes.

Seniors fall. Are your rugs secure? Does the shower have slip-proof mats? Are there grab bars? Are the tables that they will use solid so they won't flip?

Do your kids leave their toys on the floor? *Seniors lose night vision.* Are there enough night lights to get them from bed to bath? *Seniors lose strength.* Do the chairs have arms that they can use getting up? Are there grab bars near the toilet and bath? *Seniors have slower reaction times.* Is the hot water heater set so that it will not produce scalding water? *Seniors have emergencies.* Do you have smoke detectors? Do you change the batteries? Are phones accessible? Cordless phones are best.

Some of the costs associated with home care might be picked up by Medicare, Medicaid, or long-term care insurance. For example, Medicare Part A, with a 20% co-payment, will cover the cost of "durable medical equipment" such as wheelchairs, hospital beds, traction equipment, walkers, and similar devices. Medicare Part B will cover emergency ambulance services. Many of the costs of hospice care (care given to the terminally ill) will be picked up by Medicare. Finally, caring for a parent may allow you to claim an additional income tax exemption.

It may be necessary to make structural changes to your house (wheelchair ramps, widened hallways, modified bathroom facilities). If you are renting, your landlord *must* allow you to make these changes as long as you agree to take them out when you leave.

An occupational therapist can be quite helpful in making specific suggestions. For example, if the elder is a gardener but has knee or hip problems, raised plant beds can work wonders. Someone with bad arthritis will find level handles more friendly than door knobs.

At the end of the day (more honestly, at the end of the chapter), there may come a time when home care is simply too demanding: on you, on your job, on your family. Time to consider a nursing home, and you may be pleasantly surprised.

CHAPTER 33

NURSING HOMES, GERIATRIC CARE MANAGERS

"Nursing home."

What image comes to mind?

No doubt a negative one, old folks slumped in wheelchairs staring at TV static. Perhaps this image comes from movies or from long-ago visits to a grandparent, from which all we remember is beds, wheelchairs, and smells, and the joyous sense of rebirth when we left to return to our own lives.

Old images die hard. It is clearly possible to live with dignity, with meaning, and with humor in a nursing home. There are new friends to be made, new hobbies to be tried, and new books to be read. And, as we know, there is still sex.

In many ways nursing home care—at least good nursing home care—is better than home care. While residents lose privacy and sense of home, nursing homes provide better medical treatment with nurses, certified nursing assistants and sometimes physicians, on staff. Most provide extensive activities, such as exercise programs, craft classes, and field trips.

And there is a lot to be said for hanging out with folks your own age (particularly if some of them are *older* than you, and, frankly and shamefully, a tad more *disabled* than you). You can talk about Ed Sullivan, Howdy Doody, and the Honeymooners without feeling like a dinosaur. There is no need to pretend you know who Twisted Sister is (or are). And you can shuffle along at your own damned pace.

The decision to place a loved one in a nursing home is similar to the dilemma raised by child care some years earlier: no matter how loving and energetic you are, hired folks offer expertise, activities, and friends.

Many people fear dying in a nursing home. This need not be an overwhelming fear as it may be possible to return home at the time of one's last illness and receive hospice care.

If you are considering a nursing home, you have at least three kinds of concerns: cost, selection, and actual services. As to cost, nursing homes are quite expensive and very little of the cost will be covered by Medicare. Chapter 12 deals with this problem and discusses long-term care insurance and Medicaid.

One important point: children are generally *not* financially obligated to pay for their parents *unless* they agree to. When signing the initial paperwork, nursing home officials will likely ask you to sign up—refuse, even though it might put you in a "bad light."(Better in a bad light than in a poor house!)

Know that many states actually have laws requiring families (usually meaning adult children) to contribute to the care of an adult relative unable to pay for his or her own care. Those laws are generally unenforceable, both because of practical considerations and also because of federal limitations imposed by the Medicaid and Medicare programs. Times change, and with tremendous budgetary pressure placed on the states by the cost of long-term care programs, the rules may change, too.

a. The Need for Planning:
Geriatric Care Managers

Far too often, individuals are put in nursing homes on a more or less emergency basis—usually when they are released from the hospital after a fall, a major accident, or a heart attack or stroke. Such decisions, pressured as they are, may not be the best. If an elderly relative is living on their own, or in your home, it is not too early to at least begin thinking about nursing homes.

There is a new niche profession: *Geriatric Care Managers*. These folks can help you begin thinking about choices that may have to be made down the road. They usually have training in gerontology, social work, nursing, or counseling and should have extensive knowledge about the costs, quality, and availability of services in your community. They provide a bundle of services, from financial and physical assessments to recommendations of living arrangements. If you and your parents live far apart, a geriatric care manager can also help you make long-distance arrangements, and can be your surrogate eyes and ears to monitor future care.

The field is unregulated but there is a National Association of Professional Geriatric Care Managers. In making your selection, ask about training, scope of services, and letters of recommendation. For help locating a member, call the Association at 520-881-8008 or look online at www.findacaremanager.org.

If you decide to go it alone, create a network to help you decide if a nursing home is necessary and, if so, which one. The network might include friends and relatives, doctors and health care professionals, clergy and social workers.

One task is to decide what level of care is needed. Let's get some of the jargon out of the way:

> *Hospice care:* This is end-of-life care, often at home, usually (but not always) paid by Medicare.
>
> *Skilled-nursing home care:* This usually follows hospitalization and is designed for the short term; it is expected that the patient will return home. Some of the costs are picked up by Medicare—but only if the patient is deemed to have *rehabilitative potential.* Once the professionals determine that continued therapy (physical, occupational and speech) will not help the patient improve, Medicare benefits will usually end—and therapy will likely end at the same time.
>
> *Custodial care:* This is long-term. It is expected that the patient will *not* return home *unless* it is to die at home. The costs of custodial care are not covered by Medicare.

There are a host of alternatives to nursing homes, depending on the level of disability, including subsidized senior housing, Board and Care Homes, and Continuing Care Retirement Communities (CCRCs). For a discussion of these options, see Chapter 10.

b. Selecting a Nursing Home

Some nursing homes are great; others, both figuratively and literally, stink. How to find a good one? Talk to knowledgeable folks, then visit at least two homes, and, always remember, "It's the location, location, location!"

Long-Term Care Ombudsman. There are over 500 local long-term care ombudsman programs. Ombudsmen visit nursing homes, take complaints, and advocate for residents. They are a great source of information and advice. Although they cannot recommend particular homes, they can answer questions concerning:

- survey results
- number of complaints
- results of their investigations

Other good sources of information about nursing homes include:

- hospital discharge planners and social workers
- doctors and clergy
- volunteers who help the elderly

- the National Citizen's Coalition for Nursing Home Reform (www.nccnhr.org), which has published a good guide called "Nursing Homes: Getting Good Care There" (now in its Second Edition)
- Medicare itself, which by federal law must maintain a database of nursing homes and their past performance. You can locate local nursing homes and read about their history of inspections and incidents at www.medicare.gov/NHCompare/. The Medicare site includes an excellent checklist for comparing nursing homes, including both information obtained from the Medicare website and impressions from the facility visits you will be making as you read on below.)

Visit at least two (to allow for comparison) and visit each several times, at different times of day. Things you might want to look at:

Staff. Does it seem adequate to give individual attention or does it seem overworked? How does the staff treat the residents?

Mealtimes. Do residents socialize? Residents needing help should be integrated with other residents rather than eating alone.

Resident rooms. Personalized or institutionalized?

Residents. Reasonably well groomed, clean, and dressed?

Restraints and bedsores. Too many residents physically or medically restrained and too many bedsores spell trouble.

Activities. Take a look at the schedule of activities and show up to observe some. Speaking of activities, does the home have policies concerning resident sex?

Location. The more the family can visit, the better. Not only are the visits good in and of themselves, but nurses will pay more attention to residents who do not appear to be abandoned. If you have questions concerning a family member's care, you have the right to inspect medical charts. The nursing home has 24 hours to make them available.

c. Patients' Rights

The federal Nursing Home Reform Act (NHRA) applies to any home that has Medicare or Medicaid patients (a majority of such homes). The NHRA requires that a patient Bill of Rights be given to residents and their families. The most important rights:

- the right to an individualized treatment plan;
- the right to see all of one's clinical and other records;
- the right to complain and be free from reprisal;
- the right to send and receive uncensored mail and to make private calls;
- the right to refuse treatment; and
- the right *not* to be physically or chemically restrained except to prevent physical harm, and then only upon instruction of a doctor.

We cannot stress the importance of the right not to be restrained except under very limited circumstances. In some nursing homes, patients are routinely tied to their chairs. By their arms. Considerable medical evidence indicates that this actually *increases* the incidence of injuries, as patients struggle against restraints, get caught in the restraining devices, or are simply left inadequately attended to once the staff perceives that the danger of injury is reduced. If you need ammunition in dealing with a facility, look at the website of "Untie the Elderly," a project of the Kendal Corporation, a faith-based organization active in the Northeast, at www.ute.kendal.org

d. Abuse

The best way to prevent abuse is always to suspect it and to visit often. As to the signs of abuse and what to do about it, see Chapter 14. To minimize abuse and neglect, and to help improve the quality of care, adopt the "cookies and thorns" approach. Bring cookies to the facility's staff, and think of your job as being a constant thorn in the facility's side.

PART 6

DEATH IN THE FAMILY

Introduction

One of the co-authors of this book was once on the board of directors of a local nonprofit AIDS agency. At his first meeting, the three new board members were asked why they wanted to be on the board. The first gave a heart-rending story of the last months of his lover's life; the second told of her deep despair in losing a son to the dreaded disease. When it came to your co-author's turn, he meekly offered, "Well, I have an academic interest."

This Part can be approached from either perspectives. If your family is not facing a crisis, you still might want to learn of the wonderful world of hospice, the curious yet empowering notion of "dying well," and the critical need for human touch at the end of life. That's Chapter 34. Similarly, you might be interested in the topic of "pulling plugs," the debate over physician-assisted suicide, and the law surrounding cases like that of Terri Schiavo. That's Chapter 35.

Of course, academic interests eventually become compelling family stories. If a loved one becomes terminally ill, these two chapters will help.

Chapter 36, Death in the Family, has one important insight: that there is no proper way to grieve, that there are no stages of mourning, and there is no goal to mourning. Other than that the chapter deals with all of the running around one must do in terms of funeral arrangements and bill paying. The last chapter gives you the nuts and bolts of probate; despite our best efforts, we couldn't avoid it.

CHAPTER 34

HOSPICE, DYING WELL, AND BEING THERE

Art Buchwald, newspaperman, decided enough is enough. He stopped kidney dialysis. Dying, he gave one last interview, to Tom Brokaw. "Art, what do you think you will you miss the most?"

"Global warming."

There will be sadness and grief—we are dealing with terminal illness. But, as we are also dealing with people, expect humor and moments of grand transcendence. We'll discuss wonderful promise of hospice care, the curious notion of dying well, and the importance of being bedside.

a. Hospice Care

What people fear most about death is not the pain; not even what comes next. People fear dying alone.

Death in the hospital can be lonesome. And gruesome. The *Journal of the American Medical Association* studied five major hospitals and reports:

50 % of terminal patients experienced moderate to severe pain, half the time.

38 % spent 10 or more days in a coma.

31 % spent all or most of their family's savings during their final illness.

Hospice care is a wonderful and loving alternative: care at home, in a home-like setting in a hospital, or in a free-standing hospice center. Death comes, not with strangers, but with family and friends. Hospice has been an amazing success. It wasn't there for our grandparents. It was started in 1967 in England and first came to the U.S. in 1974. There are now over 3,300 hospice programs in the U.S. and about one-third of us die in hospice. (The next great death and dying movement, gaining strength today, deals with improving pain management for terminal patients, putting controlling pain right up there with controlling disease and putting aside old fears about "creating addicts.")

Hospice care is provided by a team, likely a doctor, a physical therapist, a nurse, a counselor, and a spiritual advisor. The goals of hospice are to eliminate pain (they assert that they can be almost 100% effective), to educate the patient and the family about the dying process (what to expect and how to make the most of it, and to ensure "dying well").

In the early days of the hospice movement, disease fighting medications (as opposed to pain and comfort meds) were *not* given. Recently there has been a movement, known as "open access," which allows the hospice patient to continue disease-fighting treatment.

Hospice care is essentially *free* for most patients. Congress, realizing that 25% of all Medicare funds are spent on treatments in the last year of life, and realizing hospice is less expensive than intensive care, added hospice to the list of benefits. (Despite the widespread use of hospice, the 25% figure has remained fairly constant.) Medicare pays for doctors, drugs, medical appliances (beds), social workers, home nurse visits, home health workers, short-term nursing, short-term hospital stays, and even bereavement counseling.

The kicker is eligibility: death within six months if the disease runs its normal course. Breaking the news to patients can be tricky. A doctor friend becomes something of a used car salesman. First he describes all of the wonderful aspects to the program and, once the patient commits, adds, "Well, there is one technical matter I have to discuss."

b. "Dying Well"

"I want to die like my grandfather did, peacefully, in his sleep. Not like his passengers in the back seat, kicking and screaming."

If we only hope for a death that doesn't involve a lot of pain, we are selling ourselves short; we are selling our families short. Hospice talks of dying as a growth experience.

"How can dying be a growth experience? At the end, we're dead."

We think instrumentally. Nothing is good in its own right; it is only good to the extent it becomes an instrument to be used to achieve yet other goals. We study, not because learning is challenging and fun, we study to get a better job; we exercise, not because it's great to feel exhausted, but because it will extend our lives and improve our looks. We read books, not to enjoy ourselves, but to improve ourselves (and we even get mad when the author breaks our serious quest with some reference to *The Importance of Being Earnest*).

Dying well is our recognition of the riches we have, not of things we can buy; it is our recognition of who we are, not of who we can become.

The actor Anthony Perkins, dying of AIDS, said:

> *There are many who believe that this disease is God's vengeance, but I believe it was sent to teach people how to love and understand and have compassion for each other. I have learned more about love, selflessness and human understanding from people I have met in this great adventure in the world of AIDS than I ever did in the cut-throat, competitive world in which I spent my life.*

In Robert Bolt's play, *A Man for All Seasons,* Sir Thomas More resists King Henry VIII's pressure to approve his most recent marriage despite the fact that it was bigamous according to More's religion. Henry brings more and more pressure until it is clear that More's life is endangered unless he approves the marriage. More's friend, the Duke of Norfolk, urges More to give in and thereby save his life.

> *More: I will not give in because I oppose it—I do—not my pride, not my spleen, nor any other of my appetites but I do—I.* (More goes up to Norfolk and feels him up and down like an animal). *Is there no single sinew in the midst of this that serves no appetite of Norfolk's but is Norfolk?*

Dying well involves shutting down the roles and fears and hopes we have lived—there are no more plans, no more failures, no more successes, no more appetites. Once again we are our essential selves—we are that single sinew that is Norfolk.

Of course, there will be pain. Viktor Frankl, who survived the Nazi Death Camps, wrote that people can survive pain, but they cannot survive the loss of meaning. What meaning, what purpose can there be, lying in bed, drifting in and out of consciousness, with only days to live?

You can give your family and friends the opportunity to care for you. They can express love and pay something back for all you have done for them. Caring for others is deeply human.

You can tell your stories. Children and grandchildren love to hear of times when everyone dressed up real funny.

You can drift towards greater understanding and peace.

For excellent books on this subject, see Ira Byock, M.D., *Dying Well: Peace and Possibilities at the End of Life,* and Elizabeth Kubler-Ross, *On Death and Dying.*

One caveat as to honesty. Realizing your impending death, you may want to rid yourself of long-kept secrets. Go slow. There are good reasons for secrets. In an episode of the *Sopranos,* a gangster visits his dying aunt. She is a nun and confesses that, during the war, she met a sailor and, well, she is in fact the gangster's mother. The woman he thought was his mother is really his aunt. This did not lead to tearful recognition and forgiveness: the gangster cursed both women and crippled an innocent bystander for good measure.

c. Being There

Thus far we have been looking at this from the patient's point of view. What about yours?

Dying patients crave human contact, physical contact. Read Albom, *tuesdays with Morrie,* and Tolstoy's *Death of Ivan Ilyich.* Physical contact with the dying can be yucky. It is important to get over your squeamishness: a caress, a kiss, simply holding wizened hands. Touch and hearing go last: hold hands, whisper memories, offer encouragement and love, and, to break the emotional intensity of those moments, tell a joke or offer an Art Buchwald moment:

> *Voltaire, on his death bed, was urged by a priest to denounce Satan. He refused, with, "This is not the time to be making enemies."*

Still, being bedside, won't be a hallmark moment. You will chastize yourself for negative thoughts. You will feel the urge to escape—it is instinctive to flee sickness and death. Your thoughts will turn from the profundity of the moment to how the death will affect you and, suddenly realizing that this seems to be your concern, you will condemn yourself as self-centered. Finally, there may be resentment, resentment stemming from being abandoned or from prior wrongs.

Don't be hard on yourself. None of us is as loving, as caring, as we would hope to be. We're human: it is not our fleeting thoughts that matter; what matters, being bedside.

CHAPTER 35

ENDING LIFE: PULLING PLUGS, EUTHANASIA, AND SUICIDE

a. Ending Medical Treatment

At some point you may have to consider ordering physicians to discontinue medical treatment of a loved one, knowing death will result.

Our best advice is to get family, physicians and spiritual advisors involved. Guilt and recriminations are likely, no matter the decision. Do Living Wills and Durable Health Care Powers of Attorney solve the problem? No. As we pointed out in our discussion of them, often they are ignored, in favor of maintaining treatment, if the family insists on treatment or if there is a fight about what to do. Doctors know that it is much more difficult to defend a "wrongful death" case than a "wrongful life" case.

This does not mean that you shouldn't have these documents for yourself. They can help, and sometimes make a real and powerful difference. If the family agrees to end treatment and the Living Will supports that decision, there will likely be no problem. And the documents may even help your family to reach a consensus about your wishes—especially if you talk about these complicated, personal and often wrenching issues before a crisis arises.

Back to the horrible decision you must make for a family member: although the advance directives may have only limited usefulness in many cases, if you know the treatment choices of your loved one, you support their decision, and you have the documents in hand, you have the authority to insist on their favored outcome. Get your mother, your husband, your siblings, even your adult children to sign advance directives—and to talk about them. Did we mention how important it is to have a discussion among your family members and those who are likely to be present when the time comes to make these terrible decisions?

If you are making the decision for a loved one, we even have some assigned reading for you. Find a copy of a very slim but helpful book called *Hard Choices for Loving People* by Hank Dunn, a former nursing home and hospital chaplain. You can even read the entire text online at www.hardchoices.com. It explains how people actually die, how end-of-life decisions get made, and what your legal, moral and ethical obligations are when you find yourself in this position.

And did we mention how important it is to discuss these issues with your family in advance?

But what if no instructions were given?

You may very well have to get a court order terminating treatment. State law varies and is changing.

In 1990, the United States Supreme Court backhandedly confirmed the right of a competent patient to order the removal of life-sustaining systems. It also discussed some of the rules concerning the *incompetent* patient. A guardian can order the removal of life-sustaining treatment but, before this can be done, a state can insist that the guardian *prove* that the patient, before becoming incompetent, expressed a desire that this be done. The state can require that this showing be made by *clear and convincing evidence.* But your state probably does not have such a high requirement—unless you live in Missouri, Massachusetts or New York. Your state probably allows guardians to make the decision based on the notion of "substituted judgment"—the idea that a guardian should try to do what his or her ward would do if competent.

An essential point about end-of-life treatment: *it is far easier to keep feeding and hydration tubes out than it is to get them out.* This is true as a practical matter, even though most state laws insist that there is no difference between the decision to withhold and the decision to withdraw. If a loved one is in a nursing home and the staff recommends such tubes, think long and hard before authorizing them. They have a financial interest in keeping the patient alive, no matter how dismal the prospects and no matter how painful the condition. Once the tubes are in, it may take a court order—or at least an extraordinary amount of effort and angst—to get them out.

In the absence of artificially-supplied food and fluids, a patient who cannot accept food by mouth will usually die of dehydration, not starving, and within (in most cases) about ten days to two weeks. Efforts will (and should) be made to relieve dry mouth and thirst. You reasonably wonder: is this a particularly painful way to go? A study in 1994 indicated that only 13% of those who died this way experienced discomfort. Still, some did and there may be more recent studies. Your doctor should know. And, of course, the pain of this kind of death must be balanced against the pain the patient is currently experiencing. Even if the patient seems not to be in pain, how are we to know? As Hamlet warns, what dreams may come?

Finally, Terri Schiavo. Her case set off a national debate over death and dying issues. She had collapsed fifteen years earlier and had been kept alive on feeding tubes. Physicians testified that she would never awake from her "persistent vegetative state"—an eerie condition similar to a coma, but characterized by periods of wakefulness with open eyes and apparent response to sounds and other stimuli. Her husband wanted the feeding tubes removed; her parents did not. After extensive hearings in Florida, where the judge decided that she had expressed her preference that the tubes should be removed in such a circumstance, and after hearings in the Florida Supreme Court, in Federal Court, in the United States Supreme Court, and in Congress, the tubes were removed. She died on March 31, 2005 at age 41.

Terri Schiavo did not have a living will. Had she, this case would have been much less contentious and heart-breaking. Living wills might not end the matter but they help. So get on it—Terri collapsed young, at age 27.

b. Euthanasia and Oregon's Death with Dignity Law

In 1998 an Oregon woman, dying of breast cancer, became the first person to use Oregon's Death with Dignity Law. She died peacefully in her sleep, at home, surrounded by her family. Her physician had given her medication; five minutes later she was asleep, thirty minutes later, dead.

Euthanasia involves taking *active* steps to *cause* death. It is *not* the same as removing life-sustaining help, and it is *not* the same as either suicide or assisting another to commit suicide.

This distinction, between action and inaction, between misfeasance and nonfeasance, is as old as our common law. Shakespeare skewered it. In *Hamlet,* Ophelia is to be given a Christian burial, one denied to suicides. "How can this be, unless she drowned herself in her own defense?" asked one character. The grave digger explained:

"Here lies the water; good: here stands the man; good: it the man go to the water, and drown himself, it is, will he, nill he, he goes—mark you that; but if the water come to him and drown him, he drowns not himself."

Euthanasia is murder. Helping another to commit suicide, while not murder, is criminal in almost every state and every circumstance. It is not a defense that the victim wanted to die, asked for the help, was in great pain, or would have died anyway—or that the act was motivated by love and compassion. The primary exception in this country to the ban on assisting suicide, and it is a narrow one, is Oregon's Death with Dignity Law. It allows doctors to prescribe, but not to administer, drugs that kill. The patient must self-administer the lethal drugs.

Several states have considered or are considering statutes like the one in Oregon, but none have yet been adopted. Before looking at the policy arguments, let's take a brief look at what Oregon requires. Two physicians have to certify that the patient (1) has, to a reasonable medical certainty, no more than six months to live, (2) is competent, (3) has been informed of alternatives to suicide (hospice, pain control), and (4) is making a voluntary choice in requesting the lethal prescription. If the patient is depressed or suffering mental illness, no prescription will be written. Nor will one be written until at least fifteen days after the initial request, and only then if the patient repeats the request. If all of these steps are properly taken, the physicians will not be civilly or criminally liable for writing the prescription and, if the patient takes the medications, it will not be deemed a suicide for life insurance purposes.

Since Oregon passed its law, about 40 people a year have ended their lives using its terms. Most were cancer victims in their 70's. We're not sure what it means, but two-thirds have graduated from, or at least attended, college.

At one point the federal government, in a move to kill the program, threatened doctors writing these prescriptions with sanctions under federal drug laws. The Supreme Court later ruled that this was an abuse of federal authority and the Oregon statute is up and running. Is it a good idea?

The issues are extremely complicated. In support, there is the notion that freedom and, indeed, being human, entails the right to captain one's own destiny. Why shouldn't you have the right to end your own life, and to seek medical help if necessary? Why shouldn't you be allowed to avoid the great pain and expense generally associated with final illness?

There is another less obvious argument in favor of allowing for physician-assisted suicide: it may actually reduce suicide. Many elderly, suffering from chronic illness, fear that it will eventually lead to unbearable suffering and that, when it does come, they will no longer have the ability to end it themselves. In panic, they take their own lives. The mere promise that, if that time arrives, there will be someone there for them could stay their hand and immediately relieve their consuming fear. Once again they would be in control of their future. At peace, and finding that in fact their lives never do become unbearable, most would not commit suicide. Most people who have "saved up pills, just in case," never use them.

But there are strong philosophic and religious concerns against condoning any form of suicide. No one should play God; the guiding principle of medicine is "first, do no harm," and legalized suicide, even if not widespread, will lead to a general cheapening of human life. There are practical concerns as well: if assisted suicide is available, how can relatives be prevented from dumping expensive or inconvenient relatives? From trying to accelerate their inheritance?

There is also the real concern of the slippery slope. Although most proposals to legalize assisted suicide, like the one in Oregon, are restricted to consenting adults who have a terminal illness (one which is likely to lead to death within six months), the fear is that these limits cannot hold. Why deny a consenting adult medical help in ending a life made unbearable by severe chronic fatal illness, such as Lou Gehrig's Disease, simply because that disease has not yet progressed to the "terminal stage" Although it will surely lead to death, it will not do so within the next six months. There is also the fear that condoning suicide will slowly but surely lead to involuntary euthanasia. Once the law seems to acknowledge that some lives aren't worth living, the next step may be to put severely retarded or disabled individuals "out of their misery." Fanciful? One hears arguments that the elderly have a "duty" to step aside, and a group of severely disabled individuals, fiercely opposed to physician-assisted suicide, calls itself "Not Dead Yet." We, as a society, have too much history with eugenics and social engineering to be trusted with this tool, or so the argument goes.

One final point on the general topic. Pain relief, which has the unintended result of causing death, is neither suicide nor euthanasia. For example, physicians will prescribe morphine for certain painful cancers; as the pain increases, so, too, the dosages. Increased dosages increase suppression of breathing and heart rate, and may eventually lead to death. This is known as a treatment's "double effect." It is interesting to note that the Catholic Church, a vocal opponent of suicide (and, of course, euthanasia), does not condemn the practice.

For a very interesting book on the history of the physician-assisted suicide debate, see Sue Woodman's fine book, *Last Rights: The Struggle over the Right to Die.*

c. Suicide

Of course, there is always suicide. But if you are thinking of ending your own life, go slowly, ever so slowly. If you are considering suicide, two things are most likely true: you are very depressed and you fear the pain of your illness will eventually become unbearable. Consider:

- Depression can be treated and is often transitory. "This too shall pass."
- Almost all pain can be alleviated by proper medication. The reason that many die painful deaths is not the inability of medicine to control pain, but the lack of training of most doctors in dealing with terminal illness and their reluctance to prescribe high enough dosages. Hospice, and the relatively modern pain management movement, promise adequate painkiller dosages and hence a relatively pain-free death.
- Suicide of a loved one is one of the hardest deaths to get over — guilt abounds ("Was this my fault?"). The message you send to relatives and family is of darkest human despair: "Some lives aren't worth living."

One thing for sure. Before you take any step toward suicide, talk to family, friends and spiritual advisers. If you don't, you do them a double wrong: your death and your cruel denial of their opportunity to reach out to comfort you.

CHAPTER 36

DEATH IN THE FAMILY

When a loved one dies we are shocked, deeply insulted, to find that the world goes on as it did yesterday: dogs bark, baseball is played, folks go to the movies. The world should stop. In *Funeral Blues,* W. H. Auden captures our feelings:

> *Pour away the ocean and sweep up the wood;*
> *For nothing now can ever come to any good.*

Thankfully, there will be a lot of distracting details, a lot of running around to do, a lot of business to attend to. Burial decisions, short-term financial arrangements, insurance and Social Security survivor benefits, probate. These will get you through the first several months. Perhaps, after that, things again can come to good. Not like before, but still, to good.

a. The Myths Surrounding Mourning

On T.V. talk shows, we hear that mourning is a process, with marked stages and with final goals. That has not been our experience. Mourning is different for all of us.

It is not a process you "work though" to get to some point where it is over, allowing you to "get on with your life." If there is a goal to mourning, it is not to get over the death. It is to relocate the loved one—to create a different kind of relationship with the person:

> *"So that's what the President said. I wish I could call Dad and get his reaction. What would it be?"*

Mourning is not a momentary interruption in life. It continues for the rest of your life. You won't be "OK" for a long time and memories will always rush back, unexpected.

Depression and great distress are not inevitable. Some grieve before the death and experience the actual death with relief. Expect complicated feelings—despair mixed with relief; dark, intense moments mixed with daily chores and gossip. Life is always in the *present* tense. You must figure out what to do tomorrow morning. Don't feel guilty if you find yourself distracted by plans for dinner. There are no rules, no stages, no end points. Just be with friends, neighbors, and relatives. Talk. Cry. Tell jokes.

> *An elderly couple sits on the couch. The wife says, "If I die first, you should remarry. If you die first, I'll get a dog."*

Now, the distracting details.

b. The First Few Days: Funeral Homes and Burial

Funeral homes can be called at any hour. They will know what to do. In addition to funeral arrangements, they will take care of official notifications and will arrange for several copies of the official death certificate that you may need in notifying insurance companies, Social Security, retirement plans, and the like.

Often the individual, by Will or otherwise, has indicated a preference between cremation and burial and what kind of service they wish. If not, these decisions fall to the family.

Cremation is less expensive. There will be local regulations as to where ashes can be scattered. Permanent urns are also available. Some are quite beautiful and moving, either in their simplicity or in their religious and spiritual themes. Others strike us as more fanciful, such as the ones adorned with statuettes of golfers.

> *Query: In Heaven, do you always shoot a hole in one? Or is that in Hell?*

Funerals are expensive. Several years ago Jessica Mitford exposed funeral fraud in her book, *The American Way of Death*. Funeral directors were portrayed as scum, sucking the blood of grieving families, selling them expensive coffins to "show their love for the dearly departed."

Things have improved, and dramatically, but still be wary. Funeral fraud continues in many areas. In 1984 the Federal Trade Commission promulgated the Funeral Industry Practices trade regulation rules. Funeral directors must disclose the cost of all goods and services, even over the phone, and provide a written list when you inquire in person. You have the right to purchase separate funeral products and need not buy entire packages. Although funeral directors mostly opposed those changes, they tell us that the result has been good for the industry; you may be as surprised as they were to learn that consumers spend more on funeral services when armed with detailed price lists.

The average cost of a funeral, incidentally, is about $6,500, according to the National Funeral Directors Association. That does not include the cost of a burial plot or other cemetery expenses.

> *A woman's husband left $30,000 to be used for an elaborate funeral. After everything is over, she tells her closest friend that "there is absolutely nothing left from the $30,000."*
> *The friend asks, "How can that be?"*
> *"Well, the funeral cost was $6,500. I made a donation to the church—that was $500, and I spent another $500 for the wake, food and drinks—you know. The rest went for the memorial stone".*
> *The friend says, "$22,500 for the memorial stone? My God, how big is it?"*
> *"Four and a half carats"*

A little over one-quarter of Americans choose cremation, and that's more than a 20% increase in just the past decade. One of our favorite cocktail-party statistics: Nevada, which used to be famous for divorces, is now the state with the highest rate of cremations (slightly higher than 65%), and Tennessee, at just over 3%, is the lowest. Consumer frauds to watch for:

a. Quoting one price on the phone and switching to a higher one in person.
b. Misrepresenting that state law requires embalming (embalming may be required if the cremation is not undertaken relatively soon after death, but there is no blanket requirement for embalming).
c. Misrepresenting that state law requires caskets for cremation or outer burial containers for burial (most crematories require some type of rigid container, but not necessarily a traditional casket).

It is a good time to remember your Bible. Over the long haul, no container, no plastic, can defeat life's cycle: "Dust to Dust."

You will be distraught. There will be strong psychological pressures to overspend. No one wants to appear "cheap" at a time like that. Everyone wants to show their loved one just how much they cared. We advise extreme caution.

On the first trip to the funeral home, you will be taken through the "Casket Room," complete with price listings and "warranties." (Warranties are a curious concept in this context; whose lifetime measures a "lifetime warranty"?) Don't agree to anything that first visit. That's an order. Go home and think about how else the family can use the money. Talk things over. As to showing the decedent you really cared, it is, alas, too late. You can still show your family and friends how much you really cared; consider how they would prefer to be convinced. For ourselves, we want to be invited to an Irish wake—but preferably not our own.

As to being cheap, blame us: as lawyers it is our job to be cheap. On the other hand, don't assume that funeral directors are your enemy; they can provide a great deal of emotional support and practical advice, and they have a vested interest in being helpful. They want your repeat business, and if you think they did a good job you should talk to them about making your own arrangements in advance after you get through this crisis.

Autopsies

An autopsy is simply a post-death surgery designed to determine the cause of death and the presence of diseases and abnormalities. Although gruesome to envision, an autopsy might be quite helpful to the surviving family. For example, genetic diseases unknown to the family might be revealed so that family members can take steps to avoid them. Conversely, it might be discovered that Granddad wasn't suffering from the genetic disease his family feared. For example, it is believed that Alzheimer's disease has a genetic component; family members have great anxiety as to their own futures. Autopsies reveal, however, that only about 50% of individuals believed to have that disease actually had it.

A family can request that an autopsy be performed and can insist that it be a limited one, such as a brain autopsy looking for Alzheimer's or a heart autopsy looking for heart disease. If an autopsy is done, don't expect immediate answers. What with microscopic examinations of tissue, results typically take 30 days or longer.

The good news is that most hospitals throw in the autopsy for free. Even with fierce competition for patients, hospitals seldom advertise this feature: "After your stay with us, enjoy a free autopsy."

Hospitals rely on autopsies to assure that doctors are diagnosing and treating disease correctly. Pathologists use autopsies to better understand the causes and treatment of human diseases. That we live as healthy as we do today is in large part due to the autopsies of yesterday. In this light, agreeing to an autopsy can be viewed as a contribution to our grandchildren.

Under certain circumstances, the law requires that an autopsy be performed: if the cause of death is suspicious or unknown, and perhaps, depending on state law, if the individual died within a year of surgery or died without a physician present to certify the cause of death. The decision about a required autopsy is usually made by the local Office of the Medical Examiner; if you feel strongly about not wanting an autopsy for your loved one, or want to limit any autopsy, you can talk to the Medical Examiner or staff and explain your position.

Organ Donation

Organ donations can save lives and can help in medical research and training. If the decedent opposed making a donation, then that decision should and must be respected. However, even if the decedent (by Will, donation card, or driver-license designation) indicated a desire to donate, often doctors and hospitals may still seek the family's agreement even though their agreement may not be legally required. Organ donation networks are eager not to look ghoulish, or to take organs over family members' objections. That has a significance for your own decision: if you really want to be an organ donor, best to explain that to your family while you still can, and bring them to a position of agreeing to your directive.

If the decedent left no instructions, the family can authorize an anatomical donation. State law lists, in priority order, who can make that decision: usually the surviving spouse, adult children, either parent, adult sibling, grandparent (in some states) and the person's guardian, in that order with some state variation. Some families have religious and similar objections to donations. However, some object in the mistaken belief that they would delay the funeral, or increase the cost. They generally don't do either.

Notifications

Family and friends should know as soon as possible. Phone trees work well. Obituaries in local papers can be arranged by the funeral home at a modest cost.

c. The First Few Weeks

Immediate Cash Needs and the Safety Box Ploy

Hopefully sufficient funds were kept in joint savings and checking accounts. The joint tenant can withdraw money. Similarly there should be no problem if the assets were in a Living Trust. Even if the decedent was the managing trustee, the trust will continue with notification to the back-up trustee.

Some advise keeping large amounts of cash in joint safety deposit boxes, the idea being that upon the death of one, the other can easily get to the cash and that the cash will not show up as part of the estate, thus cutting taxes. This isn't good advice. First, as to easy access, joint checking and savings accounts achieve the same goal. Second, as to avoiding taxes, it is against the law. And banks read the obituaries. In some states they may seal joint safety deposit boxes, which can only then be opened in the presence of a state official (this state practice, once universal, is now much less common). Note to aging Flower Children: Don't keep your stash in your safety box, just in case.

If the family's assets were kept in the decedent's name alone, there may be trouble reaching them. The quickest way is to immediately open a Probate Proceeding (we will tell you how momentarily) and have yourself appointed executor, administrator, or personal representative (your state has picked one, but probably only one, of those terms). You will then be issued papers by the Court, which will allow you to access the decedent's accounts. Most states provide for a family allowance—an amount of money payable to support spouses and dependent minor children—during probate. It allows the family to draw needed money before and during the probate process, which can be lengthy.

Don't assume, however, that a probate will be required. You may be surprised to find that most, or even all, assets have co-owners' names on them, or name beneficiaries to receive them upon the owner's death. And even if that turns out not to be true, most states provide a mechanism for collection of smaller estates (with quite a bit of variation in what makes an estate "small") without full-blown probate proceedings. Most of those statutes, however, require that you wait some period of time—typically a month or two—and provide a death certificate, so they do not offer much help when immediate cash is needed. One particularly ironic result: in most states a death certificate cannot be issued until the funeral arrangements are completed, but it may take a death certificate to get access to the funds needed to pay for the funeral.

Bills: Don't pay them!

It's a good idea to let things sort themselves out before you start paying any of the decedent's bills, such as hospital bills, doctors' bills, and nursing home bills. Why should you wait? If the estate is to be probated, the estate will pay the bills; if there is a Living Trust, the trustee will.

In any event, you may not be legally obligated to pay them. As a general rule, only the person (or his or her estate) who received the service is liable to pay the bill. Generally, family members (children and spouses) are not required to pay the bills out of their own pockets. This may be different in the community property states (Arizona, California, Idaho, Louisiana, Nevada,

New Mexico, Texas, Washington and Wisconsin); rather than try to figure out the answer yourself, delay payment and consult a lawyer.

Some of the bills sent to a decedent after his death may even be bogus. Scam artists take advantage of a family's distress.

If creditors are getting pushy, send them a letter explaining that the individual has died and that you will need time to sort out his affairs.

On the other hand, continue to pay ongoing bills, such as rent, utilities, and, yes, the lawyer's fees for probate. If these bills are not paid, the services will stop. You may have to obligate yourself to payment of some other bills, like funeral expenses, even if the decedent's assets turn out to be insufficient.

The Search for Documents and Notifying Insurance and Social Security

The family should search papers and safety deposit boxes for Wills, insurance policies, and other important papers. If the decedent was working at the time, the employer should be asked if the company maintained life insurance on its employees. Many do.

If you are the co-owner of any of the decedent's property, such as vehicles and real property (land and buildings), you should contact the appropriate governmental agency (Department of Motor Vehicles, Country Recorder's Office) as to how to have the title reissued in your name only.

To collect on life insurance policies, it's best to call the agent or company and see what procedure to follow.

Contact Social Security. Social Security acts as kind of a life insurance policy. The following people may be entitled to benefits:

> *Dependent children* (including adoptive children, stepchildren, and in some cases grandchildren) may be entitled to monthly payments. The children must be under 18 or, if older, disabled or still in school. These benefits are available even if the decedent had not worked very long. The decedent had to be only currently insured: had six quarters of coverage in the last 13 preceding death (or was receiving disability benefits at the time of death). If there is such a child, then the decedent's spouse is also entitled to benefits even if he or she has not reached the age of 60.
>
> *Dependent parents* in some cases.
>
> *Surviving spouse* if
> a. the decedent was fully insured (had 40 or more quarters into the program) and

b. the survivor is 60 or older (or 50 if disabled) and

c. the marriage lasted more than nine months.

Note: If you were both drawing Social Security at the time of your spouse's death, contact Social Security because it is likely that you may draw more in survivor benefits than you draw on your own account or as the spouse of an insured member.

If the couple was not married, the survivor may still get benefits if they had, or adopted, a child together.

Bottom line: If the decedent was working or had worked in jobs covered by Social Security (most jobs), call Social Security for current information on possible benefits.

There is also a small Social Security death benefit which will help with funeral expenses. It is only paid to surviving spouses in limited circumstances, and it is only $255, but every little bit helps. You will find that the best resource for understanding the Social Security death benefit will be the funeral director.

To begin a chapter with the moving words of W. H. Auden and to end it discussing a small death benefit, seems to sin against art. But maybe, when all is said and done, life is not grand moments, but rather tiny details, those coming at us every moment.

I heard a Fly buzz—when I died—
The Stillness in the Room
Was like the Stillness in the Air—
Between the Heaves of a Storm—
The Eyes around—had wrung them dry—
And Breaths were gathering firm
For that last Onset—when the King
Be witnessed—in the Room—
I willed my Keepsakes—Signed away
What portions of me be
Assignable—and then it was
There interposed a Fly—
With Blue—uncertain stumbling Buzz—
Between the light—and me—
And then the Windows failed—and then
I could not see to see—

Emily Dickinson (1830–1886)

CHAPTER 37

PROBATE

Bleak House, Dickens' great novel, gave probate a bad name. The probate of a huge estate lasted for generations. The estate went broke. The family went broke. The lawyers got rich. *Bleak House* sent law school applications soaring. There are four reasons you might want to read this chapter:

- A family member has died and you need to know if the estate should be probated. That's Section a.
- You have been cut out of someone's Will (or got less than what you think you should). That's Section b.
- You are a family member and need support money, now. That's Section c.
- You are probating an estate and need to know what to expect. That's Section d.

Unlike other chapters of this book, this one contains very little knowledge that one needs in advance, except perhaps to give you a sense of what "probate" really is and how important it may be for you to arrange to avoid it in your estate planning. If you want, you can skip the entire chapter until the need arises. (If we had a choice, we wouldn't have even written it.)

a. Is Probate Needed?

Often it isn't. If the person who died didn't have a Will, didn't have much property, and wasn't the only legal guardian of a minor child, probate probably won't be needed. The family can simply divide the personal property—furniture, heirlooms, jewelry, computers, pets, and so forth. Personal property is defined as all that stuff we own that does not have a "title" (an official piece of paper indicating who owns something).

But what of cars, houses, land, stock, bonds, and bank accounts? These items do have "title" and before the family can get ownership of them, the title must be rewritten to show the new owner.

Often these items do not present much of a problem, either. If the title shows a co-owner, indicating the right of survivorship, it is easy for the co-owner to get the title reissued. They simply show the death certificate to the appropriate official, and a new title showing them as sole owner will be issued. With cars, the appropriate official is usually the DMV (your state's name for the agency may be different), and it may not even be necessary to show DMV a death certificate, since any one of the individuals listed with an "or" can later sell the vehicle. With land and houses, file a death certificate with the County Recorder or Clerk. For stocks, bonds, brokerage and bank accounts, simply present a death certificate at the appropriate office and fill out the forms provided; the same simple process will usually allow you to collect life insurance proceeds, IRA and other retirement accounts.

What if the title is only in the name of the person who died? Well, then probate may be needed to get a court order changing ownership. However, if not much property is involved, almost all states allow for quick and inexpensive—often free—probate substitutes. Usually it involves simply filling out a form (you can probably get one from the local Bar Association, or your local Area Agency on Aging, or even at the Probate Court) and attaching a death certificate. Big time probate, *Bleak House* Probate, is usually reserved for the rich.

If probate is required, you will probably want to hire a lawyer. People can and do file and handle probates without legal help, but it is complicated and quirky enough, and your duties are difficult enough to learn about and perform, that you will probably be better served by having counsel. At the very least, interview two or three lawyers, so that you can figure out what probate proceedings look like in your state and what the lawyers think they can do to help you with the process.

b. Are You Disgruntled?

A disgruntled heir is someone who would get more under the law of intestacy than he or she would get under the Will (or Trust), or someone who would have gotten more under the Will but the lawyer who drafted the Will messed up.

Let's first look at the second situation. Say that Granddad meant to leave you a lot of money but you never got it because the lawyer drafting his Will did so negligently. In some states you can sue the lawyer as a "third party beneficiary" of the contract between your granddad and his lawyer. Complicated stuff; see a lawyer.

The typical disgruntled heir goes after the Will (or Trust) and tries to get it thrown out so that the estate passes by intestacy. In addition to the Jarndyce children (see the multiple *Bleak House* references above if you've forgotten the memorable Jarndyce clan), this raucous group includes:

• Surviving spouses

If you are a surviving spouse and are not getting at least a third of the estate (half, in some jursdictions), contact a lawyer. Sometimes "Dearly Beloved" tries to give away your stuff.

• Forgotten children

If you are a child of the decedent (natural, adopted or illegitimate) and are not named in the Will, then you may have a claim. The argument will be that the person who died did not mean to cut you out, only forgot you. "As to my son Samson, who insisted on never cutting his hair, I give nothing" at least makes clear Manoah (Samson's father) remembered he had a son. If you were expressly cut out of the Will in this fashion, then your only claim may be that the decedent was of unsound mind or under the undue influence (arm-twisting) of someone. Delilah?

• Children born, and spouses married, after the Will was written

The claim is that the decedent didn't mean to cut them out. State law may take care of that claim, providing in many cases that such "pretermitted" heirs take a share equal to that they would have received if no Will had been written.

• Children of prior marriages

Say your mother remarried and, when she died, she left everything to her new husband. This is common. However, when he dies, he leaves everything to his kids and nothing to you. See a lawyer, but don't get your hopes too high. Some couples upon remarriage agree to leave everything to the survivor with a promise that, when the survivor dies, the estate will be split between their respective children. Tempted by dark forces, the surviving spouse may renege and leave everything to his or her own children. We saw in Chapter 27 that a Living Trust can address this problem.

There is not, however, any presumption that you are entitled to receive property that once belonged to your parent after the death of your step-parent. In order to make this claim, you will need to show some agreement, and usually it will need to be more than just your parent's Will listing you as an heir if the step-parent is deceased.

• Heirs who suspect lack of capacity

"Being of sound mind" is the stock opening. (We prefer "It was the best of times, now it is the worst of times.") Despite what the stock opening says, if the testator lost legal capacity before signing the Will (or trust), it is invalid. That may not help you very much—if your rich uncle Thurston's Will is invalid, you probably won't get anything anyway. Those worthless loser cousins of yours (Thurston's kids) or, worse yet, Lovey will inherit Thurston's millions.

- Heirs who suspect undue influence

Large gifts to nurses, neighbors, and TV evangelists are suspect. Was the person in a position to assert control over the testator by threats or by withholding care?

- Heirs who suspect *murder*

In most states, a murderer cannot inherit from the victim, even if named in the Will ("Someday, son, all of this will be yours."). There is a legal maxim—"You cannot profit from your own wrong." Given the nature of the world, however, this maxim is more inspirational than descriptive.

However, if Sis can prove Bro did in dear old Dad, he can't get a nickel. There's more for Sis. There is always someone willing to profit from wrong.

If you suspect both undue influence and murder, you've got yourself a novel. Throw in a few good trial scenes and a little sex, and you won't need to inherit.

No matter your complaint, if you are a disgruntled heir, seek legal advice early. Once the probate process begins, you will be facing very tight timelines—typically a matter of weeks, not months and certainly not years. And despite all the ways we have described here to challenge the validity of a Will or trust, you should know that will contests are actually quite rare—and successful Will contests far rarer.

c. Family Allowances

Most states have legislation which allows surviving spouses and minor or disabled children to draw living expenses from an estate while it is being probated. These laws also set aside for the surviving spouse certain property (usually the family house and its furnishings). These set-asides come off the top of the estate; that is, they must be satisfied before there are other distributions, even distributions pursuant to a valid Will.

d. The Probate Process

The steps are typically something like this:

- Establishing the existence of a valid Will. (If the Will isn't valid, or there is no Will, the estate passes according to intestacy laws. Chapter 24-a).
- Appointing the executor/administrator/personal representative.
- Gathering and protecting assets.

- Settling with creditors and paying taxes (income and estate).
- Wrapping up: distribution and accounting.

Let's go through each step.

Establishing the Will. Any interested party, usually the spouse or an adult child, can petition the Probate Court to take jurisdiction over a decedent's estate. In smaller estates, a relative can do this simply by going to the courthouse and filling out the correct papers. In larger estates, a lawyer should be retained. In any event, this should be done quickly, as someone must be authorized to take possession of the individual's assets.

At the first hearing, there will be two orders of business: first establishing whether the decedent had a valid Will, and second, appointing a personal representative to take charge. In some states and circumstances, "hearing" may be a misnomer, since the entire thing may be done at the walk-up counter of the probate court without any fanfare or preliminaries.

To be valid, a Will must comport with the technicalities laid down by state legislatures in terms of witnesses and notaries (Holographic Wills, those written out by hand, need not meet these requirements in states recognizing them. See Chapter 24-b). Even if a Will is found, there may be codicils (documents that modify the original Will) and new Wills (which have the effect of voiding all or part of prior Wills). Both codicils and new Wills must comport with the technical requirements of a Will.

Naming a Personal Representative. The personal representative (in some states and in Bleak House called the executor or administrator) is the person or institution that takes charge of the estate and moves it though probate.

Usually the decedent has named a personal representative (and a backup) in his Will. If not, the court will appoint the personal representative. Usually it will be the person who filed the probate petition. Other relatives can, and should, intervene at this stage if they object to that person. State laws establish priorities as to who is appointed.

Usually the personal representative will have to post a bond so that, if he or she splits with the goodies, the heirs will be protected. Bonds cost money and that money will come from the estate. Traditionally people waive the bond if they nominate a family member or close friend.

Finding and Protecting Assets. The personal representative must search the decedent's papers, read the decedent's mail, and generally snoop around to find out what the decedent owned and owed. The personal representative will have access to safety deposit boxes and has the legal right to get information from stock brokers, bankers, and lawyers concerning the decedent's affairs. It is here you will learn that mild Aunt Mildred was, in fact, a CIA agent credited with, among other things, the fall of the Berlin Wall (accomplished by a series of poisoned, yet tasty, Peach Cobblers).

The personal representative must maintain the assets. This may involve such things as winding down the decedent's business and selling perishable assets. An inventory of assets must be prepared and filed with the court. Where appropriate, insure the assets; otherwise you might be liable for losses.

Notifying and Paying Creditors. The decedent's bills must be paid but not just yet. First discover the creditors, find out how much is owed and categorize the claimants. The personal representative notifies the known creditors and advises them to submit their claims. Usually ads must be placed in local newspapers advising unknown creditors to file their claims. If creditors do not present their claims on time, their debts are barred. However, if the personal representative knows about some and fails to list them, those creditors will not be barred.

The personal rep should not pay any bills until satisfied that they are legal. If the decedent had a good defense against a debt, the personal rep should decline to pay it, forcing the creditor to file some sort of lawsuit (it may be in Probate Court, or in some states it may not have to be). Further, if there is any question about the estate's solvency, the personal rep should not pay any bills before they all come in. Why?

Because, like Orwell's Pigs, some debts are more equal than others. Who gets to go to the trough first? State statutes list priorities, usually along these lines:

1. Expenses of administering estate (lawyers wrote the rules, and the rules say they get paid first)
2. Funeral and burial expenses (a reasonable amount)
3. The expenses of last sickness (reasonable and necessary)
4. Family allowances
5. Debts and taxes given preference by federal and state laws
6. Judgments rendered against the decedent in his lifetime in order of date
7. All other claims

If a personal representative pays lower priority pigs, leaving higher ones unfed, the personal representative may have to personally make up the difference.

Paying taxes. The personal rep will prepare and file the last state and federal income tax returns of the decedent as well as paying any federal and state estate taxes owed on earnings of the estate.

Wrapping Up. Locating assets and paying the bills should take at least four months (creditors are usually given at least this amount of time to make their claims). Probate often runs much longer, but finally there comes a day to distribute the goodies.

After distribution, the personal representative may have to file a Final Accounting with the Court, and must give an accounting to the heirs. Again, the disgruntled can object.

How to distribute the property? If there is no Will, this will be done according to the intestacy laws (but you know that already). If there is a Will, well, then, you need to know just a little more. There are three kinds of bequests:

> *Specific bequests* (objects): To my only daughter, my 1956 Studebaker Golden Hawk.
>
> *General bequests* (money): To my only son, $75,000.
>
> *Residuary bequest* (remainder): To my then living grandchildren, divided equally, the remainder of my estate.

Well and good. But what happens if there is not enough in the estate to make good on all the bequests? Say the Studebaker was sold prior to Dad's death, or that Dad gave it to the Studebaker Hawks Club? Does the daughter get nothing? What if there is a Studebaker but no $75,000? Does the son get nothing?

This gets complicated and you'll need legal advice.

If you end up getting nothing, worse things can happen. Read *Bleak House*. And that, dear friends, is a wrap.

ACKNOWLEDGMENTS

Every acknowledgment prominently lists the support of family, without which no significant project can be accomplished. Cliches are often also truisms. In addition to family, our colleagues, partners, students and co-workers all have contributed to this work in large and small ways.

We would particularly like to thank, for their contributions to this volume, Barbara Sattler and Morgan Ditch, editors extraordinaire, Perry Woods, cartoonist extraordinaire, Sherina and Michael Cadnum, title-kickers extraordinaire, and Maureen Garmon, researcher extraordinaire. Also those who helped on the substance, but not the mistakes: Drs. Jack Boyer and Scott Bromiman, police captain John Levitt, Professor Lynne Tosama, Vince Rabago, a lawyer with the Arizona Attorney General's office of Consumer Fraud, law student researchers Vicky Marcus, Christine Walters, Carl Sammartino, Robroy Platt. Special thanks go to Barbara Lopez and Melissa Haun, and, of course, a warm welcome to Marshall.

Some of the material is this book was first presented in a book Professor Hegland wrote with Allan Bogutz, *Fifty and Beyond: The Law You and Your Parents Need to Know*, and he thanks Allan for all of his insights.

The very idea of aging vibrantly was planted at an early age by grandparents, and later expanded by parents and in-laws; thousands of clients and friends continue to demonstrate the concept on a daily basis. We owe all of them —family, friends, colleagues, clients, —a tremendous and unrepayable debt. Indeed, they have a taught us how to sing in our chains like the sea.

About the Authors

Professor Kenney F. Hegland has spent his career teaching law students how to use the law to solve life's perplexing problems. In addition to Arizona, he has taught at UCLA, Harvard, and at the University of San Diego's London Program. He graduated from Stanford, attended law school at UC Berkeley, and has an advanced law degree from Harvard. Early in his career he worked in the Civil Rights Movement (in Albany, Georgia) and with Cesar Chavez and the United Farm Workers Union (in Delano, California). Two of his books, *Introduction to the Study and Practice of Law* and *Trial and Clinical Skills,* are quite popular in the nation's law schools. He has also written and produced eight law videos currently distributed by the Discovery Channel.

Robert B. Fleming practices law in Tucson, Arizona, and lectures and writes about elder law extensively, with particular emphasis on planning for individuals with disabilities and other special needs. His professional background includes a stint as the Public Fiduciary in Tucson, Arizona, and a turn as Tucson City Magistrate. In addition to an active law practice he writes and lectures extensively on elder law issues. His book, *The Elder Law Answer Book,* is one of the principal treatises on elder law used by practitioners. He maintains his law firm's website (www.elder-law.com) as a ten-year labor of love. In his spare time he is a martial artist, pilot and scuba diver.

INDEX